AF371620

Temporal Territories: An Anthology on Indigenous Experimental Cinema

Publishers: COUSIN Collective and Light Industry
Designer: Otami–ᐅᘄᒡ
Editors: Sky Hopinka, Adam Khalil,
Alexandra Lazarowich, Adam Piron
Editorial Assistant: Kaitlin Lenhard

Published in 2024 by COUSIN Collective and Light Industry
ISBN 978-0-9979102-2-3

COUSIN Collective
www.cousincollective.org

Light Industry
361 Stagg Street, Suite 407
Brooklyn, NY 11206
www.lightindustry.org

This project is supported by Nia Tero, the Robert
Rauschenberg Foundation, and the Andy Warhol Foundation
for the Visual Arts. Special thanks to Max Weinman.

"Every Picture Tells a Story" by Paul Chaat Smith originally appeared in "Strong Hearts: Native American Visions and Voices," *Aperture*, no. 139, Summer 1995. Parts of the essay "Way We Move" by Lou Cornum are adapted from "Reverse Manifest Destiny (Or, *The Exiles* and Me)," originally published in *Social Text Online*, June 2021. "Pure Legend: Dispatch from an Incomplete Search for the DeMille Indians" by Adam Piron was originally published in *Caligari*, August 2021. "To End and Begin Again: The Work of Victor Masayesva, Jr." by Elizabeth Weatherford was previously published in *Art Journal*, Winter 1995, vol. 54, no. 4, 48-52. "Indigenous Cinema and the Limits of Auteurism" by Girish Shambu first appeared on the website of the Criterion Collection, May 19, 2021. "Film Is the Body" by Sky Hopinka first appeared in the *MoMA Magazine* (online) on June 10, 2022. "The Violence Inherent: Native Videographers Shoot Back" by Adam Khalil and Zack Khalil was originally published in *The Offing*, September 20, 2016. "Desire Lines: Sky Hopinka's Undisciplining of Vision" by Diana Flores Ruíz was originally published in *Film Quarterly*, Spring 2022. "Thesis on the Audiovisual" by Colectivo Los Ingrávidos was originally published in English online in *Non-Fiction 03: The Living Journal England*. "Reflections on Language Based on the All Encompassing Sequence Shot" by Miguel Hilari was first published as "Reflexiones sobre el lenguaje a partir del Plano Secuencia Integral" in *Secuencias*, no. 49-50, 79-96. "Taking the Fiction Out of Science Fiction: A Conversation about Indigenous Futurisms" by Grace Dillon and Pedro Neves Marques was previously published in *e-flux journal*, no. 120, September 2021.

Tiare Ribeaux would like to thank the following artists for providing images accompanying her piece "To Weave With Light": HUFF Film programs, courtesy of Christopher Kahunahana; stills from *Kau ʻeliʻeli kau mai, kau ʻeliʻeli ē* courtesy of kekahi wahi; *PIKO* and *Mauna Fuji* courtesy of Nicole Naone; *Polyfantastica* by Solomon Enos; Hawaiʻi Futures by Sean Connelly.

Temporal Territories

An Anthology on Indigenous Experimental Cinema

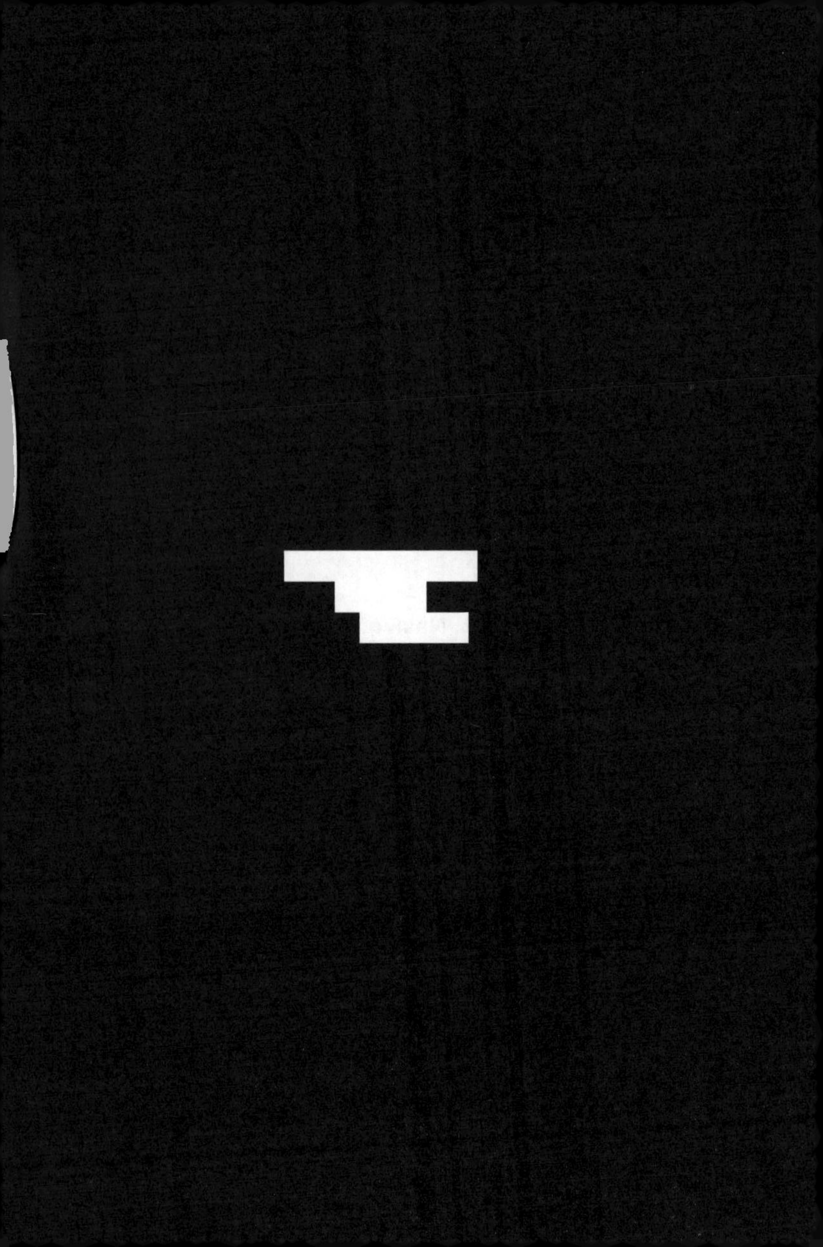

Introduction
COUSIN
Collective

In the summer of 2018, the four of us arrived at the same place
at the same time for the 63rd annual Robert Flaherty Film
Seminar in upstate New York. This was a week-long seminar
programmed by Greg de Cuir, Jr. and Kevin Jerome Everson
where 180 or so participants gathered to watch documentary
films and engage in a wide range of discussions. The irony of
four Indigenous artists meeting up at an event named after the
director of the salvage-ethnographic landmark *Nanook of the
North* (1922) was not lost on us. We had all known each other
prior to this seminar, but there was something very special
about being together for the first time in an environment
where we were able to watch the films screened in the
seminar, and talk about everything from experimental cinema
to where we were at in our own lives and creative trajectories.

This level of sustained camaraderie was unique, but
it seemed a shame that this was something we could only
experience sporadically across conferences or film festivals.
By all meeting up together, we had unintentionally carved
out a temporary space tailored just for ourselves—one
where we could share what we had seen or read, and offer
support as friends and mutual admirers, free of the burden of
contextualizing our Indigeneity, explaining what we were each
trying to do in our work. Why couldn't something like this
happen more often? We weren't in competition with each other,
we weren't racing to be the singular "token" who speaks for all
Native Peoples, as so many institutional environments tend to
compel us towards being. Rather, we spoke of the loneliness of
often being the only Indigenous person in a space such as this,
and how little care we felt from institutions and organizations.

It was during that long weekend that the seeds of
COUSIN were born. Outside of wanting to create some sort of
mechanism to aid Indigenous artists who were experimenting
and pushing formal boundaries in art and film, we didn't

really know what shape COUSIN would take. In the years since, we've been able to offer direct support to artists via grants, programmed screenings, and by connecting them to opportunities beyond our collective. While we are still a young endeavor, we're continuing to push ourselves to look beyond the expected when it comes to who and how we can support, and in what ways we can grow and become more expansive for our artists, communities, and each other. The spirit driving much of this endeavor is to allow Indigenous artists the space to make work on their own terms, and to allow that work to stand on its own merit. Much like the work of these artists, we intend the lines that define COUSIN to be opaque, flexible, and lean, and to allow ourselves the freedom to do what feels right in the given moment. This approach has brought about many unique opportunities—one of which is this very book you're reading.

In the spring of 2021, we were contacted by Thomas Beard and Ed Halter of Light Industry with an intriguing proposal. Our future collaborators and co-publishers suggested that they would like to work with us on a publication. They invited us to make a book that we wish existed. We talked a lot, and what felt right given that invitation was to present an anthology of writers, artists, and filmmakers who were each meditating and musing on the work of Indigenous Peoples experimenting with the moving image in form and concept. With the very generous support of the Robert Rauschenberg Foundation and Nia Tero, we were able to commission new essays as well as republish several key pieces that we felt were thematically and formally essential. The purpose of this collection is not to define what this movement is or is not, but rather to illustrate some of what drew us to these works and these artists, whom we admire for their creativity, their risk, and their hope. This anthology is not meant to be encyclopedic or exhaustive; far from being a comprehensive survey, hopefully it points in a multitude of new directions, and allows a reader to wander down a few rabbit holes of their own choosing.

Still, finding your way in these spaces as an Indigenous person can feel overwhelming. You don't often know where to start, and the length between waypoints can feel like vast valleys to cross. If anything, we hope this collection can be something like a celebration, a point along your path that fosters conversations and connections, as it shows some of the different ways that different Peoples are thinking about and making work as Indigenous artists and scholars. There are no rules to this thing, and you are not alone.

COUSIN Collective, November 2022

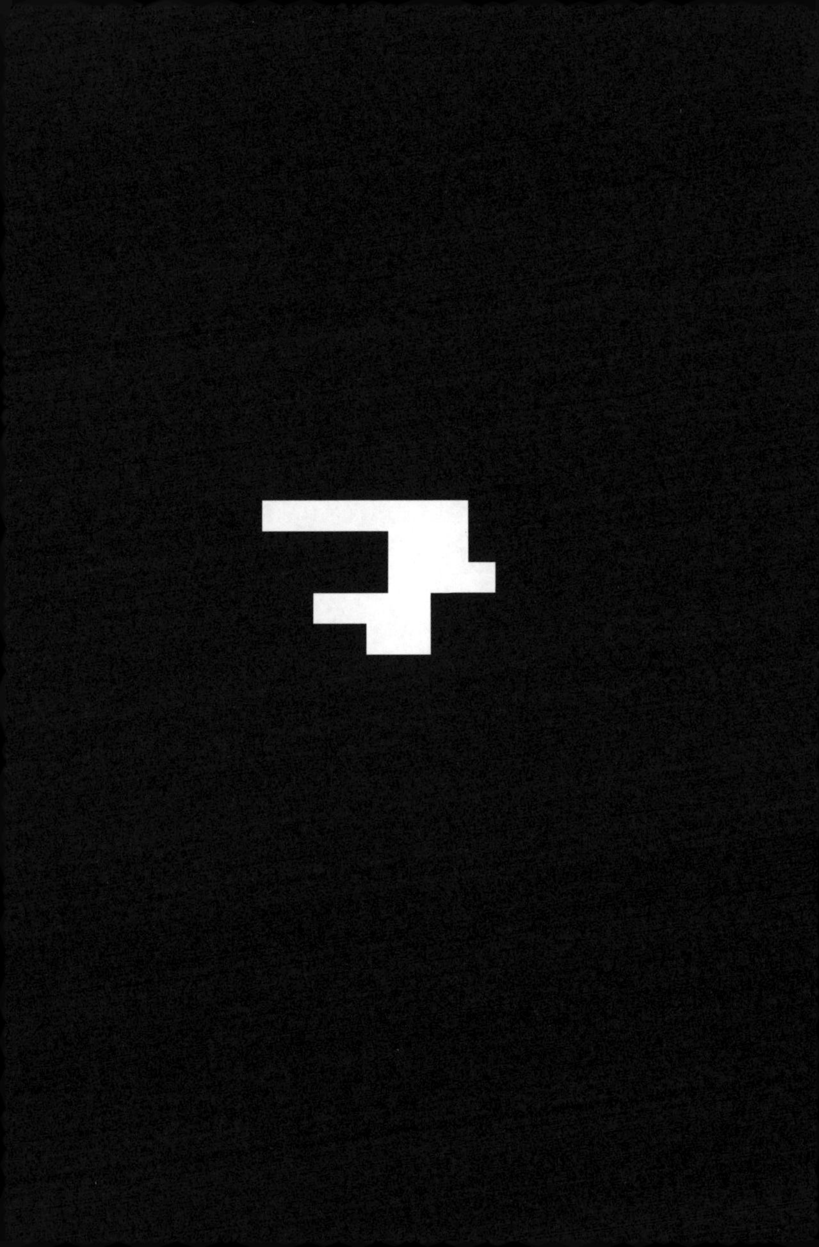

Every Picture Tells a Story

Paul Chaat Smith

History records that Ishi, aka the last Yahi, the Stone Age Ishi between two worlds, was captured by northern Californians in 1911 and dutifully turned over to anthropologists. He spent the rest of his life in a museum in San Francisco. (And you think *your* life is boring.)

They said Ishi was the last North American Indian untouched by civilization. I don't know about that, but it's clear he was really country, and seriously out of touch with recent developments. We're talking major hayseed here, at least. His keepers turned down all vaudeville, circus, and theatrical offers for the living caveman, but they weren't above a little cheap amusement themselves.

One day they took Ishi on a field trip to Golden Gate Park, where an early aviator named Harry Fowler was attempting a cross-country flight. You can imagine the delicious anticipation of the anthropologists. The Ishi Man vs. the Flying Machine. What would he make of this miracle, this impossible vision, this technological triumph? The airplanes roared off into the heavens and circled back over the park. The men of science turned to the Indian, expectantly. Would he quake? Tremble? Would they hear his death song?

Ishi looked up at the plane overhead. In a tone his biographers would describe as one of "mild interest," he asked, "White man up there?"

Twenty years later my grandfather would become the first Comanche frequent flyer. Robert Chaat was born at the turn of the century in Oklahoma, when it was still Indian Territory. It was our darkest hour. The Comanche Nation was in ruins, wrecked and defeated. The Army did a census at this time and found that 1,171 of us were still alive.

Grandpa Chaat was one of those holocaust survivors. He was a tireless fighter for the Jesus Road, who battled the influence of peyote and forbade his children to attend powwows.

Yet he also taught pride in being Indian and conducted services in Comanche into the late 1960s. His generation was pretty much raised by the Army, who beat them for speaking Indian and had them march like soldiers to school. Geronimo was the local celebrity, and my grandfather remembers meeting him before the old guy died in 1909. Fort Sill was a small place; I guess everyone knew Geronimo.

My mother remembers her dad's trips to Chicago and New York when air travel was often a two-day adventure. He sent his five children trinkets from the 1939 World's Fair, newspaper clippings about his speeches around the country, pictures of himself with the author Norman Vincent Peale.

She discovered the lantern slides on a trip back to Oklahoma in 1991. They were in a battered and ancient black case buried deep in a closet. These closets have given up more and more secrets as time has passed. A few years earlier, when Grandpa still lived in the tiny house in Medicine Park (later he would move to a nursing home in town) he produced an eagle feather from one of those closets. The feather, he told my mother, belonged to an ancestor who was a medicine man.

The forty-eight square glass slides are about three by four inches, at least an eighth of an inch thick. Each has its own slot in the felt-lined case. They're heavy: a single slide weighs more than an entire box of their modern equivalents. Generously engineered with metal and glass instead of cardboard and film, they are about as similar to today's slides as a 1937 Packard is to this year's Honda.

They show Indian lodges, tipis, Comanches of all ages in brilliant clothing, buffalo, horses, wagons, the Quanah Parker Star House, all in vivid, lifelike color.

Their meaning and purpose? Fundraising, of course. There were even a few pledge cards scattered about the case, reading: "Indian Mission Fund. I pledge to pay the sum of ___

before May 1, 19___." I could see Grandpa lugging his twenty
pounds of glass slides through airports (still called "fields")
because they would have been too precious to check, the key
to next year's budget or the church's building fund.

But what were these pictures? Mom could identify some
of the locations and people, but most of them were unknown
to her. Maybe they weren't even Comanche. Perhaps the
Dutch Reformed Church had a media consultant who put the
slides together. The label points in this direction—it says:
"Chas. Beseler Co., New York," not some outfit in Lawton or
Oklahoma City. Grandpa might have sent along a few of his
own pictures, and, for all we know, the rest might have been
from a photo agency in Manhattan.

To me, the Indians in the pictures seem dignified, friendly,
open to religious instruction and new cultural ideas. I imagine
listening to Grandpa in a church meeting room in New York
or Boston in 1937, hearing about the struggle for redemption
and a better way of life. A people at a crossroads, he might
say. The images underline his script: Indians in blankets with
papooses on their back next to Indians in starched western
shirts and bandannas, posing for the camera on their way to
a Jimmie Rodgers show. We see, ridiculously, an umbrella next
to a wagon.

Which will it be, the blanket or the Bible?

On second thought, it's obvious the Indians are resistance
fighters pretending to cooperate. See that look in their eyes?
They are American hostages denouncing imperialism in a flat,
dull voice for Hezbollah. They steal the photographer's gun
when he's not looking. At the gourd dance tonight in the
foothills of Mount Scott, they make plans for the future, plans
the city fathers won't like.

We have been using photography for our own ends as
long as we've been flying, which is to say as long as there have

been cameras and airplanes. The question isn't *whether* we love photography, but instead *why* we love it so much. From the Edward Curtis stills to our own Kodachrome slides and Polaroid prints and Camcorder tapes, it's obvious we are a people who adore taking pictures and having pictures taken of us.

So it should hardly be a surprise that everything about being Indian has been shaped by the camera.

In this relationship, we're portrayed as victims, dupes, losers, and dummies. Lo, the poor fool posing for Curtis wearing the Cheyenne headdress even though he's Navajo. Lo, those pathetic Indian extras in a thousand bad Westerns. Don't they have any pride?

I don't know, maybe they dug it. Maybe it was fun. Contrary to what most people (Indians and non-Indians alike) now believe, our true history is one of constant change, technological innovation, and intense curiosity about the world. How else do you explain our instantaneous adaptation to horses, rifles, flour, and knives?

The camera, however, was more than another tool we could adapt to our own ends. It helped make us what we are today.

See, we only became Indians once the armed struggle was over in 1890. Before then we were Shoshone or Mohawk or Crow. For centuries, North America was a complicated, dangerous place full of shifting alliances between the United States and Indian nations, among the Indian nations themselves, and between the Indians and Canada, Mexico, and half of Europe.

This happy and confusing time ended forever that December morning a century ago at Wounded Knee. Once we no longer posed a military threat, we became Indians, all of us more or less identical in practical terms, even though until that moment, and for thousands of years before, we were as different from one another as Greeks are from Swedes. The Comanches, for example, were herded onto a reservation with the Kiowa and the Apache, who not only spoke different languages, but were usually enemies. (We hated Apaches even more than Mexicans.)

The truth is we didn't know a damn thing about being Indian. This information was missing from our Original Instructions. We had to figure it out as we went along.

The new century beckoned. Telegraphs, telephones, movies; the building blocks of mass culture were in place, or being invented. These devices would fundamentally change life on the planet. They were new to us, but they were almost as new to everyone else.

At this very moment, even as bullets and arrows were still flying, Sitting Bull joined Buffalo Bill's Wild West show and became our first pop star. Like a young Warhol he sold his autograph for pocket change, and like Mick Jagger he noticed that fame made getting dates easier. He toured the world as if he owned it, made some money, became even more famous than he already was. Afraid of cameras? *Talk to my agent first* is more like it.

It was an interesting career move, even if it couldn't prevent the hysterical US overreaction to the Ghost Dance that resulted in his assassination the same month as the Wounded Knee massacre.

Some think of Sitting Bull as foolish and vain. No doubt Crazy Horse felt this way. The legendary warrior hated cameras and never allowed himself to be photographed, although this didn't stop the US Postal Service from issuing a Crazy Horse stamp in the 1980s. Maybe Sitting Bull was ego-tripping, but I see him as anxious to figure out the shape of this new world.

For John Ford, King Vidor, Raoul Walsh, and the other early kings of Hollywood, the Indian wars were more or less current events. Cecil B. DeMille, who made over thirty Indian dramas, was fifteen at the time of Wounded Knee. They grew up in a world in which relatives and friends had been, or could have been, direct participants in the Indian Wars.

The promise of film was to deliver what the stage could not, and the taming of the frontier, the winning of the West, the building of the nation was the obvious, perfect choice. Indians and Hollywood. We grew up together.

This has really screwed us sometimes, for example the stupid macho posturing by some of our movement leaders in the 1970s. (If only their parents had said, "Kids! Turn that TV off and do your homework!" we might have actually won our treaty rights.)

But maybe it's better to be vilified and romanticized than completely ignored. And battles over historical revisionism seem doomed from the start, because the last thing these images are about is what really happened in the past. They're fables being told to shape the future.

All of the lame bullshit, the mascots, the pickup truck commercials, the New Age know-nothings, I used to find it embarrassing. Now I think it's part of the myth to think all that is bogus and the good old days were the real thing. The tacky, dumb stuff about this country is the real thing now. The appropriation of Indian symbols that began with the earliest days of European contact is over, complete. Today, nothing is quite as American as the American Indian. We've become a patriotic symbol.

For our part, we dimly accept the role of Spiritual Masters and First Environmentalists as we switch cable channels and videotape our weddings and ceremonies. We take pride in Westerns that make us look gorgeous (which we are!) and have good production values. We secretly wish we were more like the Indians in the movies.

And for the Americans, who drive Pontiacs and Cherokees and live in places with Indian names, like Manhattan, Chicago, and Idaho, we remain a half remembered presence, both comforting and dangerous, lurking just below the surface.

We are hopelessly fascinated with each other, locked in an endless embrace of love, hate, and narcissism. Together we are condemned, forever to disappoint, never to forget even as we can't remember. Our snapshots and home movies create an American epic. It's fate, destiny. And why not? We are the country, and the country is us.

(What? No flash, again?!)

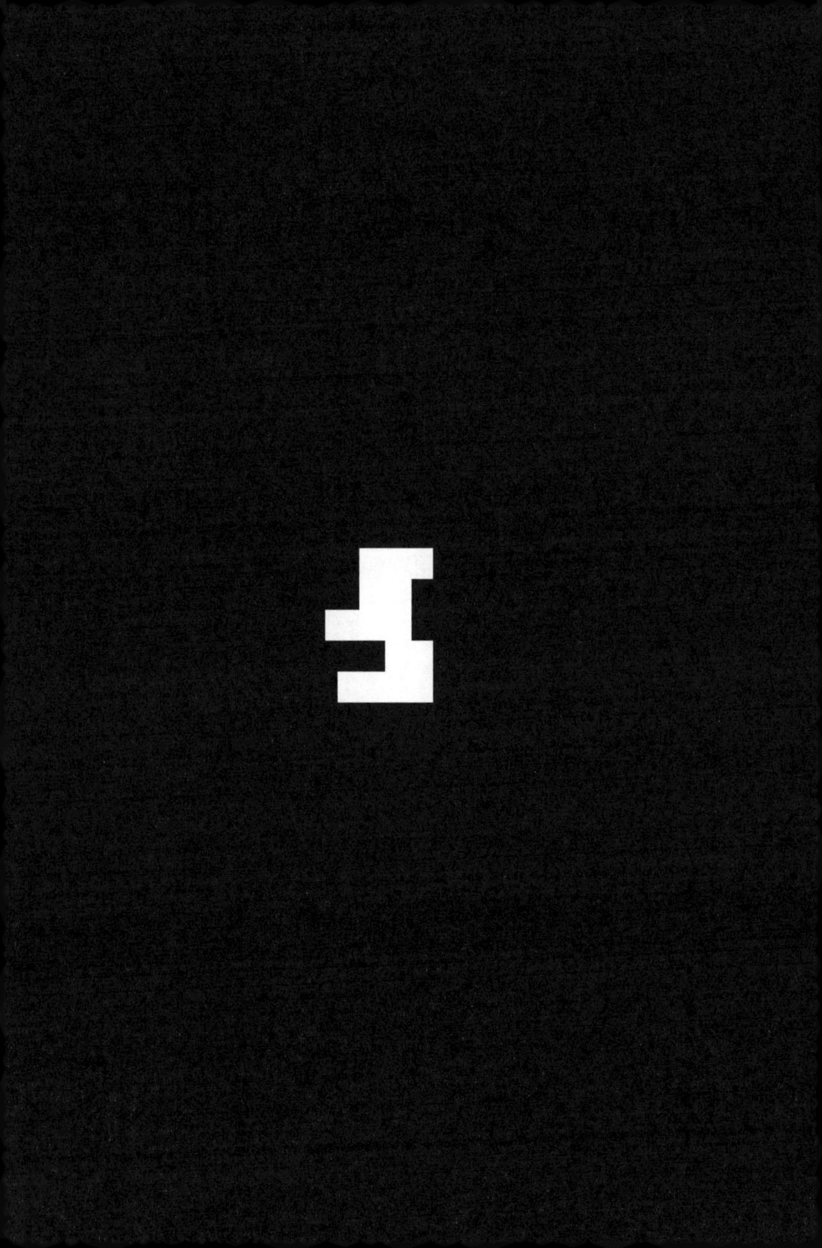

Way
We
Move
Lou
Cornum

Some of the first movies ever made were movies of Native Americans. In New York City in April 1894, those with the luxury of twenty-five cents to spend could enter a viewing parlor on 27th Street and Broadway, bend their eye to a viewing piece atop a podium-like structure and, for a fleeting few moments, watch Native figures stomping with style across a studio stage in full regalia. The film was *Buffalo Dance*, and it shared billing in the first ever commercial run of motion pictures with a variety of proto-genre flicks: there was comedy in a vaudeville act, violence and action in a cockfight film, slice-of-life realism in the barbershop and blacksmithing films—and exotic escape in the Indian movie. It was all made possible by the Kinetoscope, the recent invention of one Thomas Edison.

Buffalo Dance, *Sioux Ghost Dance*, *Indian War Council*, and *Buffalo Bill*—all of these were films produced in Edison's Black Maria studio in West Orange, New Jersey, that same year. As suggested by the last title, these early filmic depictions of Native Americans were indeed building off the popularity of Buffalo Bill's Wild West show, and several performers from the Wild West show were even employed to play the Native—that is, some projected version of themselves—for these early experiments in moving pictures. The figure of the "Indian" has been recurrent in the development of motion picture technologies. It's easy to think of these poses and performances as a macabre form of play-acting in the wake of defeat, capture, assimilation. The history of seeing on this continent has been about misapprehending Native people in order to expropriate the land they lived on—the settler surveyor sees the Indians in order to contain them. The eyepiece of a Kinetoscope becomes a portal to a way of life that the technology also enacts a measure of distance from. The Indian becomes an abstracted visual object while concrete tribal ways of life are supposedly rendered obsolete by the same devices that facilitate their representation to foreign audiences.

And yet.

I am not immune to the technologically produced sense of wonder: the chance to see Native people in motion, from more than a hundred years ago now—not the spectacle it was for its initial viewers and producers, but as a record of enduring presence. I come to the dancers not through the awkward eyepiece of the Kinetoscope but on my laptop screen while I sit on the couch. *Buffalo Dance* and *Sioux Ghost Dance* have been preserved and digitized for posterity and easy access by the Library of Congress, and uploaded to YouTube. Though I look straight at the screen, my viewpoint is crowded by the swarm of associations that come with the representation of Native. My reaction is a jumble of conflicting senses and feelings: a mix of dread, loss, compromise, desecration, as well as a transhistorical, cross-tribal desire for dignity in the midst of world-rending change and destruction.

It was a similar emotional cocktail that I imbibed while watching *The Exiles*, a 1961 film made by Kent Mackenzie, a white Brit, about a group of Native people making a life for themselves in Los Angeles, which is perhaps, not without contradiction, my favorite "Indian movie."

What makes a movie an Indian movie? It's in the way Indians move. And in this, the way Indians move the image.

I first came across *The Exiles* by complete chance in a Google Drive folder that was filled with links. It was the title that called to me; I was hailed by the collective naming before I even knew the movie was about Natives. I wasn't prepared for the first shots to be of Edward Curtis photographs, used much as they were intended as the last records of a lost race. Over images of Curtis's most iconic landscapes and portraits, the narrator of the film's prologue leads us from the end of the Indian Wars to the period of urban relocation (though none of these historical markers are named), remarking in voice-over on the modern Native who has "wandered into the cities." What came next was like an ancestral dream upon first viewing—like many dreams uncannily similar in the particulars while also completely unfamiliar and disorienting. The action follows, in the style of a dramatized documentary, a group of Natives going about their lives in the neighborhood of Bunker Hill over a period of twelve hours, from afternoon through to early morning.

I am interested in how the movement of these actors, their gestures, strides, and means of transport (usually a busted-up or overpacked car), transgresses or at the very least pushes against the binds of representation—in *The Exiles*, but also in "Native American" or "Indigenous" film more broadly, in media, and in life.

From its very first shots, *The Exiles* mediates between kinetic action and stillness. In a public market, a vendor slings potatoes with speed and agility into a paper bag while waves of shoppers swell around. Yvonne—played by Yvonne Williams, a young woman originally from the Whiteriver Apache community in northern Arizona—sits alone sipping a soda, her eyebrows ever-arched as she surveys the busy commerce around her, wearing a white sweater that gives off an ethereal glow in 35mm black and white. Throughout the film, Yvonne wanders the market and the shopfronts, a world of commodities, without anybody to talk to. We see her briefly at home plating sizzling pork chops for her layabout husband Homer (Homer Nish) and his rambunctious friends. The men are stolen by the night, hopping between bars, putting songs on the jukebox, and then driving up the hills to gather with the others around a drum, a song, a bottle.

In this cast of late-night marauders, Tommy (Tom Reynolds) is the most disappointing character. I was charm-struck by the scene in the bar where he mimes playing rock 'n' roll piano, relishing as he does the agile pantomime performance while his friends impatiently urge him to hit the road. Once Tommy and the gang get to their final destination, though, his boyish antics turn ugly and he tries to force himself on a young woman. The film, even with its occasional flights of fancy, is unflinching throughout. In comparison with the men's cruise on the edge of violence, Yvonne's evening is more contemplative. She sees a movie, window-shops, and visits a friend, the two of them eventually falling asleep next to each other.

Shortly after the film was made, Bunker Hill, the neighborhood where these Natives all lived, was razed.

Through the morass of obscured archives and lost connections, there are flashes of memory—some our own, others from others—that tell us how we came to be, or what we could become.

The poet Diane Burns became like that for me. She was born in Kansas to a Chemehuevi father and an Anishinaabe mother, and grew up in California before making her way east to New York City. Like finding *The Exiles*, finding her work and especially the 1987 short film that she features in, *Alphabet City Serenade*, felt like an excavation of an obscured inheritance. She seemed like someone I could have known if I had been born just ever so slightly sideways in time and place. I recognized her the moment I saw her, serenading with a poem the trashed lots and empty playing courts that she was walking through, streets too barren and too bustling, down and out in the Lower East Side.

Burns's voice-over: "Once they built the railroad, the buffalo fled past the horizon line. Once they built the railroad, now the railroad's gone. Brother, can you spare a dime?" She is shown from a distance, traversing an isolated, barren zone. There are multiple broken-down cars behind her on top of other twisted metal refuse and trashed objects, alluding to a continuation of the boom and bust cycles of production and death, like the construction of the railroad and the decimation of buffalo herds.

Those broken-down cars are a recurring image in Burns's output. On the cover of her 1981 chapbook *Riding the One-Eyed Ford*, she stands next to the passenger side of a Ford that's seen better days with one headlight crossed out. This illustration is superimposed over the classic photo of Geronimo in a Cadillac, taken in 1904. Burns, in a car that's always winking, and Geronimo in a top hat confusing the hell out of white America. One is riding from the nineteenth into the twentieth century, the other into the twenty-first—each bridging failures and possibilities, each moving the image of the American Indian in new ways.

The movement across country, whether it be eastward or westward, contains the often betrayed promise of movement upward in class—the frustrated dream of social (as economic) mobility. Yvonne in *The Exiles* and Burns both tread these dual meanings of mobility, and experience its frustrations. Both are restlessly searching while also seeking financial security. The difference between the two women, perhaps generational as much as temperamental, is that while Burns sneers "I hate Doris Day," Yvonne appears to be more drawn to the housewife aesthetic. In the 1960s, Native women coming to the city, be it LA, NYC, Chicago, or Phoenix, existed in a bind. They were escaping situations of immiseration or coercion—whether in boarding or vocational schools (institutions of assimilation and often abuse) or because of ostracization from their home communities—only to arrive to unsupportive urban chaos. Though in one sense these women approach "independence" (the feminist version of the American Dream), they are given few options. Yvonne's character is defined solely by her desire for a child, something of "her own" for once. Uninterested in Homer's carousing, her aspirations for love and fulfillment become aspirations for her child's imagined future, that they might attend college and have the things that she couldn't have in life.

The broken-down car becomes a war pony in *Powwow Highway*, a film from 1989 that was widely hailed as *the* Indian road movie until it was supplanted nine years later by *Smoke Signals* (as is typical in the inclusion logic of US culture, there can only be one). While, for some, the latter is perhaps besmirched beyond repair due to its association with the novelist Sherman Alexie (who adapted his short story "This Is What It Means to Say Phoenix, AZ" into the film's screenplay, and in recent years has faced multiple allegations of sexual harassment), there is at least one image worth salvaging for me, not least for the brilliant performances of Elaine Miles and Michelle St. John. They play two best friends cruising on the Coeur d'Alene reservation in a car with one particular quirk: it only works in reverse. In order to get anywhere, the woman driving must always be looking over her shoulder, surveying not only from where she may have come, but also where she is heading. What a beautiful testament to the counter-movements of Native life and history.

I thought of that looking-backwards-while-moving-forwards car from *Smoke Signals* while I was re-watching *Powwow Highway.* The film moves in a similar way, following a trip of detours from Northern Cheyenne reservation in Lame Deer, Montana, to Santa Fe, New Mexico. The driver is a holy fool trickster named Philbert, and his passenger is Buddy, a "hot-headed" activist type who wears his purple heart bone choker with an AIM (American Indian Movement) T-shirt and a denim jacket. Though they are moved with urgency to bail Buddy's sister Bonnie out of jail for Christmas, that doesn't prevent some meandering along the way, to the sacred Black Hills and the Pine Ridge reservation in particular. *Powwow Highway* is set fifteen years after the Occupation of Wounded Knee, when 200 Natives squared off with the FBI at Wounded Knee, South Dakota, site of the 1898 massacre of Lakota Sioux. As remains true today, the fractures have not healed. Despite the allusions to loss, community fragmentation, and continuing exploitation, the film also lingers not just on the movement but on movement itself. Movement through the scales of body and car, in the ways Philbert and Buddy dance and how Philbert's war pony-car, a 1964 Buick Wildcat, rips the bars off a jail window in Santa Fe. Though the movie ends with the Wildcat in flames, the group at least escapes police capture. In its zig-zag, jerking movements through space-time and the climactic midnight triumph of the rowdy Natives, *Powwow Highway* is a road movie against the grain. It also is based on a novel, by someone whose Native heritage is either murky or non-existent, and the movie was directed by a white man from South Africa. In a strange coincidence with my own interests, the writer of the original novel also wrote an autobiographic series, *The Roswell Trilogy*, about his family's experience with alien abductions and extraterrestrial encounters on army bases and other places around the world. Strange routes we all traverse to get where we are, or back to where we were, as it may be.

How can we move forward while looking backward?
To leap out of the frame of the present into the future,
that which is beyond settler enclosure and technologies of
containment, we must attend to the past. If the past is a sound
stage in New Jersey, it is also a field of yet to be realized
possibilities. There remains, as there was with Edison and his
Kinetoscope, an obsession with using the Native as a foil to

technological advancement. But it is with neither nostalgia for an unmediated past nor compliance with an engineered future that we continue the movements of those who came before us, and make way for those who will follow our dance across the cosmic screen.

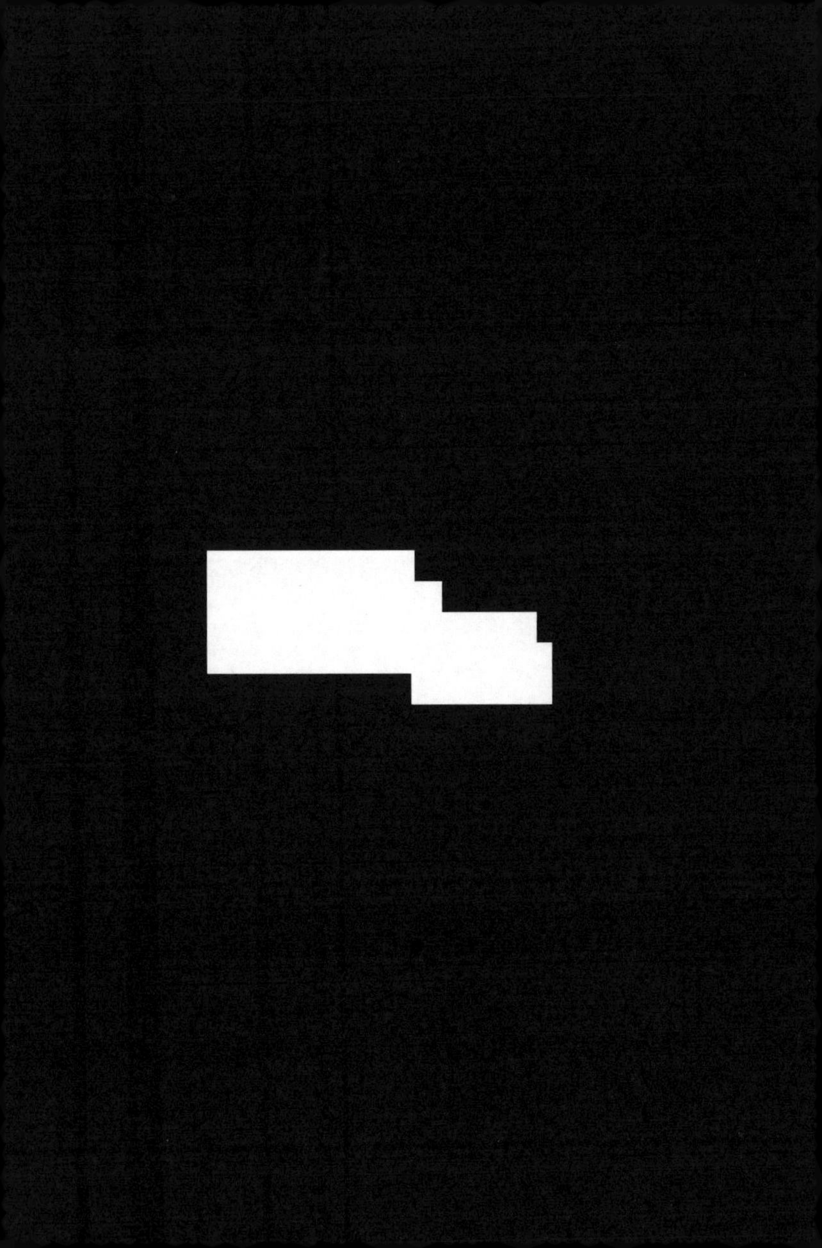

Pure Legend:
Dispatch From
an Incomplete Search
for the DeMille Indians

Adam Piron

Assigning meaning and form out of shapelessness is a uniquely, albeit consistent, human pursuit. Take, for example, mankind's recorded history of utilizing clay. In forms such as pottery through to building materials, cultural expression has been both figuratively and literally sculpted as a result of clay's extraction. Among these soil types, there exists a specific variant native to Armenia that has long been sought out for its distinct, earthy red pigment: Armenian bole. For centuries it was a popular go-to for everything from waterproofing sails to tile glazing, book binding, even alleviating diarrhea. One of its lesser-known uses, though, lay within Classical Hollywood. By dissolving this clay within water, make-up artists were able to derive a thin paste. The result was then applied, usually by means of a spray gun, to redden the pigment of non-Indigenous actors' skin in order to perform Native American roles in Western films. This cosmetic approach would later be known as performing in "redface."

A few years ago, I heard an outlandish story from my friend Adam Khalil. It was during my tenure as LACMA's Film Curator, when I was spending much time immersed in researching Hollywood's Golden Age and the Indigenous representation in American cinema of that era. A scholar in his own right on the history of Indigeneity in cinema, Adam told me about a story he had read in Michelle H. Raheja's *Reservation Reelism* about the "DeMille Indians." There had been a group of Native American performers, colloquially known as "Hollywood Indians," he recounted, who set out to petition the Bureau of Indian Affairs to form their own legally and culturally distinct tribe known as the DeMille Indians. As I initially understood it, these performers had all acted in the films of Cecil B. DeMille, a fact I later learned was not totally accurate. Adam said that according to Raheja's book, DeMille himself issued a number of commemorative pins to the members of this tribe who were using him as a namesake. What struck me about the story was that, given DeMille's ties to Paramount and its lot, these performers most likely would have been based in Los Angeles, thus making for a seemingly undocumented chapter of early Hollywood history. All of these pieces created something like a planetary alignment of my interests that led me down a years-long, and still ongoing, rabbit hole, trying to uncover any and every detail I could.

To understand this singular endeavor that the DeMille Indians had proposed—to realize an actual tribal entity within what's now known as the United States—one needs to understand what that actually means. It's not like forming a society, business, or a non-profit. It's an arduous legal process that a tribal group or community must undertake before the Bureau of Indian Affairs, a department within the federal government, for a level of recognition as a separate government that's both sovereign but at the same time subject to US law. Essentially, it's setting up for a nation-to-nation relationship. There are a number of different requirements and vetting that such a group has to face, such as proof of a consistent tribal government over centuries, an established Indigenous language, culture, etc.—which is what makes the idea of the DeMille Indians as a tribe so radical. They were a collective of Indigenous artists identified solely by a shared history of their work in relation to the moving image. Their culture was their own image and its history within cinema itself.

One bit of evidence towards tracking down the DeMille Indians lay in the story of the pins themselves. Unable to uncover any existing images of them, I was led down a path searching for any and all DeMille-related ephemera. This brought me to a series of pins commissioned by DeMille to celebrate the release of his *North West Mounted Police* (1940), a film which follows a Texas ranger, played by Gary Cooper, who rides north into Canada and helps the Mounties during the Riel Rebellion of 1885. The pins come in four variants: one of a Native American chief in profile, one of a brave in profile, another of a victorious Mountie holding a Native warrior in chains, and the last of a Texas Ranger also leading a warrior in chained bondage. Knowing what history has uncovered about DeMille's personal BDSM tastes brings an additional, discomforting layer to the already strikingly racialized images presented as promotional memorabilia. The film in question, though, was still the only surviving link that I had been able to find to anything related to the origins of the DeMille Indians.

At this point I have to give a shout-out to film critic Nick Pinkerton, who very generously let me use his newspapers. com account, which enabled me to track down a key article in the December 9, 1940 issue of the *Ames Daily Tribune* of Ames, Iowa, under the headline "DeMille's Indians Are Back Again." It's a promotional interview for DeMille's *North West Mounted Police* with Chief Thundercloud, one of the performers in the film, explaining his decision to formalize the group:

> "There are only a few of us real Indians in the film industry," he notified DeMille by letter. "Some of us frequently can't get work, although there are always plenty of Indian roles in pictures. Half the time the players who are supposed to be Indians are Mexicans or Filipinos or white men made up to look like Indians.
>
> But you always use real Indians in your pictures.
>
> Right now, I am organizing the real Indians of Hollywood into a social club, and out of tribute to you we are going to call ourselves the 'DeMille Indians,' because you have made that name almost as famous as the name of the real tribes. We think it is time there was an actual 'DeMille' tribe and we are going to be it."

According to an article in the *New York Herald Tribune* on November 17 of that same year, Thundercloud and a group of eighteen other unnamed members of the DeMille Indians were in the process of applying to the Bureau of Indian Affairs to be recognized as a legal tribe under the American government. What happened to the DeMille Indians, or their endeavors beyond 1940, is still unknown.

In the spring of 2020, a major tip to unlocking this mystery came my way. After tweeting about some of my research on the group, the filmmaker Joe Peeler reached out with a lead. At the time, Peeler was making a film on the Muscogee (Creek) Nation, and he introduced me to his subject's son: Professor Jacob Floyd, an Assistant Professor in Visual Studies at the University of Missouri who, I was told, had connected with the family of an actor that had been an actual member of the DeMille Indians. This family even had one of the elusive DeMille pins in their possession.

Once Floyd and I were able to connect roughly a year later, he was incredibly generous with both his time and his findings. Like me, he had run into a number of dead ends during his own search for more information on the group—but Floyd had found some key pieces. While he did not have an actual image of the DeMille pin in his possession, the family had shown an image of one to him. He described some of the details, namely that it featured the stereotypical profile of a Native American, and had inlaid text that said something along the lines of "DeMille Celebrates First Americans on Screen."

Floyd also informed me that the performer who once owned the pin had appeared in films under the screen name of Chief Rolling Cloud. Rolling Cloud, né Charles Brunner, was a member of Floyd's own tribe of the Muscogee (Creek) Nation in Oklahoma. Throughout the 1940s and into the '50s, Brunner found steady work in B-pictures, as well as larger studio fare such as Nicholas Ray's *Flying Leathernecks* (1951) and Budd Boetticher's *Seminole* (1953). Like many contemporary Native performers, his title of chief was concocted by the studio in order to mine an image of authentic Indigeneity as a selling point for the films in which he appeared. At the time, Brunner also ran with a crowd of Native (and some later to be revealed non-Native) actors who got similar gigs straddling studio productions, B-Westerns, and serials, including the likes of Jay Silverheels, Chief John Big Tree, George Sky Eagle, Chief Many Treaties, Chief Yowlachie, Chief Thundercloud, Iron Eyes Cody, and Chris Willow Bird.

According to Floyd's research for a forthcoming book on Indigenous performers of the era (the projected publication date is 2024, from the University of Nebraska Press), Hollywood in the 1920s–1940s was home to a melting pot of Native performers, many arriving in Los Angeles thanks to the production boom brought on by Westerns. They took on roles as actors, extras, stunt people, and cultural consultants. A major meeting location for many of them was the American Indian Art Shop on Hollywood Boulevard, across the street from Grauman's Chinese Theater. Originally founded by performers Chief Yowlachie (né Daniel Simmons) and his wife White Bird (Mary Simmons), this shop provided a hub for performers to sell their wares, as well as a space for cultural gatherings and for advocacy groups to meet— such as the War Paint Club, an organization meant to protect the rights of Native American actors and to discourage non-Native actors from playing Native roles. It is unclear whether the DeMille Indians were affiliated with the American Indian Art Shop or the War Paint Club directly, but these performers certainly occupied the same space and shared concerns during an era that saw Indigenous performers demanding increased agency, better working conditions, and more accurate representations onscreen.

One of the great ironies of the DeMille Indians lies with the case of Chief Thundercloud himself. It was later uncovered that this seemingly de facto spokesperson for the group was not even Indigenous at all. He was a charlatan. Born Victor Daniels in the then-territory of Arizona, he had falsely claimed that he was from Oklahoma, and alternated between identifying as either Cherokee or a descendant of the Muscogee aristocracy, of which there has never been such a thing. He continued to play Native roles and went to his grave denying the accusations and the proof surrounding his appropriated identity. After a series of legal troubles, he spent his final years performing in live Western shows for tourists at the Corriganville Movie Ranch in Simi Valley, before eventually succumbing to stomach cancer in 1955 at the age of 56. His final screen appearance was in John Ford's *The Searchers* (1956), released shortly after his passing.

After looking through the Bureau of Indian Affairs' archive of petitions for tribal recognition, there's no record nor even a mention of Chief Thundercloud, the DeMille Indians, or DeMille himself. It's another dead end, and further indication of what both Floyd and I have come to suspect: that the story about the formation of the DeMille Indians into an actual, legal tribe was probably the fantastic creation of the Paramount Pictures publicity machine. Much like the chieftain titles contrived for performers, this was probably another attempt to sell an audience an idea of Indigeneity, or at least a performance of it. Still, the pins themselves existed, and Brunner's own participation shows that there were actual Native performers involved. What did they think of all of this? Was it all advertised showmanship, or was it also something else? Why mention the Bureau of Indian Affairs when such a specific legal process would have gone over the heads of 99% of non-Native audiences? Today, there remain more unknowns than there are surviving fragments of the truth. Much like the plots of Westerns themselves, the DeMille Indians are the stuff of pure legend.

In part, you could say that the DeMille Indians would not have existed, even as an idea, were it not for Westerns. The need for the Indigenous image in these films spurred many Native performers to heed the call from productions looking for stoic villains, scouts, warrior extras, and behind-the-scenes cultural consultants. It was steady work that paid better than what they could find at home. Many found something like a home among their own in the backlot camps of Inceville early on, and later at the aforementioned American Indian Art Shop. Being away from one's tribal community was a new and uncertain identity that many Native performers had to navigate—something of a double-edged sword for those negotiating both their place and image within the larger Hollywood machine. Much like the idea of the DeMille Indians, the very notion of such a tribe questions who gets to determine what is and what isn't the Indigenous image.

Admittedly, even knowing that the proposal of such a tribe was probably nothing else but a joke to hype a DeMille film (of all things), it has created something of a feedback loop in my head that I haven't been able to escape. There's an apocryphal beauty to all of it. It asks how we as Indigenous people can define ourselves, and what our sovereignty can mean when we affirm it beyond the dynamics set forth by the terms and conditions of our settler colonial states. Coupled with cinema, it also presents a radical notion: inverting the concept of a national cinema by forming an actual nation shaped by a history of the moving image. It's an ouroboros of self-determination, control, and cinema's power; a cycle of death and rebirth. The DeMille Indians may have not been an answer to anything, let alone film's exploitation of Indigenous people, but in a way they're something like a starting point.

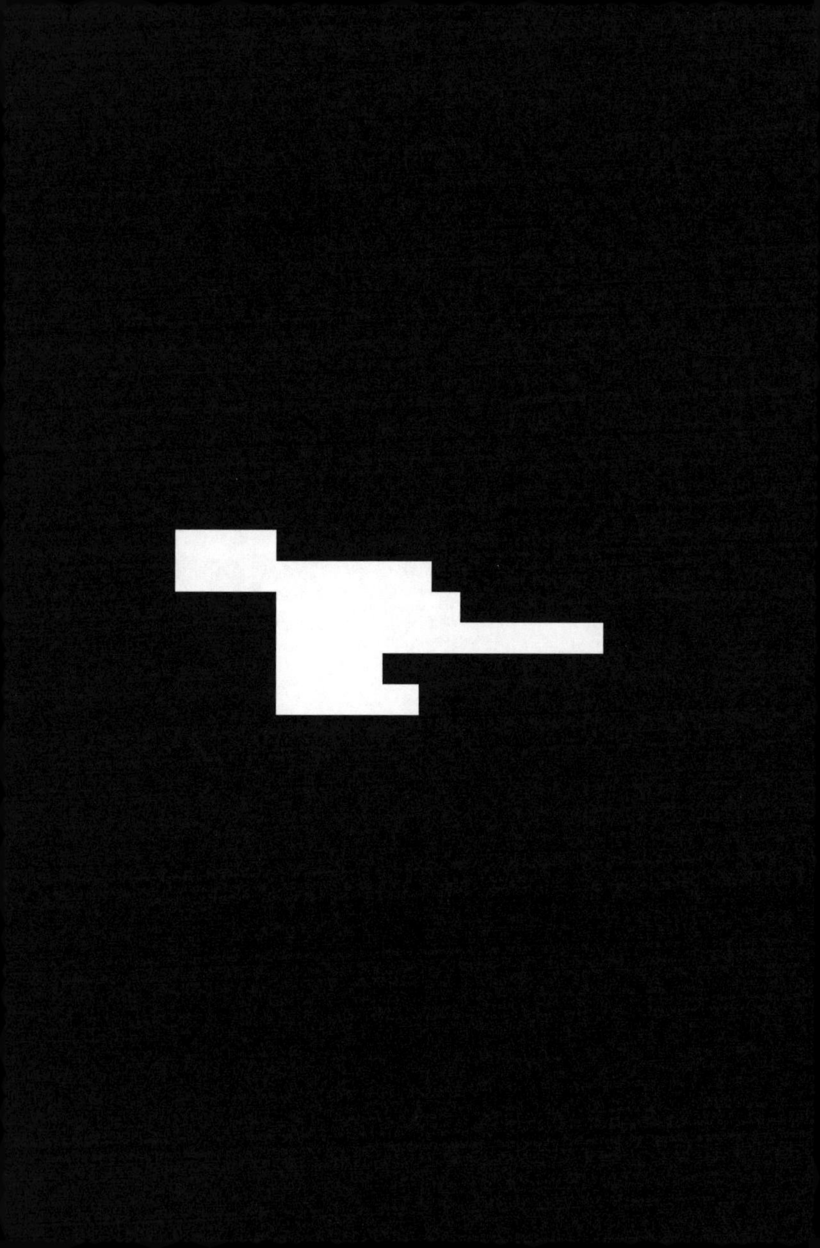

To End and Begin Again: The Work of Victor Masayesva, Jr.

Elizabeth Weatherford

From his earliest involvement with media production in the
1980s, Hopi videomaker, filmmaker, and photographer Victor
Masayesva, Jr. has displayed a complex sensibility and
a strong sense of community-based purpose. Living in the
Hopi community of Hotevilla, Arizona, and participating in
a range of media activities, Masayesva integrates experiences
of a strongly traditional American Indian world and the
various discourses around Native American media found in
artistic, academic, and media production. For the growing
circle of Native producers, Masayesva is a major figure for an
additional reason—he is personally engaged in creating ways
for an Indigenous media movement to emerge in the United
States and internationally. Masayesva is energetic in creating
projects to further this aim, and in recent statements has also
considered the means by which Native American producers
can best create an aesthetic specific to their own cultural and
artistic outlook.

Masayesva is independent in perspective and
practice, and in his work avoids the didacticism typical of
documentaries. Often viewers come to these works with
fixed notions of how Native Americans should be represented
and their histories and cultures explained. Masayesva does
not believe that Indian cultures can be reduced to simple
metaphors for the purpose of discussion, a frequent strategy
of popular anthropology.[1] He contends, for example, that the
quest of ethno-filmmakers with the Hopi has been to present
them as the "people of peace." But in at least one of his
productions, *Itam Hakim, Hopiit* (We/someone, the Hopi, 1984–
85), Masayesva opens his story with a Hopi historian's narrative
about a bitter and bloody historical struggle among Hopi. Also,
Masayesva reveals information in a developmental way, as if
mirroring Hopi patterns for instruction in which initiation into
the implications of knowledge is a precondition for being the

recipient of further information. Information is unfolded, to be apprehended at different levels of understanding according to the viewer's familiarity with Hopi or general Native American knowledge. Though strongly based on interviews, his *Imagining Indians* (1992) also presents the experiences of numerous Indians whose accounts mount a case about the intrusion of film into Indian communities.

With an experimental attitude toward media, Masayesva seeks rich, associative combinations throughout the visual track. In *Pott Starr* (1990) he experiments with animation in the opening sequence of a video concerned with a major museum exhibition on Pueblo pottery. In this sequence, a Native woman in traditional dress carrying a water pot is seen sinuously walking to the water, a sly reference to the eroticized feminine image with pots often seen on picture postcards of the Southwest. Masayesva uses animation to express something complexly sacred, reorienting the viewer to what Pueblo pottery means in *Pott Starr* by depicting bowls and their symbolic motifs whirling through the Indian landscape in which chasms, peaks, and waterways are often places of sacred history. In *Ritual Clowns* (1992), he animates symbols from Hopi design, and figures representing various Hopi sacred clowns, to portray the key protagonists in traditional Hopi history with its emphasis on the disruptive and creative aspects of existence.

Masayesva's artistry extends to other video techniques. Implying the multileveled states of being that are represented in the Hopi stories of origin, Masayesva devised in *Ritual Clowns* an elaborate graphic tableau through which images of harmony and disruption are projected. His experiments with colorization highlight some of his presentations. *Itam Hakim, Hopiit* features a long interlude of repetitive images of invading conquistadors, in color shades distorted through digital manipulation.[2]

Masayesva is an active participant in the highly traditional Hopi community at Hotevilla, yet he has been exposed to many

     Elizabeth Weatherford

aspects of the world outside the Hopi mesas. As a teenager he was awarded a scholarship to attend a well-regarded prep school in New York, and he continued his education at Princeton University. While there he was encouraged to explore the cultural history of the Hopi for his coursework. Masayesva found himself unwilling to write a major paper in any language other than Hopi. From early on he asserted that his expressive capacity would be best served in languages other than English—visual language and the Hopi language are his tools for eloquence.

When he returned to his own community, Masayesva became engaged in a series of photography projects.[3] In 1980, under the federally funded Ethnic Heritage Program, a short-lived initiative for the development of culturally specific curricula, Masayesva created a project with the Hopi community schools in which oral histories of elders would be used to teach Hopi language and values, as well as to demonstrate the adults' knowledge of traditional skills. For the project he began by using a video camera and trained an all-Hopi crew of high school students in video production. Ironically, Masayesva recently found these early tapes thrown out by the school. In recounting this story he does not hesitate to wryly comment on what this tells the videomaker about the importance of his work. Perhaps this action demonstrates the difficulty of sustaining interest in tribal heritage among today's Indian youth. But perhaps it is also a revealing look at values articulated by the Hopi and other Pueblo groups—the preservation of objects is not important; rather, importance is placed on the continuation of traditional practices. For instance, the masks of ceremonial dances are to be buried with their user upon his death, rather than preserved in his absence. For the Hopi, videotapes have an ambiguous relationship to lived reality and could be seen as inappropriately preserving the elders' images past the duration of their own lifetimes.

Masayesva's early videomaking was undertaken in a context of a community that has had great concern about the process of being documented. From the first days of photography in the nineteenth century, photographers and tourists saw the Hopi and their dances as a compelling subject. The distinctive qualities of their communities, which include the oldest known community in the United States, Oraibi, led anthropologists and popular writers to try to penetrate the Hopi philosophical system, while missionaries and teachers attempted to alter that philosophy forever. The filming of the Hopi has been vigorously pursued by white documentarists, museums with Hopi art collections, and anthropologists. Some elders, given the charge to convey the Hopi prophecy, have seen in film a chance to spread their message worldwide. Masayesva's work has developed as a response to these mediations of Hopi belief and worldview created for outside audiences. But there is in the community a wariness about media, even internally. Masayesva has pointed this out himself, commenting on how he has been perceived in his community in his role as photographer as a "katcina, a spiritual being, one of that category of katcinas who involve themselves with buffoonery, burlesque, and social commentary,"[4] and that some Hopi see him as obnoxious. Even his acts of mediation are being held in question. But Masayesva tries to strike a different note in his work, by staying focused on Hopi knowledge for Hopi audiences, rather than on the interpretation of Hopi-ness by and for outsiders. This radical shift frees the filmmaker.

In addition to his portraits of elders, Masayesva produced two highly original videotapes from footage shot during the Ethnic Heritage project. *Hopiit* (1981) is a montage of different views of Hopi landscapes and people during the cycle of a year. In every scene the view is unusual, and no narrative is supplied. He shows visually stunning views, such as the concluding image of an old woman stacking numerous ears of blue corn like cordwood.

Inspired by one of the elders' strong interest in being involved with the video production, Masayesva produced his first long video, *Itam Hakim, Hopiit*, three years later. In this innovative work one of the last members of the Hopi historians' clan, Ross Macaya, recounts various epochs in Hopi history. The production consists of visual sequences and frequent close-ups, with a narrative audio track that is complemented, although not specifically illustrated, by what is seen. The vignettes, including scenes of landscapes, cascading blue grains of corn, and a captive eagle in the rain, strike the viewer as still photographs prolonged through time and motion by being on video.

The production opens with a clear assertion that Masayesva is presenting an unidealized view: a close-up shot of Macaya's feet in old sneakers as he goes to fill a bucket with water. The elder is dressed in his own worn clothes and lives in a simple house without many amenities. Macaya evokes four epochs of history, beginning with his own life story as it was affected by his father's insanity. He then recounts the origin of the Hopi and explains how, through the intervention of Ma'asaw, a sacred culture hero responsible for creativity and for death, they came to be. The Spanish invasion and the Pueblo Revolt of 1680 (to which the program is dedicated) are depicted by using repetitive images of horseback-riding conquistadors, accompanied by an endless loop of Renaissance music, juxtaposed against contemporary images of Hopi ritual runners (the uprising occurred simultaneously in all participating communities because of the effectiveness of Pueblo runners in contacting them).

Macaya's tale concludes with a particularly Hopi type of history: the Hopi Prophecy. The apocalyptic nature of things out of kilter is suggested by scenes, in normal and sped-up time, of Hopi social dances (including dances that spoof the apparent chaos of Indians from other tribes who have taken on white clothes and culture). This is followed by a final scene, the serene image of two people at work in the fields; according to the Prophecy this is how the creative cycle continues—the world will end and begin again.

Throughout this work Masayesva carefully chose imagery to correspond to the elder's account. Frequently the visuals present symbols particularly meaningful to a Hopi audience. For example, as the elder tells of the origin of death, the tape shows a captive eagle in close-up. What the Hopi audience knows is that the eagle is to be ceremonially sacrificed in order for feathers to be obtained for use in acts of prayer. Children are seen, probably on a cultural heritage visit to Macaya's cabin, but they are rowdy or bored and play dangerously with a kerosene lamp. The tone reflects the chaos and unpredictability of life, and the unfolding quality of human experience in which life's lessons are to be learned.

Although produced in the Hopi language, clearly with a Hopi audience in mind, *Itam Hakim, Hopiit* received funding from German national television (ZDF). Its screenings in the United States were initially in Hopi.[5] Yet opportunities for distribution and new audiences pressed Masayesva to create a version in English. For the next several years, the implications of the white-dominated cultural world's increased interest in his work would also become its central theme. Masayesva's productions began focusing on the many ways in which whites have misunderstood Hopi culture, while continuing to insist on the right to interpret it. He began to be contacted for commissions. Two productions—*Pott Starr* and *Siskyavi: The Place of Chasms* (1991)—were made for museums. He also received one of the first Intercultural Media Fellowships from

   Elizabeth Weatherford

the Rockefeller Foundation, which enabled him to work with computer animation and graphics.

Masayesva has never received funding from the Corporation for Public Broadcasting's (CPB) Native American Public Broadcasting Consortium, whose mission has been focused on support for productions that might gain a broadly based American TV audience, rather than on experimental media. However, in the first year of the Independent Television Service, a new CPB initiative urged into being by the independent film and video arts community, Masayesva was granted funds for the production of a major work. The time was ideal for further reflection on the implications of white intrusions on Native realities, and Masayesva turned his attention to filmmaking itself. In 1993 he released *Imagining Indians*, a unique work that draws its energy from its layered inquiry into the effects of white intrusion upon Native individuals and communities. His principal focus is a strong critique of Hollywood movies as projects instigated by outsiders who not only disrupt, but inevitably exaggerate differences within the community. Interviews initially were held with many Native Americans who had participated in Hollywood productions, and then with Native American media-makers and cultural critics. Early on, Hollywood decided to shoot films on location on Indian lands with Indian extras to create a feeling of authenticity. What commands most attention in *Imagining Indians* is the examination of films as social projects, sowing disruption while perpetuating the myth that Indian cultures are easy for whites to understand.

Masayesva intercuts interviews with a fictional scene in which an Indian patient (acted by Patty Runs After Swallow) suffers through the ministrations of an intrusive dentist. The piece, like his other work, creates a mounting indictment of white attitudes. It is also witty, and in the presentation of the broadly stereotyped dentist mirrors what he has been saying about the usual way that images of Indians are frequently substituted for more authentic portrayals.

Masayesva provides a critical look at Indian accommodations to white ways. For example, his inclusion of footage of powwow dancing, with the components of competition and colorful public show, is a critique of some Indians having lost the thread that connects dance with spiritual practice. In such scenes as the meeting of Hopi leaders concerned about permitting the filming on their lands of a movie based on the Tony Hillerman novel *The Dark Wind*, he shows the Hopi community divided over an agreement to permit the filming. He exposes the most dearly held of white attitudes—the non-Native's professed love of the beauty of Indian ways, an affection that fails to comprehend the complexity and Native definition of these ways. Masayesva examines his own position as a media-maker with this same, even gaze. Thus at the end of *Imagining Indians*, the dental patient herself drills into the camera lens (Masayesva's camera!), and the very well-intentioned Indian portraits painted by George Catlin in the 1840s dissolve into little color particles. The film ends with the sounds of Indians speaking in their own languages.

Masayesva is committed to exposing the *bahana*, or white-man mentality, which has so strongly affected Indian lives. The clearest statement of this white world view is found in the privileged place it gives to acquisition, ownership, and appropriation. To Masayesva, Indian creativity is appropriated when arts are purchased for white collections; in *Imagining Indians* the freedom of white filmmakers to use Indians to "authenticate" their films is likened to the art buyers at Indian Market and at the antiquities marketplace. Even more profound, the source of all future creativity is depleted when

     Elizabeth Weatherford

whites devalue through appropriation the traditional language, songs, and histories from which the Indian community would continue to draw its arts. Finally, reflecting carefully on the image-making enterprise, Masayesva is concerned with the process by which whites feel that they own Indian knowledge and therefore can freely represent Indians in films, scholarly works, and discourse.

For Masayesva, knowledge is always best gained through exploring ideas in their original context. In his recent work he has been even sharper in his metaphoric critique of whites converting Native cultural practice and belief into collectibles.[6] Every artifact is embedded with a knowledge of sacred sites and symbolic representations of Indian philosophy. In *Imagining Indians*, by adding scenes of Indian Market's satisfied white customers to his critique of the way Hollywood employs Native actors and locales, he completes the circle of associations.

By the early 2000s, Masayesva reached the end of a long period of concern with *bahana*, with the impact of white mentality on Indian lives and arts.[7] He began to stress in forums, such as various film festivals and symposia, that a Native American media-maker's first obligation is to their community, and that he believed the source of all future Hopi creativity is to be found within the community.

This is perhaps one of Masayesva's concerns that is most difficult to grasp for people outside contemporary Indian community life. In the non-Native world, progressive media has been associated with widening the distribution of information and viewpoints generally suppressed from the public. For Native Americans an alternative view is that their media can focus on aspects of culture that can affect public opinion, but that privileging Native access to anything internal to their own communities is the right of each Native community. In recognizing this, Native media makers ideally would be given the primary responsibility of mediating Native situations, above all because they would best understand the processes by which community elders would hold them accountable for their media works.[8] For Masayesva, Native Americans rooted in their community appreciate knowledge as something achieved, not something to be distributed equally. This mirrors the Hopi process by which young people become initiated in stages into full adult awareness and knowledge.

Masayesva's attention has been drawn to concerns with Native filmmakers and communities, and their own communication with each other. A founding participant in the movement to form inter-American Indigenous media-makers alliances and a founder of the North American Producers Alliance in the United States, Masayesva is currently working to help unify independent Native media-makers and to further their access to resources for making productions that reflect a deeper version of Indian experience. Masayesva recognizes media-making as a creative social project as well as an artistic one, although, always skeptical, he does not assume that media is always beneficial and nurturing. He sees deep benefits, however, in Indigenous-to-Indigenous communications, and is currently exploring new projects reflecting this. He is developing productions in collaboration with other Native filmmakers in both the United States and Mexico, thus conveying Indian stories with strong shared meanings across borders that may have been artificially imposed.

For Masayesva, the purpose of his work includes making space for the development in Native terms of an aesthetic, even a technology, for the future. The source for the development of a uniquely Native aesthetic resides in filmmakers drawing from their own people's knowledge, tribal stories, and languages. But he is also exploring a fast-dwindling option, and he knows it: "Native American filmmakers have run out of the luxury of access to the creative old-timers for whom language and song was the ultimate human creation."[9] With the sense of this valuable "community property," Masayesva has been active in developing protocols for the future production of Native images within Native communities. He is also defining the application of "cultural copyright" protection, a sphere in which, through moral suasion and community agreement, the investigator respects the community's ownership of knowledge and practice.

In this atmosphere, Native Americans are given the opportunity to have first access to the work of their culture's interpretation. In Masayesva's view, their creativity will flow from their actions toward those in the community most conversant with the people's historical versions. He asserts that Native filmmaking, if it succeeds, will do so because Native Americans will know when their topics are appropriate for public circulation, and when their subject matter may be too private.

As with his own work, Masayesva considers Native audiences as the primary audience for Native work. His documentaries, always provocative, have reserved the right to teach without didacticism, as in the best Native storytelling, in which the audience's knowledge is counted on for filling in details that are lightly suggested in the narrative. The shift in the notion of audience creates for the non-Native viewer a chance at achieving a truly alternative perspective, and at becoming aware of how events are seen by Native Americans. This same shift moves the discussion of Native Americans as a minority to allow a way in which Native media can free itself to be itself.

This brilliant, innovative media artist retains the independence of the elders, to create, to explore a prophesy of recreation in the future, and to be truthful about internal as well as external forces pushing Native communities. His concerns have drawn him to deeper commitments to nurturing other young talented film- and video-makers and their critical voices.

Afterword (September 2022)

Over the last two decades, Victor Masayesva has been active with new projects that focus on community and the diverse perspectives that occur, especially around potentially controversial events. Committed to recognizing how many variations make up any community's "history," Masayesva is a strong participant in the education of young people, encouraging them to learn in depth, within the community and from its elders, about their own culture and its practices.

His newest projects have included working with Indigenous filmmakers from other tribes in collaborations that explore distinctly Indigenous cosmologies. The idea is to use tools of media-making to create a space for Indigenous ways of thought. In *Waaki* (2019), a co-production with Mariano Estrada Aguilar (Tzeltal Maya) and José Luis Matias (Nahuat), the story focuses on Hopi, Nahua, and Mayan communities, and the ritual practice and thought—and the agricultural knowledge—that produces maize/corn. The connections and interrelationships of the people to corn are confirmed in each community's traditions of song and ceremony. *Pensoyungham: People with the Pencil–Hopi Prisoners at Alcatraz 1894-95* (2022), a production intended for the Hopi communities of the Third Mesa in Arizona, explores a still painful historic event. The viewer is given direct knowledge of diverse positions about what are the best actions to take when powerful outsiders intervene within community practices. The only commentary is the animation framing each "chapter" of the film of a metaphoric mockingbird, who represents how slippery interpretation can be. The video intends also to serve as an inspiration for young Hopi community members to learn their own history, and to refocus on the hard-won right to have education in their own community.

Recently, Masayesva has been engaged in a project initiated by Earth Timekeepers, an international group of Indigenous timekeepers who have been meeting every two years since the advent of the current Maya count in 2013. Masayesva has agreed to develop media, and to express through it the Timekeepers' deep concern about environmental "sorrows" coming on the Earth, with a forecast of thirteen years for course correction. The purpose—as in much of Masayesva's work—is also for community youth to learn how they are connected to the cosmos.

The first production, created for projection on a dome, is intended for Otomí community screenings in Mexico's Central Plateau. In 2022, the pilot was shown at a planetarium in Toluca for an audience who could provide feedback regarding the appropriateness of dome/VR technology for the conveyance of Otomí traditional knowledge. It was greeted with approval and two more screenings are anticipated in remote Otomí communities using a portable dome for projection. The project will continue into full production, and interest has already been expressed in working on cosmological projects with Hopi, Kiowa, and possibly Maori, Navajo, and Cree.

1. An excellent recent article about Masayesva's work is Fatimah Tobing Rony, "Victor Masayesva, Jr. and the Politics of *Imagining Indians*," *Film Quarterly* 48, no. 2 (Winter 1994-95): 20-33.

2. At this time a growing movement of Native American artists resulted in the formation of ATLATL, a professional organization. Its founding director, Erin Younger, worked with Masayesva on Victor Masayesva, Jr., and Erin Younger, eds., *Hopi Photographers/Hopi Images* (Tucson: University of Arizona Press and Sun Tracks, 1984).

3. For longer descriptions of his works produced before 1988, see Elizabeth Weatherford and Emelia Seubert, *Native Americans on Film and Video*, 2 vols. (New York: Museum of the American Indian, 1988), 2: 36-37, 42-43.

4. Masayesva and Younger, *Hopi Photographers*, 10-11.

5. The work had its New York premiere at the Museum of the American Indian-Heye Foundation's Native American Film and Video Festival. Shortly thereafter it was selected for the video series Video Viewpoints at the Museum of Modern Art, New York, and an illustrated transcript was supplied to the audience. The video art distributor Electronic Arts Intermix then took on the production in its English language version. See Masayesva's statement in the catalog for the Imagining Indians: Native American Film and Video Festival presented by the Scottsdale Center for the Arts in Scottsdale, Ariz., June 2-5, 1994. Masayesva was Creative Director of this festival.

6. Victor Masayesva, Jr., acceptance speech for the American Film Institute's 1995 Maya Deren Award for Independent Film and Video Artists, February 2, 1995, Anthology Film Archives, New York.

7. Victor Masayesva, Jr., "Through Native Eyes: The Emerging Native American Aesthetic," *Independent*, December 1994, 27.

8. Ibid., 21.

9. Ibid.

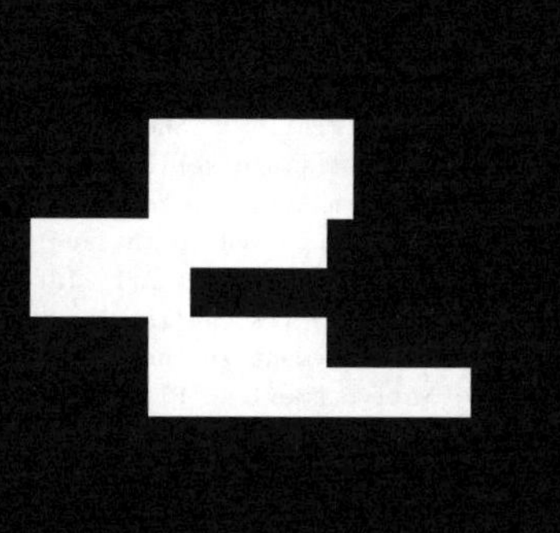

Cousins and Kin:

A Conversation
Between
Fox Maxy
and Shelley Niro

The following post-screening conversation between filmmakers Shelley Niro and Fox Maxy took place on June 14, 2021, hosted by the San Francisco Cinematheque, as part of Cousins and Kin, a series curated by COUSIN Collective—both a survey and a culmination of the moving images that we've presented, individually and collectively, over the years. The question of how to find other Indigenous filmmakers who were making work that is experimental and exciting was where we began. How to support and share their films is where we were building towards at this moment.

Program Three in the series centered on Niro's *Honey Moccasin* (1998), which has stood as a high-water mark of experimental Indigenous cinema for over twenty years. Set on the fictional Grand Pine Indian Reservation, Niro's film looks at the world and tribal members around its titular character, played by Tantoo Cardinal. Whether the film is jumping from performance art sequences to a mock cable access show or to a tongue-in-cheek crime mystery, it melds an irreverent cinematic language from elements of pop culture and a distinct brand of Native humor.

Honey Moccasin defies any notion of traditional categorization. Niro takes no authoritative stance on questions of identity nor delivers any kind of thesis on Indigeneity; rather, her invitingly playful and exuberant film weaves its way through a multitude of approaches to present a surreal spectrum of subjective meanings. The film's own open-endedness—and the nuance born of this open-endedness—has cemented its reputation as an underground classic of '90s Indigenous cinema, and as ultimately timeless in its accessibility and concerns. A forerunner to the recent blossoming of experimental work by Indigenous artists, Niro's film embodies the ethos of work by Indigenous artists that COUSIN Collective seeks to champion through its mission.

The conversation that follows was live-streamed through the San Francisco Cinematheque website. It has been edited for length and clarity. *—Adam Piron*

ADAM PIRON: For everybody tuning in, Shelley's work is something that was really inspirational for all of us at COUSIN, and with our formation. Around when I met Sky Hopinka for the first time—I want to say it was back in 2015—he shared *Honey Moccasin* with me. It really blew my mind, not only seeing formally what Indigenous artists have been doing for a while, but also that there's a legacy for this type of work. And also just as a source of inspiration, seeing other Indigenous filmmakers and artists making these types of works. So it's a huge honor to have Shelley here. With this program in particular, it feels like a lot of stuff has come full circle. Again, thanks, Shelley. So: how did this film come about? How did it get made, and how was it conceived? I want to know everything about it.

SHELLEY NIRO: Well, this was my second film. I made another short film called *It Starts With a Whisper* in '92. I did that with a partner, but this one I had wanted to do by myself. So I sat down and started writing it in '93, I think. That's the great thing about writing, you don't know what's going to appear on your computer. As one thing starts to develop, things take you to other places as well. I started out by thinking about the end of World War II—'95 was the 50th anniversary. It's not that I wanted to make a point of saying, "Okay, now we're at the end," or, "Now we're going to celebrate the 50th anniversary," but I wanted to touch on that very briefly.

And I wanted to see what *wasn't* being discussed in Native film. At the time, there didn't seem to be too many two-spirited people involved in any kind of film. I thought, "Well, I'm going to put a two-spirited person in this picture and make them one of the main characters"—as it turned out, that character was the culprit as well. As far as the story goes, they're the one who is stealing the powwow clothes from people on the reserve, and people on the reserve are going crazy about it: "Somebody's taking our stuff, and a powwow is coming on, and we don't know what to do!" But then one of the elders comes on board and says, "We have these materials, we can sit down and make our own outfits again." That's the basic storyline. [And then] there's an experimental film within the film. The character Mabel Moccasin [Florence Belmore], she's a filmmaker just getting out of film school, who wants to share with her community the things that she's doing. [Her film uses] a poem by Daniel David Moses—Daniel, he passed away last year. So because his poem is in there, and he makes a small appearance, it's now about archiving him, his voice and his poetry. There's so many things going on in this film. I don't know where it came from, I don't know how it really ended, but it was like, I'm just going to put as much in there as I can.

AP: That's one of the things I find super inspiring—also for the work that I'm trying to shift towards now, too. There's such a, I hate saying "free-flowing," but there's such ease in the way that your film shifts gears throughout. And because I think—probably similar to what you were saying around some of the stuff with Native film, or some artists—that there tends to be a propensity to make a statement of "This is what it's like to be Indigenous," and, like, for everybody. One of the things that's so great about this film is that it's not interested in taking any authoritarian stance on identity. It's more saying, "Hey, these are some of the folks that I know. And I'm kind of like this person, I'm kind of like that person, we're all different kinds. We don't agree on everything, and we look different, etc." Even going back to what you were talking about in terms of the creation of this film, that is so unique about it. I know that touches on some of your other work, too. Could you talk about that a little?

SN: Yeah. I do photography, I do some painting, some sculpture, and I try to incorporate beadwork into my work as well because beadwork is probably the oldest tradition of Native art-making in North America. I grew up doing beadwork and it's like comfort food. It's something that you can always return to because you know how to make something look good if you're using beads. And for me, beadwork was one of those things that was looked at as kind of a sellout; if you're making beadwork to sell, it's like, "Oh, you're just doing it for tourists." But in some regards it was the only way of making money at the time. So I like to bring honor to people who have done beadwork. I like to remind people that there was a time when beadwork wasn't always an accepted artform. Now if you look at beadwork, it's amazing. People have really taken that one little bead and that little needle, and they've managed to make these monuments, little monuments, but they're still quite extraordinary pieces of work.

And photography is just something that I can use to archive people around me. Archives are a big, important part of my art-making, although I've only realized it in the last few years, because as you go through your art-making life, you're building up these images. Then after, what, 30, 40 years, it's like, "Oh, I do have these images of this person, this person, this person." And you can see them changing from a youthful person to a much older person. The same thing goes with filmmaking. I try to put people in my film so that you can see them, and you can always return back to that image. Because I used to think that watching films, you get to see, like, stars—you get to see them age, and go through different cycles of their life. And now we are having that. We are seeing people. In my films, I like to put people in those positions as well.

AP: Can you talk a little bit about what your process is like, working under or across so many different mediums? Is it different for each project, or what does it look like for you when you approach a project, and then as you work your way through it?

SN: Well, filmmaking takes so long. You start with the script, and it takes forever to develop it to a point where it's like: I think it's good, I can film this now. You get to the point where you start looking for your production crew, and you start getting all those details down. It takes so much time. It takes so much energy because you're working with so many people. And the financial part of making a film is also really demanding. When I finish a program or a project, I feel like, *whew*. And then I just want to draw with a pencil, sit there and just do the most simple act, as far as art-making goes—could be with a pencil or it could be with beadwork—but it's a way of shaking a lot of that stress away. I think if you're making a film and you're not stressed, you're probably not doing it right. At the same time I think it's just your brain—I know I'm only using half my brain, so I have to think of something else to use the other half for. It's a way of shifting, and stimulating, and becoming excited about what you can do, because filmmaking is something you can't do by yourself. You have to have people around you, you have to have actors around you. You have to have all these people, which is pretty exciting on its own, just to be able to communicate your ideas with all these people. But when that is done, it's really relieving to know that you don't need all these people to make something. You can just do it on your own. So I just shift everything around.

AP: Fox just joined us. Hey Fox, how's it going?

FOX MAXY: Hi everyone. My apologies. I had some family business, but I'm here in my car, ready to talk to you guys, and I'm so happy to be here.

AP: Awesome.

SN: Hi Fox.

FM: Hi Shelley.

AP: Fox, I was talking to Shelley about making her work,
which is also across many different mediums.
I was wondering if you could talk a little bit about
your process as well? I was just speaking to
someone earlier today who was mentioning your
films—a mutual friend of ours, Woodrow Hunt,
shout out to him if he's listening in. We were
talking about the sheer volume of work that you
make, and that there's such a clear voice behind
it, which in a lot of ways is... there's definitely
some crossover with Shelley's work in the sense
that it's not making any authoritative statement on
Indigeneity, or speaking for anybody other than
yourself. You just finished a film too, right?

FM: Yeah. I just finished a film called *Gush* and it's a 30-minute
film about rape and being a survivor of these
things. I feel like my process is very emotional,
so it's definitely a way to work on things, and
a way to just be with my own self, and be with my
own questions, and my own thoughts. I think you
mentioned this before, but I really don't have any
answers to anything. So I feel like making a film
is a great way to process, to be asking questions,
and to be safe in that because there's not a lot of
people who personally I can go talk to. Making
a film is doing that for myself, and it's real important.
That's one of the first things that I got to learn from
people in different Native communities while I was

at Standing Rock: I listened to a lot of people, and they were saying the only thing that we can do is really speak for ourselves. That stuck with me, and has been huge for my filmmaking, because it's a very sensitive thing to tell somebody else's story or put words in other people's mouths. I'm just trying to focus on my own thoughts and things like that. That's the process, I guess.

AP: One of the other things in both of your work is, maybe I'm projecting this, but how it references a lot of other media that you've watched, and which has perhaps been an influence. Shelley, with *Honey Moccasin* there's the mystery aspect, the detective story, there's some hints of Wonder Woman even in there, superheroes—and performance art as well! And Fox, you have a lot of archival footage, and stuff from social media, too. Do either of you want to talk about how other media has affected your work, or how you approach that?

SN: I can step in here. I grew up in a reserve. We were really poor, and I often think about how me and my sisters and brother would sit around the TV on a cold winter night watching *Vignetting* or something. For us then, film was like magic. It was just magical being able to watch something. And then of course there were Westerns, which were always on TV then, and [we were] still fascinated by the whole thing. But then as I got older and I made my own films—now I'm really interested in entertaining. I imagine my family watching films.

It's like, "Would this make them laugh? Would this speak to them? How would they react to this?" And sometimes that was a little bit weird—like when Mabel Moccasin is presenting her film to her community and they're sitting there, looking at it, wondering, "Is it good?" Yeah, I guess it's good. But they're still entertained, they're still stimulated. I think they're curious about what they're looking at. So I try to bring those feelings into the work. It feeds me when I'm trying to think, "How should the story go? Where should we go from here, and what elements do I want to bring forward?" And hopefully the audience who's in my own imagination, how will they respond? So that's how I go through the process of making a film. Take it away, Fox.

FM: I think that is my favorite scene in [*Honey Moccasin*]... Oh my God, that one sticks with me. I love the idea that people were just silently reacting. Like it wasn't a big thing... Nobody really had any negative or positive things to say. It is just in their faces, what was going on. And I love that. I've had a little bit of experience receiving that feedback before, so it feels really familiar. But yeah, I love reality TV. I grew up with, I guess, the birth of that—I'm thinking of really trashy, horrible, rock-your-brain kind of TV that I wasn't allowed to watch. I was not allowed to watch TV growing up at all, my parents wouldn't let me. I was a pretty crazy—they said "violent"—child. They attributed that to TV, so they wouldn't let me have any of it. But when I would go to friends' houses, I would sneak off and watch things. To me, it was like, "Oh my God, what is this weird world? Obviously this is reality TV, but this isn't real. This *can't* be real. Somebody has to be making these events happen, and provoking these fights or this drama or whatever. It's not real drama." That always sat with me, and really just inspires me, even though right now I'm making my own little world of visuals, I hope to one day work out writing my own little skits and making my own reality TV, in a way. But I like performing, I like doing performance art. That's the way I broke out of my shell. I was super shy. And then I moved to New York City. I had a group of friends and we called ourselves The Space Cadets. And we just performed and did really wild things based off of skeletons, based off of aliens, based off of ghosts. We loved ghosts. And there were just things that we wanted to explore, and performance art was the way to do it. You could get weird, and that's what I liked. You could do whatever you wanted and just be like, "Oh, well, it's performance art. If you don't get it, that's the point."

AP: Segueing from there, Shelley, one of the things I always think of when I think of *Honey Moccasin* is that really great moment, right in the middle of the film, where there's the performance art piece. Could you talk about that, and how you have found working in "Indigenous film," or what that even— I don't know... that can mean so many different things. There's a lot of agency that your film takes, along with your other work, of rejecting any label

   A Conversation Between Fox Maxy and Shelley Niro

and really digging in. Even with this film, which is part-film, part-performance art; it's part so many of these things...

SN: Like I mentioned before, I lived on Six Nations Reserve and our house was isolated from all the others, like every other house there. You had to find ways of entertaining yourself and each other. And sometimes that combination of youthful, I don't know, experimentation can get a little crazy, but it stays with you. It just really hooks into you. It's like, "What if I do this? Will this get a reaction?" By becoming an artist, it's like I can take that energy and I can do things with it that aren't being done. And so—are you talking about the part with the song "Fever"?

AP: Yeah, yeah.

SN: That song's so weird. I must have been sitting on my computer and that song came on. I started listening to the lyrics, and they're like "John Smith and Pocahontas had a wild affair and it gave me a fever." At the same time I thought, "That's the Native experience in North America." Everything they've done has literally given us a fever, and some people have died because of the fever, some carry that fever forever and pass it on to the next generation. It just kind of feeds something. And you start thinking about all the images the lyrics are bringing up in your own mind. With that, I started developing what I'd like to see. I hired Jeff Thomas who's a well-known Canadian photographer living in Ottawa. He was close to the national archives [Library and Archives Canada] and he was able to go in and find these photographs of residential school kids, and nuns, that kind of imagery. And so we put [those images] together with the song itself, and then it was screened on a teepee, with Mabel Moccasin's face coming through that teepee, and steam was coming through. Everything just came together really well.

AP: Awesome. Fox, a lot of your work is also questioning, you could say the influence of pop culture, but—similar to what Shelley was talking about with the song "Fever"—how much violence against Native people is also just part of pop culture. It's just kind of a given, and it's something for us to dissect in terms of how we approach some of this stuff. Could you talk about that a little, in relation to your work?

FM: Because I make things so personally, and so much based off of what I'm working through mentally at that moment, there's a lot of anger. I was adopted out and grew up in a real quiet environment where I was not allowed to be angry about anything. So then when I left that environment, I exploded. I had a lot to express, and I still do, and find a lot of safety in expressing my anger and putting that into art because that's the safest way for me. And, oh hell, there's a lot to be angry about, and there's so much to cover. Even to just explain what the fuck happened, or how we came about, or even just how my family is here, you know what I mean? Even just to explain that there's a lot of anger, and there's a lot of violence, and a lot of shit that just doesn't sit well with me. Even in my own community, it's really interesting to share my work or have it seen because a lot of people are like, "Oh, damn. I agree with that, but I've never been able to say that, or I've never been able to have a place to talk about that before."

AP : Kind of going off of that, do both of you want to talk about how you've found your work has been received by both non-Indigenous and Indigenous audiences? Shelley, I heard a little bit about a screening that you had, I believe it was at NAU, or up in Flagstaff somewhere?

SN : Yeah. I was invited to show *Honey Moccasin* there—in 1999, I think. And the audience was Navajo students. The theater held maybe 400 people? I'll say 400 Navajo students were there, and they laughed so hard every time anything happened. And it was so great. It was like, "Wow, this is a really great audience." I think they were just so happy to see a film that was trying to make them laugh, and then they responded with laughter, and it was very, very nice. It was one of the best screenings ever.

AP : Fox, how about your work? I know you've had a different experience with things really popping off in the last year, during the pandemic.

FM : Yeah. It's been crazy. The first screening that I ever had was in-person, maybe two or three years ago.

It was in New York, for a Native art festival. And so half the audience was Native and half was non-Native; it was about 200 people. It was the first time I screened anything in front of an audience. And it was just crazy, because I never could have predicted the way that it feels to show your work to people. Right now, I don't really know what's going on, because all the screenings are online and I never meet people. And this right here is not ideal; I would like to meet Shelley, and I would like to hang out with everyone. But that screening was the best thing ever because—oh man, I was so nervous. I felt like I was going to throw up. I was not ready for that. And then the minute it started playing, half the audience would laugh and half the audience would cry. Just to hear these reactions, I mean, I could've never predicted that people would be... I thought people wouldn't get it, or wouldn't like it, I just didn't know. As it turned out, everyone had some part that they could relate to. And it was all different parts—the audience would light up, or cry, or react in different ways at different times. And I could tell, oh, that's a white person over there laughing at that. Or, oh, that's definitely a Native girl laughing at that. I will never forget it. It was the best thing I've ever been a part of. I hope in the future I'll get to screen more things in real life and to experience that again because, ooh, it's a powerful feeling for sure.

SN: That's great, Fox.

FM: Thank you.

AP: Shelley, I'd love to hear more about what you're currently
     working on and what you have on the horizon.
     Same with you, Fox.

SN: I'm working on three projects. One I can't talk about
     because it's not really formulated yet, but one is
     with Elizabeth Hill, Jordan Wheeler, and Darlene
     Naponse. It started out as a narrative around
     Pocahontas and Joseph Brant—it's not really
     revisionist history, but we want to take those
     characters and really examine their personas.
     Because those two people have had such a huge
     influence in North America and they're used in
     not the best way; they're always kind of looked at
     as a joke, not taken seriously, that sort of thing.
     So we've really pulled apart their existence, like
     where they started in history and how they ended
     up in a certain way in history. And it's been really
     great. It's really interesting. February 2022, we're
     having a reading of those scripts we're writing
     in Thunder Bay, Ontario. So if you have nothing
     to do, come to Thunder Bay. Another project I'm
     working on is called *Café Daughter*. It's based
     on the life of a woman born in the '50s whose
     father is Chinese and whose mother is Cree. And
     so her mother always told her, don't let anybody
     know you're Indian because Indians weren't very
     well treated, especially around the prairies. No,
     anywhere—they weren't treated well anywhere—
     but the story takes place in the prairies. It's about
     her growing up, she was the smartest kid in her
     high school. She became a doctor and then later
     on she ended up being a senator in the Canadian

government. It's loosely based on her life—it's not my original project, it's based on a play written by Ken Williams, but I think it's a really good project.

AP: Fox, how about you?

FM: Well, I just finished *Gush*, and I have an artist spotlight screening that's virtual online at BAM (Brooklyn Academy of Music). They're going to play four of my films, and give me a bit of help because I'm fundraising and organizing to make my first feature, *Watertight*. It's a hybrid documentary experimental film. And it's going over my personal story with adoption, and my family's history with boarding schools, and my experience with suicide, and my mother's suicide, and my family's experience with mental health and health in general. I'm also talking to many of my friends and their families about their experiences, and I'm going through California, New Mexico, North Dakota, South Dakota, and New York City. So it's a real opportunity for me to connect with a lot of different artists and tell so many important stories. It's also an opportunity for me to get experience making little fake commercials and fake reality-TV moments, and slip in these little dream sequences and narrative items in-between the interviews. My goal is to make the movie feel like you're just flipping through channels and seeing lots of different things going on. Right now it's really important to fundraise, or even just gather support, whether it's equipment, food, or whatever the hell people want to offer, because it's the first time I'm going to have a crew, and it's a fifteen-person crew. I want to pay everyone proper wages and really make sure people are taken care of and safe while we're traveling. So that's my priority right now.

SN: Good for you.

FM: Shelley, can I ask how you came across or how you chose the film about the half-Cree, half-Chinese woman?

SN: I was approached by the playwright Ken Williams and his partner who's a Chinese guy, and they were both very interested in getting this story told. They came to my house and asked if I'd be interested in directing it, and I said, "Yeah." And then [they asked], "Do you know anybody who could write the screenplay version?" You just dive in and try to do the best job that you can. I called the woman the story is based on, and talked to her for a long time. She has a brother—he's not in the screen or the stage play, but I called him and he had stories to tell. Talking to them, they both filled that script up more than what I had, and they just made it more... what's the word? More real, because there are two people who I didn't know before, but after talking to them, it became a much richer experience. And if it wasn't for Covid, I would've gone to Saskatoon and spent more time with them. So yeah, it's a really great project.

FM: I'm excited for you. That sounds super cool. And I want to say thank you because in our last talk, you gave really helpful advice about just being a director, and being open to what your crew members have to say and what they have to contribute to the project, how it's such an exchange between you, the project itself, and the people who are in it—even the actors, the people behind the camera, everything like that. That influenced me a lot, and you had me thinking about so much since we last talked. So I appreciate that.

SN: Oh, that's nice to hear. You're a great director.

FM: If Shellcy thinks so, then I'm good to go.

SN: You are, I can hear it in your voice. When I was first directing, I didn't go to film school or anything. And so when it came time to say action, I'd be like, "Oh, yeah. Okay. Go. I mean, action. Stop, I mean, cut." I still have trouble with all those.

FM: I was going to ask: the terms, the whole film world language, is that something that you think is necessary?

SN: There's people who go to film school and the ones who are technical stick to all those little things. I don't know, I don't like working with those guys. I like working with the people who, even if they have gone to film school, work organically, and like to work with each other. And after a while, if you work as a crew, it almost becomes telepathic. You won't have to say too much to them. They'll know what direction you want to go in, and then it magically happens. But it's all about being really tight with your crew, and really respecting them, and then they'll respect you. I think that's the main thing.

          A Conversation Between Fox Maxy and Shelley Niro

FM: Do you have people on your crew you've worked with since
day one?

SN: Yeah, I have one person I've had all the way through, in
most of my films. If you can hold onto your crew,
it's really great. Of course, they have their own
lives, too, and you just have to keep finding those
people who are like-minded and who are good to
be around, because you're there with them 24/7
for as long as it takes to finish that film.

FM: You seem really organized; you've got all your ducks in a row
before you film, it seems like. Do you ever get on set
and then go in a different direction because you're
like, "Oh, I see something new, I see something
different," or because you get instant inspiration?

SN: Yeah. Sometimes you see something you could have put in
your script. And it's like, "I didn't write this down,
but now that we're here, I see I could include this."
If it doesn't take too much time and if it's just easy,
you can slip it in—I do that. But you can't do it all
the time, the crew will get mad. It all comes down
to spirit. What kind of spirit do you have on your
set? Everybody is working in that spirit. It makes it
so much easier because if you get somebody who's
not in the spirit with everybody else, it throws a
lot of sour milk in there, and you don't want that.
You've got to be good to your crew.

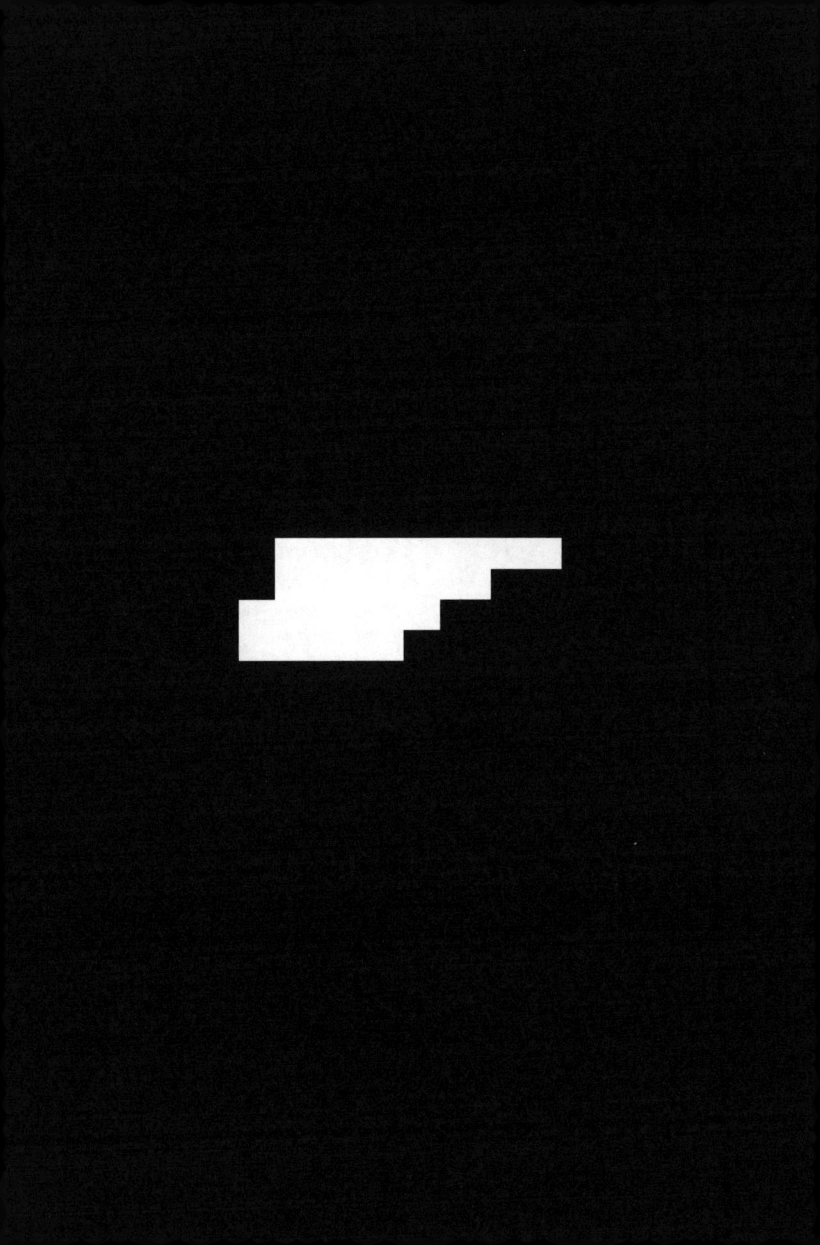

Indigenous Cinema and the Limits of Auteurism

Girish Shambu

For the last twenty years—until the pandemic broke my streak—I drove each fall to spend a week at the Toronto International Film Festival (TIFF). Before making the trip, I took care to avoid reading anything about the subjects, characters, or narratives of the films; they did not matter. Instead, as my eye scanned the festival program, I took note of all the auteurs whose work I admired. Any year with a new film by Agnès Varda, Claire Denis, Hou Hsiao-hsien, or Christian Petzold was a good year. The films on the festival program that sparked my interest fell into two groups: auteurs of whom I was already a fan; and auteurs whose work held promise, beckoning me to explore further.

This was the way I approached all film festivals until a few years ago, when I first attended the imagineNATIVE Film + Media Arts Festival—the largest festival of Indigenous film and media in the world—also held each fall in Toronto. If auteurism had long been the principal cinephilic lens through which I engaged with the medium, imagineNATIVE broke its dominance in my viewing life. It did this by showing me how, when used exclusively, or even predominantly, auteurism diminishes the richness of cinema by curtailing its possibilities. What's more, this applies especially to cinema made by marginalized people: women, Indigenous, Black, LGBTQ, disabled, and POC filmmakers.

The Black Lives Matter protests of 2020 and the starkly differential impacts of the pandemic have thrust into public consciousness—have made it impossible to deny—the pervasiveness of systemic exclusion. Such exclusion has always existed in the cultural sector. Specifically, in film culture, the machinery of auteurism has worked for decades to sideline nonwhite and non-cismale filmmakers. Because its primary focus lies in tracking the style and themes of a relatively small number of directors accorded the status of auteurs—

in Eurowestern film culture, mostly hetero, white men—
auteurism prizes not just individual "good" films but a
filmmaker's entire body of work, to which it returns obsessively.

This ceaseless multiplication of discourse around a
privileged group of filmmakers spreads out and occupies space,
installing itself centerstage in film culture. Meanwhile, moving-
image artists from marginalized communities, having suffered
drastic historical exclusion from funding opportunities, are
prevented from building a corpus of work of any significant
size. Since auteurism functions by identifying patterns of
continuity across an auteur's career, marginalized filmmakers,
first disadvantaged by funding systems, are harmed again, this
time by the aesthetic system that is auteurism. As a result, their
work—if they are lucky to be permitted to make any—generally
languishes outside the field of visibility and attention.

There are at least two more reasons why marginalized
filmmakers are not well served by auteurism. Since its origins
in France in the 1950s, auteurist cinephilia has always
privileged text over context: formal/aesthetic analysis over
serious consideration of all the contextual factors—such
as those related to representation, production practices, or
reception—in the appreciation of a film. It's not that auteurists
are uninterested in context, but that they give it scant weight in
the evaluation process. Today, this still has strong implications
for which films end up in social media conversations, on end-
of-year lists, and in the canon.

In point of fact, all films would benefit from increased
contextual understanding, but when it comes to marginalized
filmmakers, grounding their work in context becomes even
more important. This is because audiences have typically had
less exposure not only to this work—which often has culturally
specific dimensions—but also to background knowledge
relating to representational histories or production practices

　　　　　　　　　　　　　　　　　　　　　　　　　　Girish Shambu

that might help them make full and rich sense of these films and the contexts that envelop them. For Indigenous filmmakers, such contextual knowledge becomes crucial because the industry has historically given them so few opportunities to tell their own stories on-screen.

Finally, the individualist ethos of auteurism perversely opposes the essentially collaborative nature of this art form. The imagineNATIVE festival highlights this fact by frequently framing the festival's offerings as collective creations, indebted not only to teams of moving-image makers but also to the communities represented in them—and without whom the work could not exist.

The festival was founded in 1999 by Cynthia Lickers-Sage, a Mohawk, Turtle Clan visual artist from Six Nations. Her collaborators included the Toronto nonprofit artists' center and video distributor Vtape, and the venture was driven by an urgent imperative to raise the visibility of work by Indigenous artists. For me, one of the great pleasures of attending this festival has been the experience of engaging with an astonishing range of moving-image forms: not just fiction, nonfiction, and experimental work, in the shape of features and shorts; but also digital and interactive media, audio works, and gallery exhibitions, including a group "art crawl" through downtown Toronto. Many of the screenings are free, the rest are subsidized and affordable, and Indigenous artists from around the world are frequently on hand to give valuable, culturally specific accounts of their aesthetic practices.

Looking back on my years of attending imagineNATIVE, I realize that the most memorable films for me have had at least one thing in common: they have embodied, in deep and multitudinous ways, the idea of community. They have done so visibly on-screen, and also invisibly in the cultural and production practices that have fed into and animated their making. It is thus impossible to fully understand, analyze, and appreciate these films without serious recourse to context.

I now want to take up a few examples of these films, viewing them through the theme of community, and situating them within certain contexts that turn out to be revealing. It is a framework that does not abandon auteurism but instead de-emphasizes it, in order to make room for other approaches that expand the possibilities of what can be learned about and from these films—and their embeddedness in the world.

The Canadian drama *One Day in the Life of Noah Piugattuk*, by Inuk director Zacharias Kunuk, played at imagineNATIVE in 2019. Most of the film's reviews so far have approached it through an auteurist lens, Kunuk having directed a small but distinguished body of fiction features including the widely celebrated *Atanarjuat: The Fast Runner* (2001), the first feature film ever to be written, directed and acted entirely in the Inuktitut language. But it is every bit as rewarding to consider his latest film in light of its contexts: that of settler-colonialist history, language preservation, and the institutional conditions of the film's production.

A few words first about the film's narrative. *One Day in the Life* takes place on a single day in 1961 and follows Noah (Apayata Kotierk) as he sets out with his band and their dog team on a hunting trip. Along the way, they make a stop for rest, and encounter a white man named "Boss"—the Inuit call him "Isumataq," meaning "he who thinks for us"—who is accompanied by an Inuk youth who will serve as translator between Noah and Boss. During their conversation, Boss (played by Kim Bodnia, the Danish actor well known from

the TV series *Killing Eve*) tries to persuade Noah to relocate
his family from their ancestral homeland in Kapuivik, Baffin
Island, to a government settlement. Noah refuses, repeatedly.

At the heart of the film is the extended conversation
between the two men, mediated by the young translator.
As we watch and listen, a strange and wonderful dynamic
emerges: the words of both men are not rendered to each
other smoothly and faithfully, but instead are frequently
mistranslated, peppered with pauses, made bumpy by
awkwardness. Boss's words are often direct and unrelenting;
he only cares about one thing: moving Noah and his family.
But the translator bends and softens the white man's words,
likely not wanting to offend and insult the elder Noah.
The sequence is amusing, ironic, and poignant.

There exists one other explanation for the
mistranslations: that the translator is a young man, and he
does not have the same facility with the Inuktitut language
as his elders do. This point speaks to intergenerational loss.
Settler-colonialism has brought dispossession, displacement,
and disenfranchisement to the Inuit; as a result, their
cultural heritage and legacy, which includes their languages,
have suffered seriously from lack of preservation. Younger
generations have acutely felt this severing of links to cultural
practices of previous generations.

The film was co-written by Kunuk with Norman
Cohn; together, they cofounded Isuma, Canada's first Inuit
independent production company, in 1990, with Paul Apak
Angilirk. Isuma's mission, from the start, was to produce
independent community-based work—first films and TV,
and then internet media. The collective has its own internet
broadcasting channel, and an online library of nearly
eight thousand media works, in eighty languages. Cultural
preservation and transmission are at the core of Isuma's

mission, and so the theme of cultural legacy and practices in *One Day in the Life* turns out to be crucial: they hold the key to unlocking its meanings and laying bare its stakes.

—

If auteurism was one possible, if limited, paradigm for approaching *One Day in the Life*, our next film, *Waru*, reduces that possibility nearly to zero. *Waru*, which opened the imagineNATIVE festival in 2017, is an omnibus film made in a collective spirit by eight directors, all Māori women. It comprises eight "chapters"—each directed by a different filmmaker, but each shot in a single, unbroken, ten-minute take. The action in every chapter takes place on the morning of the funeral for a young boy who has died at the hands of his caregiver. The film is named for the boy (his name also means "eight"), and his voice is heard at the beginning and the end: "When I died, I saw the whole world." Even though we never see him, we feel his spirit throughout.

The characters we encounter across the eight chapters vary widely in their proximity of connection to the boy. Some are family members and relatives, but many have little or no link to the narrative proper; they help constitute a portrait of the community that is affected by his death in some way. As New Zealand critic Sarah Watt explains, at the heart of *Waru* lies the Māori idea of *whānau* (or "community"), in marked distinction to the *Pākehā* (white New Zealander) conception of "nuclear family." She adds, "It is our whole community that suffers when one of our children dies."

Kerry Warkia, one of the two producers who spearheaded the project, has said that a specific *kaupapa* ("collective vision") drove the film, and that she wanted the weight and burden of this *kaupapa* to not be placed on a single individual but shared by a group of Māori women directors. This underlying vision was to address a serious social crisis: the high rates of child abuse in New Zealand. The writer Rachel Williamson argues that the resulting, kaleidoscopic form of the film is rich and rewarding for two reasons. It brings multiple perspectives (all female and Māori, and thus non-hegemonic) to bear on the story; and it uses the inherently heterogeneous form of the omnibus film to differentiate these perspectives. The splintered structure is held together both aesthetically (by the use of the extended, single take) and politically—by a specifically Māori worldview based on collectivity. Critic So Mayer points out, in their useful analysis, that "the result is a film that differs profoundly from the Strong Female Character isolationism beloved of supposedly 'progressive' Hollywood films."

Waru was not a one-off; its producers, Warkia and Kiel McNaughton, returned to the festival in 2018 with another omnibus film, *Vai*, directed by eight Pasifika (Pacific Indigenous) women. Shot in seven different countries, it consists, like its predecessor, of eight short films that are narratively linked, nearly all of them shot in single takes. Each of *Vai*'s eight segments narrates a moment in the life of the female title character, from the ages of seven to eighty. The diverse vignettes that make up *Vai* have a common theme: the trauma of displacement experienced by Indigenous people—and the way this displacement endangers individuals, communities, traditions, and histories.

The filmmaker Sky Hopinka, whose work has featured regularly at imagineNATIVE, is among the most admired of contemporary experimental moving-image artists. Hopinka conceives, shoots, and edits his films himself, thus instantly inviting the application of auteurism. And while auteurist analysis undoubtedly yields insights into his work, it is also possible to see that widening the circle of context— specifically, by mapping the work's connections to Indigenous languages and cultural practices—opens it up for us in new and unexpected ways.

Although Hopinka made his first feature recently, he is best known for a succession of short films—between five and twenty minutes long—that have a strong documentary basis, and that he likes to categorize as "ethnopoetic." The word is deliberately chosen, to distinguish his approach from that of ethnographic film: the dominant approach historically used by white scholars and artists to capture documentary images of Indigenous peoples and cultures.

Hopinka has a biography that is both culturally varied and instructive. He is a member of the Ho-Chunk Nation of Wisconsin, and a descendant of the Pechanga Band of Luiseño Mission Indians. Now thirty-eight, he spent his teens and twenties in Southern California, then moved to Portland, Oregon, where he became actively involved in the project of Indigenous language revitalization. He began learning, then teaching, the language Chinuk Wawa. Coincidentally, around the same time, he took an introductory video class with Portland Community Media, moving on to YouTube tutorials and blogs to teach himself the rudiments of filmmaking. He sees the two activities as analogs: both involve a long process of acquiring proficiency while enabling and requiring constant experimentation.

Community as a theme is central to Hopinka's work, where it appears not directly but routed through language. Hopinka has said that when he got his first proper camera, the first thing he shot was a language lesson between him and his teacher. He remembers his teacher's words: "Ninety percent of what we do is community-building, and ten percent is language." It served as an important reminder that language is neither developed nor learned on one's own; it demands to be spoken, tried out, and tested in a process of exchange with others.

Hopinka's six-minute video *wawa* (2014) begins with a Chinuk Wawa language lesson in which he is a participant, and then moves to two interviews with Native elders who speak the language fluently. This simple description, however, belies the way the video builds up, layer by layer, into a thick and dense assemblage of image, translated on-screen text, and overlapping voices on the soundtrack. Meanings become destabilized, and communication disperses, turning playful and unmoored from certainty.

Hopinka's father, who was a Ho-Chunk songwriter and singer, and played the powwow circuit, is at the center of his video *Jáaji Approx.* (2015). The primary element of the soundtrack is audio recordings of his father singing and speaking, made over a decade-long period. The images are of landscapes that the filmmaker and his father traversed, either together or separately over the years. Hopinka's signature approach of layering is both seen and heard: in superimposed images of landscapes—some of them inverted, creating a strange, unsettling effect—and in multiple voices speaking at the same time. The *jáaji* of the title is an approximate translation for how to directly address a father in the Hočąk language.

Hopinka has said that he tries to tell contemporary stories of Indigenous experience without romanticizing Native life or dwelling on trauma. In doing so, he is also countering two other ways in which dominant culture tends to view Native American culture: as a single monolithic entity, and one that exists in the past rather than thriving and transforming in the present. The title of Hopinka's film about Standing Rock, *Dislocation Blues* (2017), signals his reluctance to speak authoritatively for all Native people, and he has taken pains to position it as simply one personal, non-definitive film about that momentous event and movement. Because of his itinerant life, marked by frequent displacement, Hopinka has spent considerable time filming and learning languages in Native communities that are not his own. "I try not to have a voice for all Native people," he has said, "and speak on their behalf."

And yet Hopinka emphasizes that he does not view these communities as an outsider. His films participate in—and engage in a dialogue with—the community and culture they depict. Take, for instance, the importance of myth in various Native cultures. His films have explored this theme, not to merely reflect or document myths as they currently exist, but to perform inventive variations on them. *Fainting Spells* (2018) begins with direct-address subtitles asking someone to tell the story of Xąwįska, or the Indian Pipe Plant, used by Ho-Chunk to revive people who have fainted. The film then stages a remembrance of this Pipe Plant, and an imagined myth of how the Ho-Chunk people came to use the plant.

Likewise, his first feature film, *małni – towards the ocean, towards the shore* (2020), which is set in the Columbia River Basin and is spoken largely in Chinuk Wawa, centers on and departs from the Chinookan origin-of-death myth. *Małni* (pronounced "moth-nee") follows two real-life Pacific Northwest Natives, Sweetwater Sahme and Jordan Mercier, whose Chinook identities (as Hopinka puts it) "steer their conceptions of life, death, and rebirth." The film's long takes follow these two characters in parallel, often in exterior settings, as they speak to the unseen Hopinka, who is behind the camera. As in so much of his work, landscape and language—Hopinka's two great themes—are a felt presence throughout.

It's true, auteurism remains a valuable lens through which to think about and enjoy a wide spectrum of cinema, including Hopinka's. This is not a cry to "cancel" auteurism. Instead, in film culture, we have a different, twofold task before us. First, there is a need to recognize that while auteurism is potentially neutral, its actual outcomes have been drastically uneven. To continue using auteurism will mean consciously decentering those who have benefited disproportionately from it, while centering filmmakers from marginalized social groups. Second, auteurist film criticism must be self-reflexive in practice: aware of its two key limitations—an under-emphasis on contextual factors and a valorization of individualism—as it goes about fashioning an expansive, new auteurism to correct for them.

Before I made that first, fateful trip to imagineNATIVE, I believed that stories, characters, subjects, and themes— and the social, cultural, and aesthetic contexts from which they emerged—were less important than the auteur whose sensibility and "genius" spun them into a sublime cinematic form. These days, in my viewing and reading life, I find myself much more drawn to films, filmmakers, and worlds—often those of marginalized people, such as women and people of color— that a lifetime of auteur worship has diminished and hidden from me. Prime among them is the rich and heterogenous universe of Indigenous cinema.

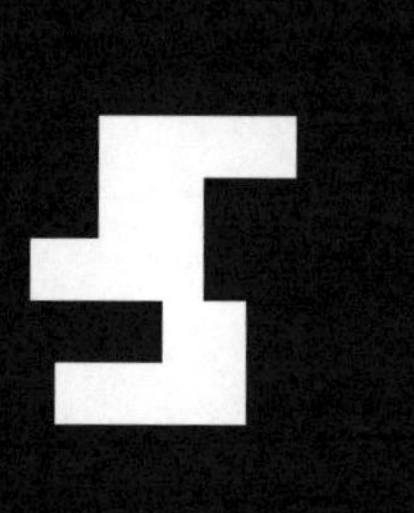

Film Is the Body

Sky Hopinka

You'll forget all you've been taught and you'll abandon everything that hasn't worked for you or your family. I'm tired again and it's starting to be a bit warmer outside. I'm tired of the words and the voices that never relent, and I'm tired of my own thoughts and sounds of my ahs and ums that punctuate those spaces when I can hear myself thinking through answers of the questions that no one is asking. Sometimes it's easier than others, yet still I'm caught in those moments at the end of the day when I've got nothing left to say and all kinds of silences to fill. Fill them with sounds of the television or words on a phone, or if I'm feeling happy then I'll fill them with old recordings of friends and family—alive, or gone. It hasn't been too long since I thought about the middle of nowhere being the center of somewhere, yet that still feels aspirational.

Being decentered from a land and a home burdens many of us, and I'm not entirely sure where the salve can be found that soothes those aches and that hurt that punctures deep into the body of what we remember and what our ancestors experienced. It's hard to parse out the pain of the Elders and pain that's your own. It's all our own, though. There's no theirs and ours, or then and now. I think of my mother and my father, and their pain and their joy. I think of my grandmothers—maternal and paternal. Grandma and Grandmother, and the love they gave and the love they held onto for themselves. I don't know my maternal grandfather or my paternal grandfather, and neither did my mother nor my father. Intergenerational suffering becomes a transgenerational reckoning.

**You are the grandchild of great love, and you're the
grandchild of great violence.**

Someone said this to me a year or so ago and it's stuck with
me, a prayer I've said to myself many times as I've tried to
understand the implications of what it means to have a mother
who never knew who her father was, and a father who never
knew who his father was, and to have grandmothers who
felt too much weight to share those answers. Those lives and
those deaths and those secrets can define so much of how
our parents view themselves, how their children understand
themselves, and how we and our siblings and our cousins and
our kin navigate the questions posed by centuries of love,
violence, and resistance. "Survival" as a word never felt like
enough to encompass the fortitude needed, that was passed
on intergenerationally to flourish. We're an aggregate of those
traumas and resiliencies. Elastic in movement and lines and
trails and trials on the road of life and death. Flourishing in
mind and bodies that are our own.

> To survive is not to escape death or to go on living after
> death but to die alive. We die alive. In fact, everything,
> every trace dies alive and what dies alive survives. [2]

That quote above comes from Kas Saghafi writing about
Jacques Derrida's definition of survivance, which feels not that
different from Gerald Vizenor's, and the ways in which merely
survival or to survive is ever enough. As Saghafi describes,
"survivance" grammatically exists suspended between the
active and the passive voice, and so do we. Somewhere
between an active and passive presence, we're all contending
with intergenerational and transgenerational effects of pain,
resistance, stress, love, and joy. Forgetting and remembering

                                                           Sky Hopinka

the impermanence of our existence on planes of being that are both in and out of our body and our control.

"I'm tired of being temporary"[3]

Soma is the body and what we have apart from our soul and our vagaries. I hold a camera and I hold a pen and I type on this keyboard thinking of mind-pictures and stories I don't have the words for. Film is the body and photographs are the body and words are the body and as Crystal says the body is the body; in English, in Ho-Chunk, in Chinuk, on celluloid or in pixels or on paper and I hope they mean everything I can make them mean. Indigenous cinema is a cinema of the ineffable dreams suppressed for so long. Indigenous art is the art of the indescribable things that you can't think of in English. The meaning isn't in the shape of words, but rather it's found in those crevices between the facts and the information that we've been taught to understand of ourselves, those slick spaces where the spirit slips through that I don't have the words for, that you don't have the words for. All the things that surprise us—by not only our humanity, but the humanity of others.

I've exhausted a place called home.[4]

The body is still the body and it needs these other elements and factors to give its shape and its form and its memory meaning. I feel myself in my body everyday and I look to my chosen Elders to guide me in understanding it as a child does, for we're all children learning and trying to become more than what our appearances are prescribed to us by the histories in place. I see my mother in her space and her life, now and today, growing and becoming and loving and making things with her hands and her heart. I saw my father, tired in his own way before his death, finally at peace next to his feather and his children. We return to the land and return to our homes and we exhaust our minds and our spirits, seeing and being in the grass and the water and the dirt. Exhausted and free to remember what we need to know, as now the time has come.

1. Lee Maracle, *I Am Woman* (Vancouver, British Columbia: Press Gang Publishers, 1996), 15.

2. Kas Saghafi, "Dying Alive," *Mosaic* 48, no. 3 (September 2015), 21.

3. Julie Niemi said this one day last summer.

4. Not unlike Georges Perec.

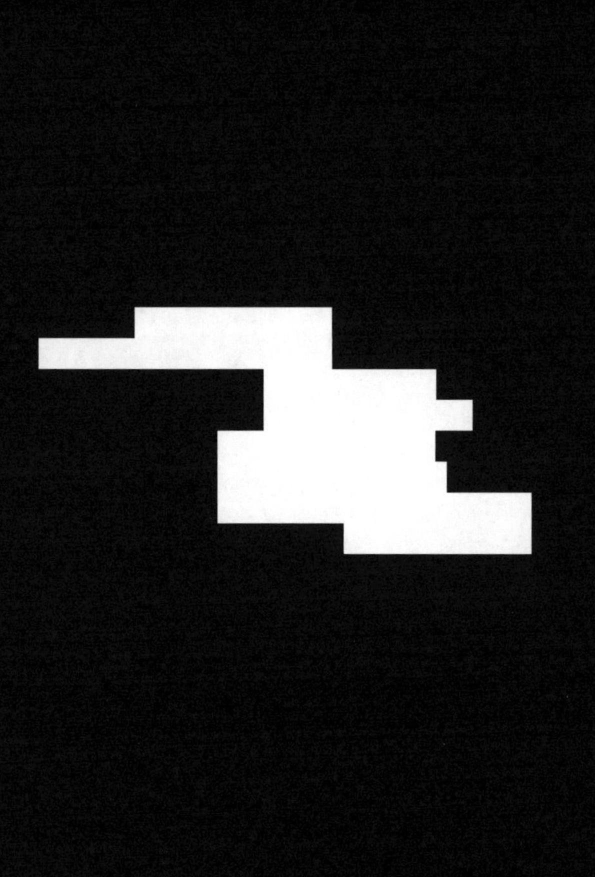

Anticipation of a Remembrance: The Politics of Continuity in Indigenous Found-Footage and Archival Cinema

Michael Metzger

Experimental cinema has always been understood, in part, as a "counter-cinema," posed against hegemonic industrial models and their corresponding formal conventions. Against the linear narratives, commodity structures, and heteronormative myths of mainstream film, experimental cinema has fostered a bevy of subversive techniques, privileging amateurism, nonlinearity, ambiguity, and disinhibition. Such oppositional strategies have made experimental cinema a robust site of queer, feminist, and anti-capitalist representation for decades—none more so than found-footage and archival filmmaking, seen as quintessentially subversive in its repurposing of commercial material for artistic and political ends. But the myth of the avant-garde's countercultural essence has also obscured the degree to which BIPOC filmmakers have remained largely excluded from, or marginalized by, these techniques. Again, the principle of archival appropriation is illustrative: the two works most widely identified as the origins of found-footage filmmaking, Joseph Cornell's *Rose Hobart* (c. 1936) and Bruce Conner's *A Movie* (1958), both pointedly traffic in primitivizing stereotypes and scenes of anti-Indigenous violence.

Taking up the strategies of found-footage and archival filmmaking, Indigenous filmmakers not only demonstrate the enduring radical potential of these strategies, they also reveal ways that earlier, predominantly white avant-gardes reproduced oppressive paradigms of their own. Two works by contemporary Indigenous artists—*Mobilize* (2015) by Anishinaabe/French Canadian filmmaker Caroline Monnet and *Kicking the Clouds* (2021) by Ho-Chunk/Pechanga filmmaker Sky Hopinka—demonstrate how Indigenous perspectives complicate the underlying assumptions of experimental film conventions. Working within and adjacent to traditions of found-footage and archival filmmaking, these films invite being read through the lens of scholarship on experimental approaches to appropriation and historiography. In so doing, the films reveal the degree to which settler colonial logics are sedimented within both these idioms, as well as in the theories that have emerged to account for them. The very gestures that would position these films in their respective genres also trouble their categories: can acts of reclamation from state archives be characterized as "appropriation"? Are family photographs and audiotapes "archival" if they serve more as vehicles of anticipation rather than of memory? Challenging mainstream and experimental traditions alike, these films expose the settler colonial logics that undergird the very concepts of "found" and "archival" media in the first place.

Temporal Disparities

The archive is an imperious concept in the discourse of experimental cinema. Once reserved—tenuously, perhaps— for films working explicitly with material drawn from official collections of image and sound, the "archival" tag has expanded to encompass a range of practices involving found, gathered, appropriated, and reused content. As the scholar Jaimie Baron has observed, the collapse of the distinction between "found" and "archival" footage is a relatively recent one, coinciding with the emergence of online repositories for sharing vast amounts of content.[1] In this source-agnostic media environment, the specific mechanism of content retrieval (licensed, sampled, remixed, stolen) is less relevant than the effect produced by montage: "it is the viewer's experience of the 'foundness' of certain documents— whether found in an official archive, an online database, or in someone's closet—that produces archival documents as such within appropriation films."[2]

                                                      Michael Metzger

The archive claims whatever it finds on the basis of "foundness." In the colonial archive, objects are "found" when they are plundered and inserted into a historicizing context, the archive, which overrides the situated condition of their origins. Withdrawn from—lost to—their lifeworlds, they become "found" artifacts; abducted, they become fragments of the archive's historical mosaic. In this new context, according to the scholar Ariella Aïsha Azoulay, such objects become addressable within a "universal" history according to a temporal logic which organizes cultural production along a "progressive, linear timeline... in which colonized people and colonizers occupy different positions and roles."[3] Whether art objects, ceremonial tools, or human remains, such objects, once "found," extracted, and archived, are used to produce a form of historical temporality that cleaves the moment and context of their production (then, prehistory) from their moment of reception and study (now, modernity). As Azoulay argues, "the archive was established as a neutral threshold separating the past and the present, history and politics."[4]

For Baron, that quality of "foundness" at work in archival films is rooted in perceptions of difference. "Temporal disparity" describes the ways that appropriated material asks viewers to make distinctions between a "then" and a "now" in a film, relying on depictions of subject matter changing over time, or relying on a viewer's sensitivity to material distinctions between source materials, such as grainy 16mm and high-definition video.[5] While accepted as a given in the experience of viewing found-footage films, such operations of temporalization and discernment take on a different resonance in the context of Indigenous experience. As scholars like Jean M. O'Brien have observed, white settlers relied on myths of Native extinction to construct the category of modernity. Their mechanisms of discernment were notions of "blood purity" on the one hand,

and on observation of cultural change on the other: "Indians who changed did not comply with non-Indian expectations of their authenticity. These ideas produced a lethal brew: non-Indians insisted that Indians could only be ancients, they could never be modern."[6] Mechanisms for establishing temporal disparity have been instruments of violence towards Native people, especially in the realm of ethnographic media: colonial projects of "salvage" ethnography presupposed a temporal disparity between "authentic," pre-modern Native cultures and the present, prompting ethnographers to build archives recording traditional lifeways—which subsequently became evidence used to portray contemporary Indigenous communities as inauthentic.[7] The strategies of temporal discernment used in found-footage films are not identical to these anti-Indigenous practices, but they compound the dangers faced by Indigenous filmmakers drawing on those very ethnographic archives. How might Indigenous filmmakers employ archival strategies that counteract tropes of "the vanishing Indian," without reproducing archival temporalities that divide past and present?

Mobilize: Wayfinding Footage

Monnet's short film *Mobilize* repurposes material from the archives of the National Film Board of Canada (NFB) to contest those representations. In the opening moments of the film, Monnet cuts between shots of hands threading snowshoes, and of snowshoe-clad feet moving swiftly over snowy terrain. While the footage of traditional Indigenous crafts recalls (or indeed might originate from) those salvage ethnographies, Monnet implies a continuity between the latticework techniques of the snowshoe-makers and her own deft editing. Monnet's immediate alignment of film montage with snowshoe-making signals her rejection of the logic of temporal disparity;

instead, her film constructs its Native subjects as "a people that mobilizes itself and that is far from being stagnant. [A people who] are contemporary, culturally rooted and constantly on the move."[8]

The overall impression is of speed and synchronicity, shuttling across parallel spaces and forms of Indigenous labor to the rhythm of singer Tanya Tagaq's insistent soundtrack. Archival montage, like the snowshoes, canoes, seaplanes, and snowmobiles she alternates between, allows Monnet to cover a lot of ground quickly. But the film celebrates Native mobility in both spatial and temporal terms, cutting between canoes, seaplanes, and snowmobiles, juxtaposing high-rise construction with cabin-building. Although the film is broadly divided into two sections—the first focused on rural, the second on urban settings—Monnet's edit dovetails these spaces, bypassing linear narratives of irreversible modernization to stress Indigenous circulation in time and space. "The sequencing of the images speaks a bit about my own family history," Monnet has remarked, "where my grandparents were living in the bush, and throughout the generations, we became more and more urban. However, this does not mean that I cannot go back to the bush and learn all these things."[9]

In the first section, the film emphasizes its temporal fluidity by foregrounding the image of Cree hunter Sam Blacksmith navigating turbulent waters in a canoe, filmed with a camera fixed to the vessel. Drawing from a range of 16mm films in the NFB library, Monnet arrays fleeting glimpses of nature, industry, and play around this central image, surveying a complex landscape of Native representation. *Mobilize* steers through this terrain, like Blacksmith, through keen observation and navigation. Monnet doesn't "find" footage, she finds a way through it. As the mounting thrum of Tagaq's music gives way, and Blacksmith's canoe comes to rest, Monnet pauses on an image of light rippling at the edge of a grassy river embankment, offering another figure of fluidity before launching into an exhilarating montage of Native urban experience. This sequence mirrors the first by focalizing an array of clips around the perception of a mobile figure, a young Indigenous woman in Mod attire absorbing the sights of 1960s Montreal. Her expression, a mixture of curiosity and vigilance, suggests another form of wayfinding in an environment of both opportunity and oppression—a form of looking critically at the production of the film itself, which steers around the pitfalls of working with colonial archives, producing powerful and subversive cinema.

By modeling its fluid cinematic language in Indigenous crafts, wayfinding, and observation, *Mobilize* emphasizes continuities and convergences rather than linear historical structures. Though assembled from footage from the 1960s and '70s, *Mobilize* addresses itself to the present through the urgency of its montage, and the specific choice of exclusively using color film material, a decision that disrupts the strategies of temporal discernment that would have produced an archive effect. Monnet has said that she "wanted audiences to wonder if I shot the footage myself or if it was really found footage," complicating authenticity claims as well as temporal disparities.[10] That's because *Mobilize* is not an essay about an earlier historical conjuncture when its appropriated materials were originally produced. Its on-screen figures are not positioned as pre-modern predecessors or ancestors, but as surrogates for a contemporary Indigenous audience, whom it addresses with an incitement to take action with both "modern" and "traditional" tools. The language of montage models a form of perception that transcends temporal disparities; unlike most found-footage films, there is no sense here that contemporary viewers should see the world any differently from the figures on screen.

This continuity between the profilmic subject and the audience confounds another convention of found-footage filmmaking, which Baron describes as "intentional disparity." Intentional disparity arises from the viewer's perception of a rhetorical or contextual difference between the material's origin and its present use.[11] This disparity is contingent upon the perception of a difference between the intended recipient of the material and the filmmaker: "Like the historian, the appropriation filmmaker who draws on found documents is always an unintended—or, at very least, an unanticipated—reader."[12] This model of history again aligns with the strategies of the colonial archive: Azoulay describes the ways that imperial plunder claims "the right to discover, uncover, penetrate, scrutinize, copy, and appropriate" objects, redistributing the rights of access to those objects "between those [colonizers] who are capable of such discoveries and are authorized to name them, and those [colonized] who may be discovered, or worse, be neglected or relegated to a bygone past."[13] Through the acts of appropriation, recontextualizing, and renaming objects, the colonizer becomes the unanticipated recipient of an object, while the community that produced that object is denied rights of access to them, on the pretense of their temporal disparity from the colonial present. *Mobilize* bypasses this by reorienting its reappropriated materials around their Native protagonists rather than their (predominantly white) producers, restoring the rights of the producers as the recipients of knowledge. Another work of Indigenous experimental cinema, Hopinka's *Kicking the Clouds*, challenges the assumption that history should be written by an unintended reader by activating familial artifacts through intergenerational dialogues, memories, and dreams.

Kicking the Clouds: Heirlooms of Anticipation

Hopinka's film opens with flashed 16mm footage depicting children playing on a beach, images that ground the work in the materiality and contingency of analog film, the visual language of home movies, and the Pacific Northwestern landscape. Cutting to scenes of driving on a forest road, Hopinka introduces audio from tapes of his great-grandmother giving Pechanga language lessons to his grandmother, material he intermittently returns to over the course of the 16-minute film. The women's voices on the tape debate whether to start in the middle, with words "that the kids would be using," or to proceed "from the beginning and go through, lesson by lesson." The exchange points to different models of retelling; to the ways that heritage is *intentionally* passed along pathways of kinship; to the ways that the form of transmission is shaped through relations to intended recipients; and to the role of language in shaping access to memory. The film's title appears over landscapes of the waters around Washington's Lummi Bay, followed by words that lay out something like a pretext for the meditation to come: "We were at a loss for language except what we could speak, and we spoke and spake our way right out of this place. It's cool here still and as the clouds never lingered too long on the past, we don't remember what was a memory and what was a dream." Like the Pechanga lessons, *Kicking the Clouds* resists narratives of loss—of language or of heritage—by imagining new modes of communicating facets of Indigenous experience, modes that elude articulation and confound archival temporalities.

Though it incorporates inherited media, *Kicking the Clouds* is not a found-footage or archival film. Every image was produced by Hopinka on a Bolex camera. Much of the film is given over to images of clouds, foliage, and sunsets, ephemeral impressions of light on celluloid. As the language lesson tapes and oral histories play over these images, gathered in the environs of his hometown of Ferndale, Washington, the effect mimics the tension between memory and dream announced in the on-screen text. The juxtaposition speaks to the persistence of Indigenous ancestral knowledge, language, and presence in the landscape, but also to the impermanence of the world we inhabit. The film's numerous shots documenting family heirlooms and photos act as a counterpoint to those evocations of ephemerality—yet the effect is not one of temporal disparity, but of continuity across generations. These images accompany interviews that Hopinka recorded with his mother, discussing her relationships with her great-grandmother and grandmother, as well as her own experiences as a mother to Hopinka and his siblings. Such objects, the film suggests, are agents of memory, mnemonics used for the retelling of family stories and the active transmission of knowledge, and are thus critical sites of cultural identity.

Unfolding visual and sonic heirlooms alongside intimate contemporary recollections, *Kicking the Clouds* flirts—yet contends—with the conventions of the archival film through its mobilization of what is increasingly referred to as a "family archive." In experimental cinema, films built around family archives and oral histories can realize a "history from below," offering representations of communities often excluded from official and dominant narratives.[14] The informality and irregularity of such collections, shaped by specific experiences and communities, could be seen as upending the universalizing historical conventions of institutional archives. But why would we refer to such non-institutional collections of objects, endowed with private meaning and maintained within networks of kinship, as "archives" at all? If Foucault's formulation of the archive as the law that determines what can be said—and, by extension, what can be seen and heard—

still pertains, then to call something a "family archive" is to insist on the availability of the objects it contains to vision and enunciation.[15]

If all collections of inherited and gathered media have come to be described as archives (family or otherwise), this reflects above all the ongoing ramifications of colonial knowledge structures, which impose regimes of preservation, legibility, and access on spaces of intimacy. The ongoing subsumption of inheritance within the logos of the archive is an outgrowth of the colonial museum's anti-Indigenous foundations, whereby private heirlooms, sacred objects, and ancestral remains were forcibly displaced and rendered public through acquisition, display, and articulation. If, as Baron argues, films made from home movies produce their archive effect by transposing material "from a perceived intended private context of reception with a private or limited audience to an actual public context of reception," then might we argue that archival films reproduce the logics of displacement, compulsory visibility, of mandatory articulation?[16]

In his essay "Film Is the Body," Hopinka describes why Indigenous cinema necessarily works outside such archival logos:

Indigenous cinema is a cinema of the ineffable dreams suppressed for so long. Indigenous art is the art of the indescribable things that you can't think of in English. The meaning isn't in the shape of words, but rather it's found in those crevices between the facts and the information that we've been taught to understand of ourselves, those slick spaces where the spirit slips through that I don't have the words for, that you don't have the words for.

If *Kicking the Clouds* is a language lesson, it is one that seeks to decenter language among the many ways of accessing experience. Objects provide one such conduit—or rather, meaning arises in the relationship between objects, orality, people, and space, a meaning that cannot be rendered "public" and detached from its intended recipients. In "Film Is the Body," Hopinka also specifies holding a camera as another strategy for expressing those fugitive and confidential meanings. Even more than in its texts and voices, *Kicking the Clouds* grounds its challenge to the archival logos in camera practice.

Across all of Hopinka's work, the manual operation of the camera is a central axis of meaning: in films like *Dislocation Blues* (2017) and *malni – towards the ocean, towards the shore* (2020), Hopinka's moment-to-moment decisions about what to show and where to show it from determine the viewer's conditions of access to spaces of Indigenous experience. In *Kicking the Clouds*, Hopinka exercises the same discretion in the way he presents close-ups of moccasins, photo collages, hand-decorated drums, and his grandmother's elaborate beadwork. In many of these shots, Hopinka's camerawork skirts the edges of abstraction, trading focus for proximity, granting access to the detail but witholding the whole. Hopinka is the "intended recipient" of these objects, but he positions the viewer, knowingly but conditionally, as a recipient as well. When we do see complete objects, as in the film's signature image of an outstretched hand holding a vibrant beadwork rose, they are presented as an offering to the camera. In the place of the public exposure of conventional archival films, these offerings are semi-private, consensual, and partial; in the place of the archival film's retrospection, these offerings situate inheritance within a dilated present of active memory.

As in earlier work, Hopinka's mobile frame measures negotiations of privacy and access. *Kicking the Clouds* finds the artist now working with analog film, a shift that demands surrendering the strict and immediate control over the image offered by the DSLR, but that allows for a different relationship to temporality. Often privileged for its ability to preserve indexical traces of the past, analog film nevertheless possesses a proleptic dimension as well. The photochemical nature of the medium means that the status of the image is always provisional in the moment of filming, contingent upon the successful development of the film strip at a later point. In the hands of an artist as responsive as Hopinka, adopting analog film means inviting anticipation, expectation, discovery and surprise into the construction of the image. Shooting film doesn't simply mean capturing traces of what was, it means watching, waiting for things to develop, to see if the intention behind the image carries forward to its reception. The film's juxtaposition of inherited sounds and images with spontaneous impressions, its play of impermanence and survival, extends to the materiality of the medium itself. Like passing down language lessons and preserving family heirlooms, shooting film is the anticipation of a remembrance: it is the commingling of dream and memory.

Instead of intentional disparity, *Kicking the Clouds* exercises intentional agency; instead of archival dislocation, the film situates the objects it documents within their proper domestic and natural environments. Instead of archival permanence, the film privileges ephemerality and anticipation. Like Monnet, Hopinka effectively turns the conventions of archival filmmaking against the very concepts that those operations typically reinforce. They are films that draw on material from the past to propose forms of continuity with the present, which fundamentally challenge the neat delineation of past and present in the first place. Fittingly, we don't have the language to describe this kind of filmmaking, because the terminology we do have—found footage,

                                    Michael Metzger

appropriation, archival film—cannot exist independently of the settler colonial logics that these films uniquely confound.

Continuities

The majority of scholarly treatments of appropriation and archival filmmaking have been predominantly concerned with the form's application as a form of alternative history-writing.[17] Monographs like Catherine Russell's *Archiveology: Walter Benjamin and Archival Film Practices* and Jeffrey Skoller's *Shadows, Specters, Shards: Making History in Avant-Garde Film* celebrate archival and found-footage strategies for the way they privilege the fragment over the whole, thus making history visible as an assemblage of artifacts and ruins.[18] These texts validate found footage in the light of Walter Benjamin's discontinuous model of history, posed as a challenge to the bourgeois concept that the history of humanity has been one of continuous progress. Seeking to articulate a genuine materialist history, Benjamin saw historiography as montage, casting the light of the present on the fragments of the past, a method that demanded the violent rupture of past and present: "in order for part of the past to be touched by the present instant, there must be no continuity between them."[19] Theorists of archival filmmaking similarly uphold the threat that archival and found-footage films pose to dominant models of history by making a virtue of discontinuity. Yet, whether practiced in cinematic montage or in historiography as Benjamin espoused, these techniques of discontinuity, of collecting and decontextualizing, of fragmenting and atomizing, also reproduce logics that have served the causes of empire.

A theory of found-footage and archival poetics grounded in the temporalities of films like *Mobilize* or *Kicking the Clouds* would need to move beyond the fragment as the basic unit of meaning; to evaluate montage for its synchronic potential; to imagine ways that appropriation might recover, restore, and repatriate material to its original context, rather than displace it. Such a theory would also demand a reckoning with the images of anti-Indigenous violence which have been a staple of the form going back to its very origins, and would uplift neglected figures like Raphael Montañez Ortiz—whose 1958 short *Cowboy and "Indian" Film* modeled a found-footage technique on Yaqui ritual—to their rightful place as originators. Such a theory would be grounded in the aesthetics of filmmakers like Colectivo Los Ingrávidos, who scratch and burn through sentimental entertainments of Mexican cinema's Golden Age to bring the present brutality of femicide to light; like Fox Maxy, whose work collapses distinctions between shot, gathered, and borrowed material, using the tools of nonlinear editing to construct films teeming with connections and linkages across the variety of Native experience; and like New Red Order, who infiltrate and detonate spaces of archival display in the name of an unbroken, centuries-long campaign of anti-colonial militancy. Or, perhaps, that theory already exists—and has already existed—long manifest not in language or scholarship but in the films themselves.

1. Jaimie Baron, *The Archive Effect: Found Footage and the Audiovisual Experience of History* (London: Routledge, 2014), 7.

2. Ibid. 49.

3. Ariella Aïsha Azoulay, *Potential History: Unlearning Imperialism* (London: Verso, 2019), 76.

4. Ibid., 42.

5. Baron, *The Archive Effect*, 17-20.

6. Jean O'Brien, *Firsting and Lasting: Writing Indians out of Existence in New England* (Minneapolis: University of Minnesota Press, 2010), 5.

7. On ethnographic salvage and cinema, see Fatimah Tobing Rony, *The Third Eye: Race, Cinema, and Ethnographic Spectacle* (Durham, NC: Duke University Press, 1996); Wanda Nanibush, "Outside of Time: Salvage Ethnography, Self-Representation and Performing Culture," in Anna M. Agathangelou and Kyle D. Killian, eds., *Time, Temporality and Violence in International Relations: (De)fatalizing the Present, Forging Radical Alternatives* (London: Routledge, 2016), 104-118.

8. Kier-La Janisse, "Q&A: Caroline Monnet on NFB Remix 'Mobilize,'" *Spectacular Optical* (12 September 2015), http://www.spectacularoptical.ca/2015/09/qa-caroline-monnet-on-mobilize.

9. Ibid.

10. Kristine Pregot, "Quick Chat from Sundance: *Mobilize* Director Caroline Monnet," *postPerspective* (3 February 2016), https://postperspective.com/quick-chat-from-sundance-mobilize-director-caroline-monnet. Quoted in Andrew Burke, *Hinterland Remixed: Media, Memory, and the Canadian 1970s* (Montreal and Kingston: McGill-Queen's University Press, 2019), 169.

11. Baron, *The Archive Effect*, 23-27.

12. Ibid., 25.

13. Azoulay, *Potential History*, 54.

14. See Efrén Cuevas, *Filming History from Below: Microhistorical Documentaries* (New York: Columbia University Press, 2022).

15. Michel Foucault, *The Archaeology of Knowledge* (New York: Routledge Classics, 2002), 145.

16. Baron, *The Archive Effect*, 89.

17. Leo Goldsmith has identified the dominance of this scholarly approach to found footage, articulating some of the limitations of (and alternatives to) this model in Leo Goldsmith, "Fragmented Screens: Found Footage and Image Circulation," PhD dissertation, Department of Cinema Studies, New York University (2018), 18-22.

18. See Catherine Russell, *Archiveology: Walter Benjamin and Archival Film Practices* (Durham: Duke University Press, 2018); Russell, *Experimental Ethnography: The Work of Film in the Age of Video* (Durham: Duke University Press, 1999); Jeffrey Skoller, *Shadows, Specters, Shards: Making History in Avant-Garde Film.* (Minneapolis: University of Minnesota Press, 2005).

19. Walter Benjamin, *The Arcades Project*, trans. Howard Eiland and Kevin McLaughlin (Cambridge, Mass. and London: Belknap Press of Harvard UP, 1999), 470.

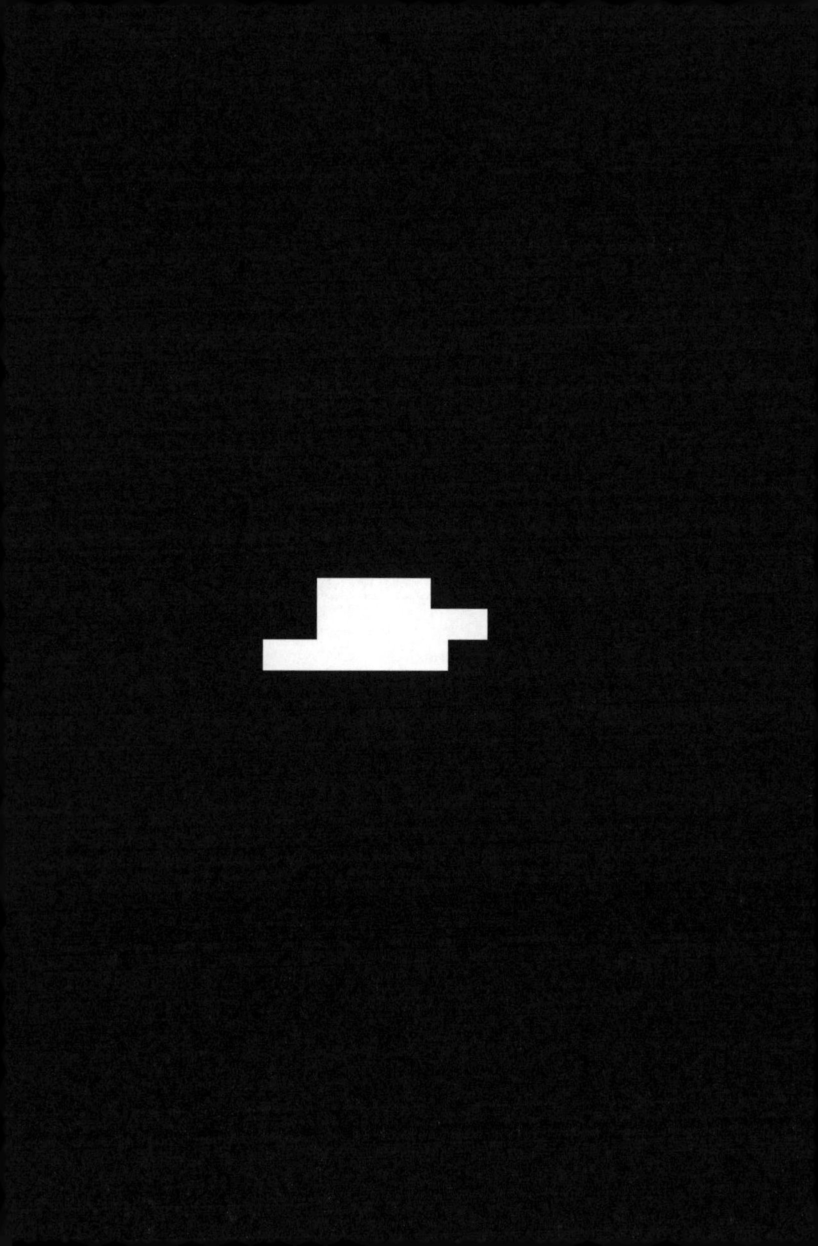

Vehicle
to Memory
Caroline Monnet

I first became interested in the power of moving images when I saw Alanis Obomsawin's *270 Years of Resistance* (1993) at the age of twelve in a very small cinema in Douarnenez, France. Growing up, I used to spend all my summers in Brittany, where my paternal family lives. It struck me later that I had had to cross the Atlantic Ocean to be able to see Indigenous people onscreen for the first time. No doubt that Obomsawin's documentary is powerful, but still, the whole viewing experience transformed me in ways that only today I can grasp. I remember sitting in the darkened theater, understanding at that moment how moving images can be a tool for education and empowerment. It filled me with energy but also anger, paired with a strong desire to contribute positively to the world around me.

Years later, fueled by a drive to create change and bring positive Indigenous representation to the screen, I started making my own short films. I wanted to become a filmmaker because I realized how moving images allowed me to grow intellectually as well as emotionally. All my senses were engaged; I could abandon all expectations.

As a young Anishinaabe woman beginning to explore artistic endeavors, I felt a strong need to take up space, to be physically present and seen. At the time I believed that this was a way to counter oppression, assimilation, and to heal generational traumas within, at least, my own maternal family. It was a political act. I was naïve, but following my instincts.

After making several short films, I no longer wanted audiences to be passive in front of the images that I was creating, nor did I want them to be confined to a dark space for a limited time span. I saw in installation art the potential to not only expand my practice, and to put my work in dialogue with the space it occupies, but also to explore vital ideas around land, geography, identity, and memory. I am curious to study how we occupy space, and how these environments affect us in return. I wanted to challenge the colonial organization of land, bodies, and time by exploring how universal modes of communication can bridge vast physical and psychological divides. I wanted to speak to the interconnectedness and the diversity of views that shape our place within the world, shedding light on the given historical and cultural complexities of our contemporary colonial context.

With installation art, I found a way to merge my interests in video and sculpture to create a more immersive environment. The intention remains to create an experience— whether physical or emotional—that can trigger a deeper understanding of Indigenous lived realities as well as start conversations around issues that are important to me.

Installation art felt particularly suitable for Indigenous ideas of transmission. Instead of seeing the work as a technical thing, we might consider it a social process, focusing on what it does and what it can become, rather than what it is. Does installation art have the capacity to resurrect the spirit in the moving image? And do spirits change depending on the space in which the work is presented? Could it work as a vehicle to memory and act in a spirit that encourages remembrance and perpetuity?

I strongly believe that installation work can channel forces of possibility and renewal. Everything is to be re-invented each time the work is presented because it must adapt to the space. An experience of the work is determined not only by the artist, but also by the setting, the curator, the movements of the audience. Each space has its own ideological and architectural determinations that must be taken into account. It's not uncommon for video art to be a somewhat collaborative process, but it's interesting that the finished work can also continue collaborating with its surroundings and players, mimicking a

                                                                    Caroline Monnet

sense of community. It becomes a social environment where the work unfolds for the viewers like a conversation, a space that can challenge and invigorate.

I love the idea of the spectator moving throughout a gallery, consuming at their own pace images that, for the most part, are not designed for sequential viewing. Depending on when you step in or out of the installation, it's never the same experience for anyone. The audience is left with the choice of walking away at any given time. Landing somewhere between the cinematic experience and that of the video installation, the hybrid dimension of installation art is built on the relationship between the time lived by the spectator and that of the work itself. This constitutes a remarkable difference from the spectator in a movie theater, who sits immobile for a given duration.

While my practice encompasses multiple mediums, I recognize that my continuing desire to explore installation art is a way for me to branch out into new areas I have not yet explored. This allows me to grow as an artist and as a person. It seems I am not alone in this. I am witnessing a video art renaissance that is most likely derived from the increasing range of exhibition methods, improvements in technology, wider institutional acceptance of the medium over the last two decades, and the growing ambitions of artists. Video art has become a requisite for any collecting contemporary art institution, while Indigenous filmmakers have enthusiastically taken up the artform, situating themselves in an in-between zone with shifting limits. Perhaps this is because video installations can make for a unique, immersive environment that is more in tune with Indigenous worldviews. They emphasize creative experimentation and a multidisciplinary approach to making art. They challenge the viewer's ideas about the world that surrounds them. They can be meditative and contemplative.

This experimental approach to storytelling results in an infinite array of stories that often embrace different views, incorporating language, culture, technology, land, spirituality, and traditional teachings. The phrase "all my relations" is often used to explain the interaction of all things within an evolving, ever-changing social, cultural, scientific, and cosmological dynamic, and it can certainly be applied to the current landscape of installation art. It's interrelated, and part of a larger Indigenous worldview. It exists as media, as a message and a form of transferable knowledge. Indigenous artists are able to extend their projects, blurring the boundaries between onscreen images and the viewer's surroundings. Museums, galleries, and other such public spaces feature works that have the power to orient, shape, and engage with issues currently facing Indigenous peoples, so that these issues cease to be the distant problem of a distant country, and can help bring about a world in which Indigenous communities finally cease to be marginalized. A great piece of art moves you, possibly even literally.

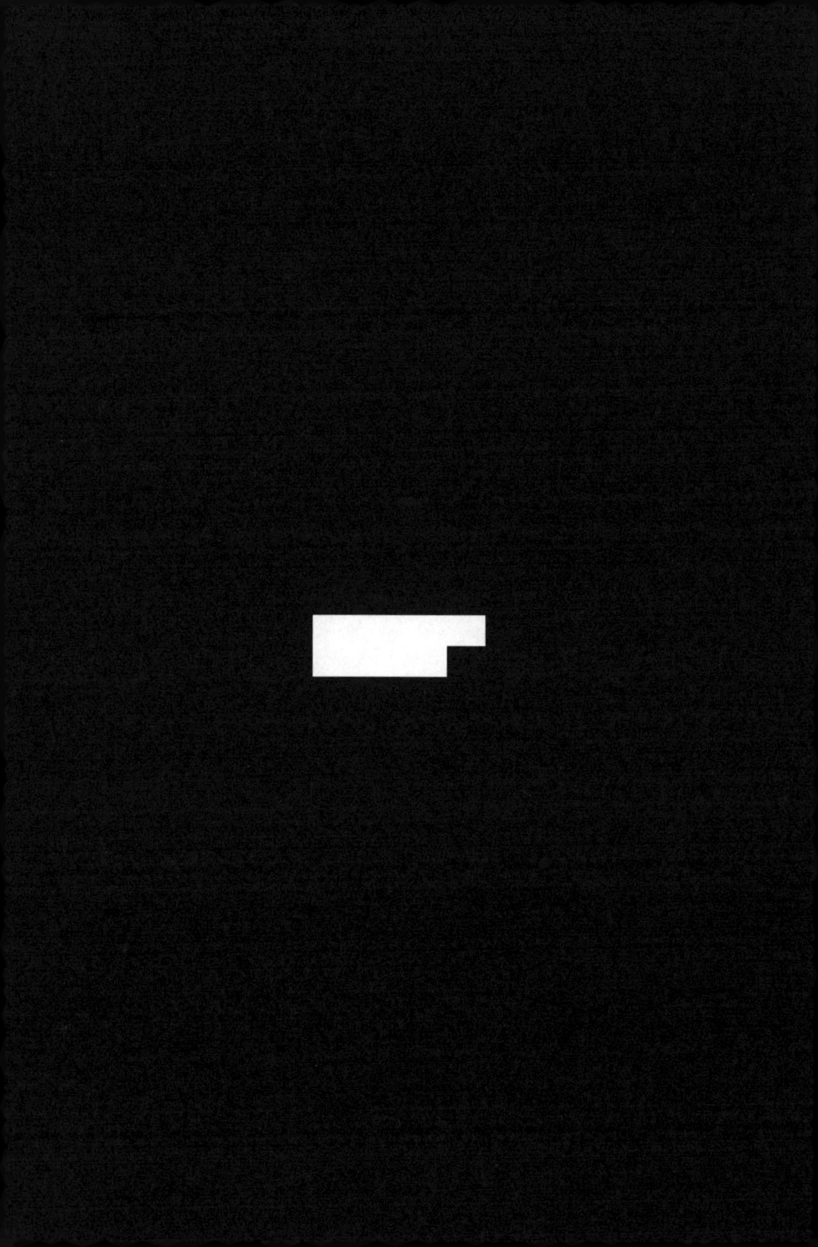

A Comic

Walter Scott

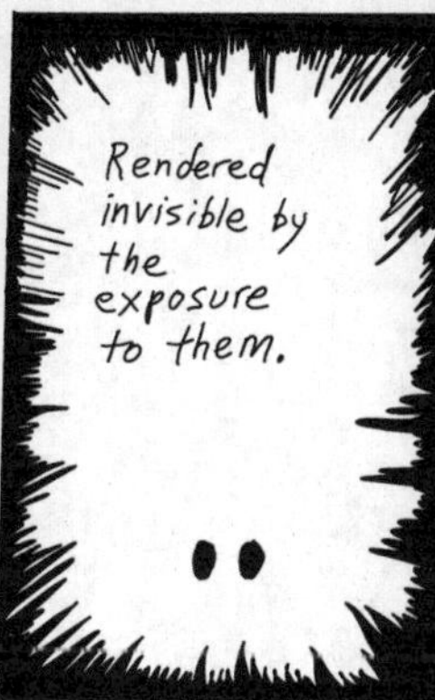

LIVING IN THE WORLD OF IMAGES
Rendered invisible by the exposure to them.

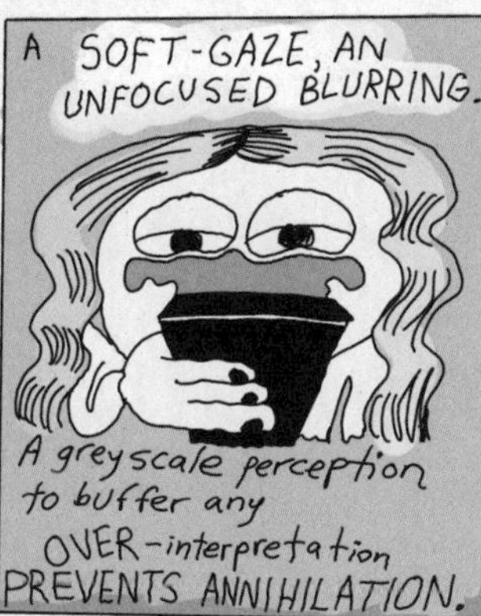

A SOFT-GAZE, AN UNFOCUSED BLURRING.
A greyscale perception to buffer any OVER-interpretation PREVENTS ANNIHILATION.

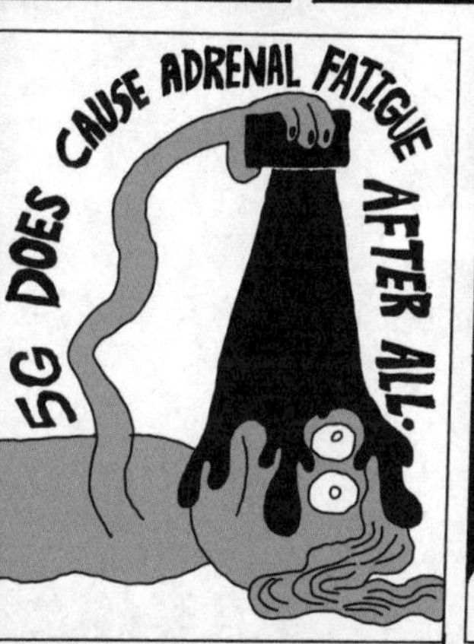

5G DOES CAUSE ADRENAL FATIGUE AFTER ALL.

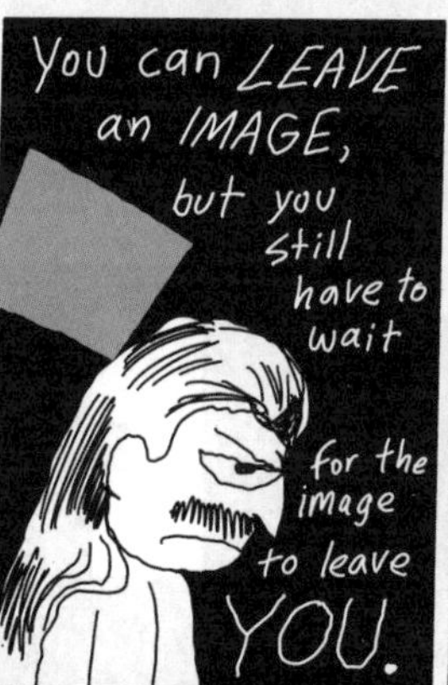

You can LEAVE an IMAGE, but you still have to wait for the image to leave YOU.

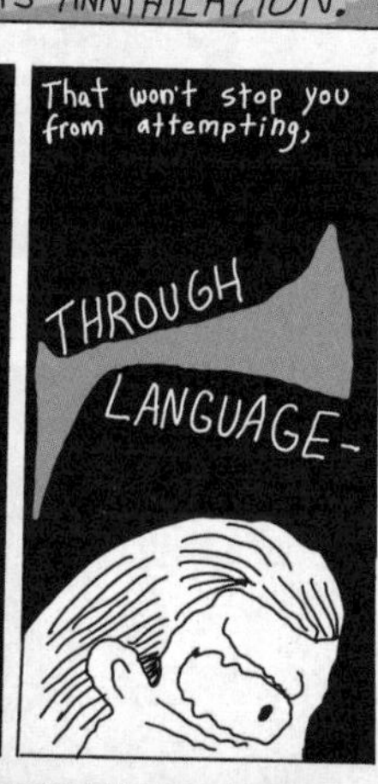

That won't stop you from attempting,
THROUGH LANGUAGE-

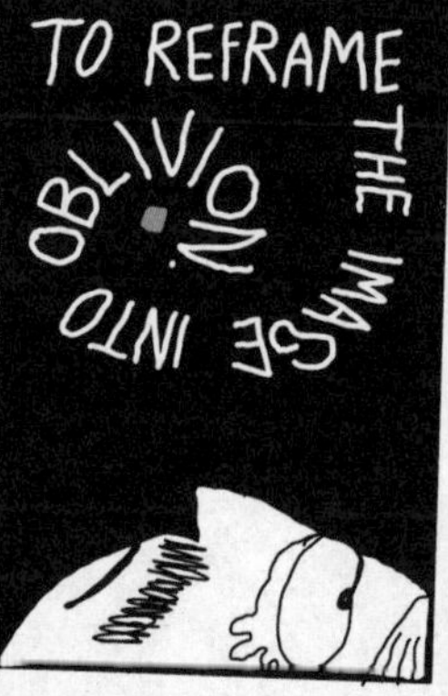

TO REFRAME THE IMAGE INTO OBLIVION.

And in the darkness made by words,

you will be left with-

- a description of yourself.

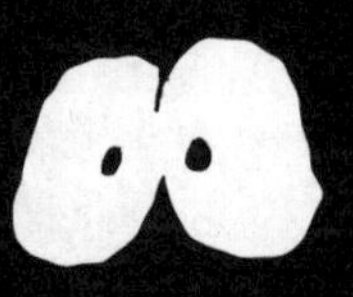

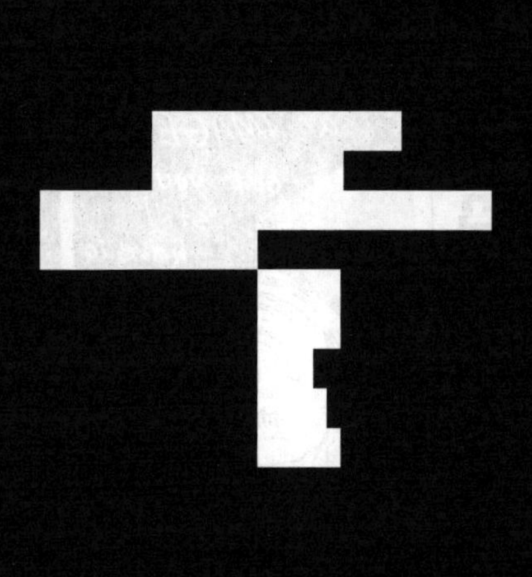

The Violence Inherent: Native Videographers Shoot Back

Adam
Khalil
and
Zack
Khalil

"He surprised me by suddenly emerging from the dense forest on my right, pointing his loaded shotgun at me. He was threatening me. At that instant by luck, I was recording a tape.

"Instinctively I pointed the camera at my potential assassin as if it were a firearm, with that aggressive gesture, that imaginary threat, which we video artists use as a warning that the camera also is a dangerous weapon, as if bullets could come out of the lens."
—*Juan Downey, The Laughing Alligator (1979)*

While doing research for a film about the history of our tribe, the Ojibway of Michigan's Upper Peninsula, we discovered this video by Chilean video artist Juan Downey called *The Laughing Alligator*. The diaristic video chronicles the year that Juan, his wife, and daughter moved to South America to live with the Yanomami, one of the Amazon's most infamous isolated tribes. What intrigued us about his video was not his depiction of the Yanomami, but his own brutally honest interrogation of the ethnographic impulse, and the violence inherent in his camera's act of representation.

The camera is a dangerous weapon for Indigenous peoples, one that has been wielded against us since its inception. Images of Indians dancing for white audiences in Buffalo Bill's Wild West show were some of the first moving images to pass through Thomas Edison's laboratory in 1894.

Anthropology's obsession with preserving images of our "vanishing" cultures—through ethnographic films or archives filled with boxes of our ancestors' remains—has long been a tool used to colonize and oppress Indigenous peoples. By relegating our identities to the past and forcing us to authenticate ourselves via this past, our existence as contemporary individuals living in a colonized land is denied.

The anthropologist's encapsulating gaze ignores the fact that, for Indigenous communities, tradition is not an immutable set of truths handed down by revelation, but a set of ever evolving social practices whose continuity cannot be repaired by preservation—only elaborated through struggle, and finally achieved under conditions of genuine self-determination.

In our tribe, the Ojibway, this struggle for self-determination manifests in the Seven Fires Prophecy. The Seven Fires Prophecy is a story about the history of our tribe which both predates and predicts first contact with Europeans. The story not only foretells the arrival of Europeans, but urges the Ojibway people to begin a great migration westward to avoid them. It goes on to narrativize the colonization of our people, while also providing direction for the recovery of our way of life in the future. It functions as both historical record and prophecy, and it was added to and amended as time unfolded, passed down through an oral tradition—though at different points it was also recorded as pictographs etched into birch bark.

When the Christian missionaries came and Ojibway beliefs were outlawed, the scrolls were gathered and hidden by Ojibway spiritual leaders so that our ceremonies and stories, such as the Seven Fires Prophecy, would not be lost or forgotten.

These scrolls eventually served as inspiration to Ojibway painter Norval Morrisseau, who mimicked their stories and style—but instead of depicting them on birch bark, he painted them in incredibly vivid colors on huge canvases. His unique style revitalized interest in the Indigenous art scene in Canada, and he was dubbed the "Picasso of the North."

Morrisseau created an entirely new style of painting, while simultaneously pushing Ojibway traditions and stories

　　　　　　　　　　　　　　　　　　　　　　　　Adam Khalil and Zack Khalil

into the future by adapting them to a new medium. His act of perpetuating traditions through formal innovation—rather than the anthropological act of preservation—proved a far more effective way of allowing Ojibway people to move their traditions into the future, and served as a model for our 2016 debut feature film *INAATE/SE/ [it shines a certain way. to a certain place./it flies. falls./]*.

We are at a cultural moment where Native videographers are able to exercise self-determination and shoot back against the historicizing gaze of anthropology. Directly inspired by both Morrisseau's work and Juan Downey's anti-ethnographic sentiment, our film is a retelling of the Seven Fires Prophecy, and an attempt to reclaim it from the archives and museums that would confine it to the past.

The impetus for the film was a poem written by our late mother and Indigenous scholar, Allison Boucher Krebs, titled "Native Videographers Shoot Back":

Native videographers are armed and dangerous:
ready willing and able to shoot back,
taking no captives,
aiming straight from the hip
to the heart of the unsuspecting audience.

Native videographers wind the thin corn silk
of storytelling genealogy –
layering
image,
word,
sound,
and silence –
challenging the purposeful amnesia of American History.

Native videographers lean into and snap apart
the imaginary lines separating history from prehistory,
reach across the permeable boundaries
drawn tentatively on maps of modern nation states,
sweep aside the borders that
dot dash dot
across the terrain,
and speak in tongues to the land
who breathes a sigh of relief to hear our voices
resonating back through the once breathless silence.

Native videographers open the aperture
extending the depth of focus
beyond the doctrine of discovery,
the Papal Bulls,
manifesting a destiny of space time continuum
embedded in a metaphysic
of resonance,
resilience,
persistence and
performance,
repeating itself patiently
in looped frame insistence
that while everything has changed,
nothing has.

—Allison Boucher Krebs, "Native Videographers Shoot Back"

Adam Khalil and Zack Khalil

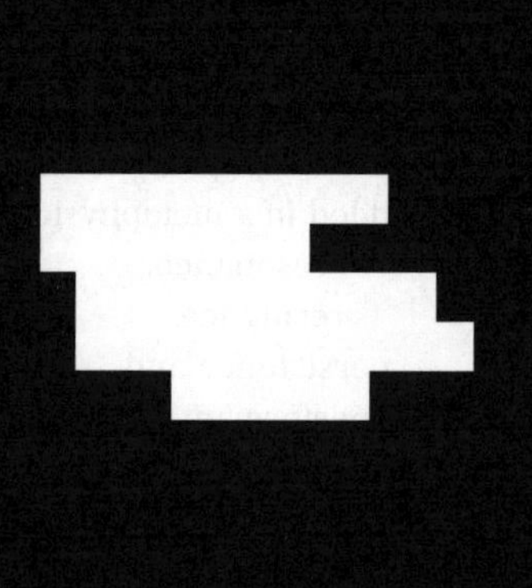

Catching Fire:
INAATE/SE
and the Limits
of Documentary

Adam Spry

Adam and Zack Khalil, the creators of *INAATE/SE/ [it shines a certain way. to a certain place/it flies. falls./]* (2016), have described the experimental film as an attempt to articulate an "inherently Ojibway form of cinema."[1] Shot almost entirely in the Ojibway community at Sault Ste. Marie (on the upper peninsula of present-day Michigan), it in many ways is a heartfelt portrait of the land and people that comprise the Ojibway world. It is not, however, the fidelity of the depiction of this community that makes *INAATE/SE/* a work of Ojibway cinema, but rather its willingness to interrogate the idea that their people can be adequately represented on film at all.

INAATE/SE/ is loosely structured around a traditional teaching called the Seven Fires—a series of seven prophecies that "both predates and predicts first contact with Europeans," as the Khalil brothers write in the piece that appears in this book, which warned the Ojibway about the looming threat of the "light skinned race." The first half of *INAATE/SE/* focuses on the first six sections of the prophecy in the familiar cadence of ethnographic documentary—using talking-head interviews, archival footage, and narrative voice-over to relate each fire to a specific period of Ojibway history. We learn about the early missionary history of Sault Ste. Marie and its eventual transformation into a major artery of American industry with the construction of the Soo water locks. Along the way, we see the damage colonialism has done to the Ojibway community at the Sault, in the form of shocking scenes of substance abuse and heartbreaking testimony by residential school survivors. Over its first half hour, *INAATE/SE/* perhaps gives the appearance of being just another

1. Louisiana Channel. "Artist Adam Khalil on Why Irony Has a Radical Potential," YouTube.com, (12 April 2022). https://www.youtube.com/watch?v=Bg5KQk0TNUM.

2. Adam Khalil, Zack Khalil, and Leo Goldsmith. "Adam & Zack Khalil with Leo Goldsmith," *The Brooklyn Rail* (March 2016). https://brooklynrail.org/2016/03/film/adam-zack-khalil-with-leo-goldsmith-March16.

3. Louisiana Channel. "Adam Khalil on Why Irony."

social issue documentary—albeit one with a slightly more hip aesthetic than what you might see on PBS.

In interviews, the Khalil brothers have been vocal about their distaste for such documentaries, with Adam stating, "Native doc for the most part is fucking terrible." For decades, the Khalils argue, documentaries have flattened contemporary Native existence to the binary of "the drunk Indian or the medicine man," leaving no room for the exploration of other kinds of Indigenous subjectivities. Instead of challenging audiences to think about Indigenous peoples differently, such documentaries only work to reinforce existing stereotypes about Native victimhood and cultural exoticism. As Zack explains, "When you present information like that, people stop thinking about it because they know what they're supposed to understand."[2]

The lack of critical engagement from the audience undermines whatever political project these films might have because, as Adam puts it, "the audience can leave with a sense of having done something, when really all they've done is consume something."[3] This critique is mirrored in *INAATE/SE/* in the words of a traditional healer: "We've seen, whenever we share something with non-Natives, it's theirs. They take off with it... They've taken something that we hold really sacred to us and made it into a show."[4]

The irony, of course, is that *INAATE/SE/* is a show, too—an irony that the film both acknowledges and playfully

4. This critique of documentary is reminiscent of Peter Bürger's observation about art's pacificatory role under capitalism: "Through the enjoyment of art, the atrophied bourgeois individual can experience the self as personality. But because art is detached from daily life, the experience remains without tangible effect, i.e., it cannot be integrated into that life. The lack of tangible effects… characterizes a specific function of art in bourgeois society: the neutralization of critique." Peter Bürger, *Theory of the Avant-Garde*, trans. Michael Shaw (Minneapolis: University of Minnesota Press, 1984), 12-13.

begins to explore in its more experimental second half.[5] As the film finally reaches the Seventh Fire—the generation who is meant to restore Ojibway culture to wholeness—the tone of the film begins to transform. The score becomes more synthetic and harsh, the editing devolves into disorienting series of smash cuts, and the content shifts from ostensibly documentary scenes to a series of fictionalized sequences that imagine the final, violent fulfillment of the Seven Fires prophecy. As the film makes its hard turn towards the experimental, *INAATE/SE/*'s project becomes clear: it is not a documentary, per se, but rather a self-conscious parody of the form—exaggerating the genre's tendency to reduce the complexity of Native life to simple narratives of loss and resilience that can be easily digested by non-Native audiences.

The turning point of *INAATE/SE/* comes with the introduction of the Tower of History a little more than halfway through. A brutalist monolith built by the Catholic church as a shrine to the region's missionaries, the tower looms over the skyline of Sault Ste. Marie—a visual metaphor for Euro-American dominance that would be too on-the-nose if it weren't a real place.[6] Inside the tower, we see murals and dioramas of traditional Ojibway life frozen in time, while a chipper tour guide cosplaying as Jacques Marquette proudly explains, "These are actual, real artifacts. They are not imitations." (fig. 1)

The Tower of History acts as a dark mirror that reflects back onto *INAATE/SE/* itself, revealing how the same desire to preserve and share Ojibway culture that animates the Khalil brothers' film can easily become the kind of

5. Although the film offers a poetically literal gloss of "inaatese" as "[*it shines a certain way. to certain place./ it flies. falls./*]," the commonly understood translation is "it is a certain kind of movie or television show." "Inaatese," *Ojibwe People's Dictionary*, eds. Nora Livesay and John D. Nichols. https://ojibwe.lib. umn.edu/main-entry/ inaatese-vii.

6. Full disclosure: I've paid admission to visit the Tower of History—it's weird.

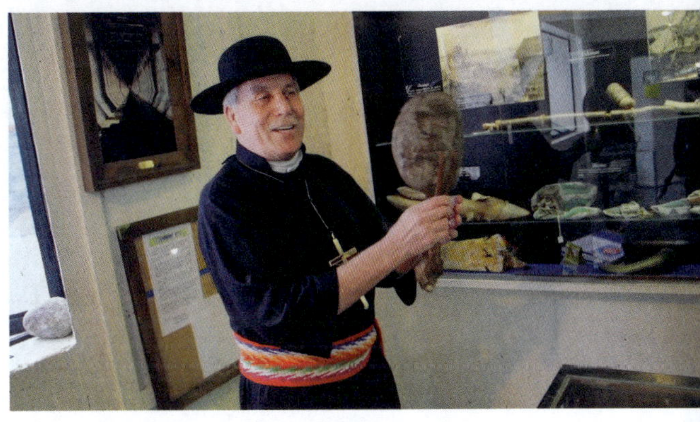

exploitative display we see in the Tower—the reduction of Ojibway life to a kind of static diorama.

Once *INAATE/SE/* introduces this element of ironic self-awareness, the tenor changes dramatically, shifting away from the pretense of documentary objectivity, and leaning into an exaggerated sense of artifice. The final sequence of *INAATE/SE/* is centered around a hallucinatory confrontation between a young Ojibway woman named Alicia and a monstrous figure of a priest (dressed suspiciously like the Tower's tour guide, see fig. 2). At the climax of the scene, Alicia draws a gun on the priest and says, "Bakinaage, bitch!" as she pulls the trigger (fig. 3), vanquishing the colonizer once and for all. The scene offers a powerful fantasy of decolonization, but whatever radical potential it might express is simultaneously undercut by a persistent awareness of its artifice. The style of this scene seems to self-consciously, even parodically, mimic the aesthetics of '80s action movies—from the protagonist's pithy one-liner to a score clearly inspired by John Carpenter's *Escape from New York* (1981). Even as one version of Alicia prepares to fire her gun, the film cuts to another version of

Adam Spry

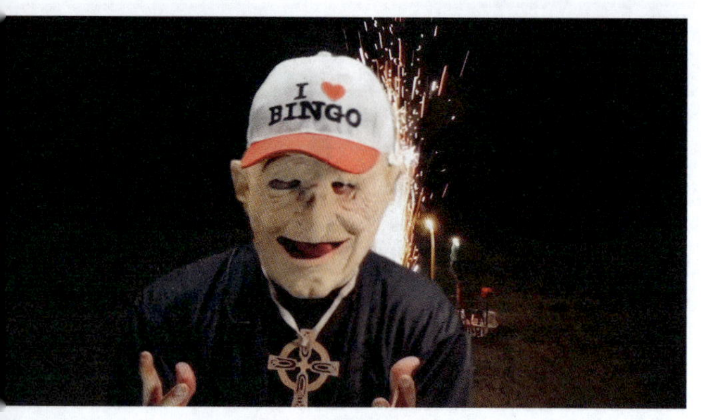

fig.2

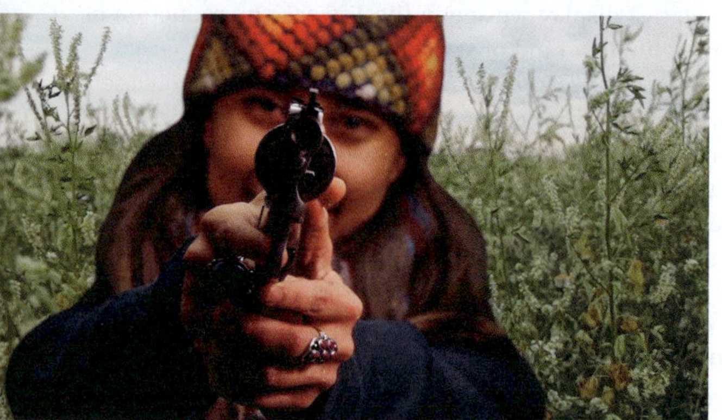

fig.3

Alicia standing atop the Tower, vacantly staring, slack-jawed, into the camera (fig. 4)—a pose that mirrors the passivity of the viewer. As the scene plays out, it becomes clear that the Seven Fires prophecy has been fully transformed into a "show"— a spectacle of wish-fulfillment that offers the audience a sense of narrative closure, without demanding anything in return.

Like a souvenir bought at a museum gift shop, the cinematic fantasy of decolonization on offer in *INAATE/SE/*'s climax may provide immediate gratification, but its artificiality becomes apparent in the final scene of the film. After Alicia shoots the priest, *INAATE/SE/* cuts to the image of three young Ojibway superimposed over a kitschy painting of an historical Ojibway village (fig. 5). The promise of the Seven Fires having been attained, the Ojibway seem happy to have been "returned" to traditional life, smiling and waving at the audience. But as the shot continues for over thirty seconds, their smiles fade, and the awkwardness of the scene becomes impossible to ignore. The three figures are not free—they're stuck in a carefully constructed image of Ojibway culture, aesthetically (and ideologically) identical to the cheesy dioramas in the Tower. In this moment, *INAATE/SE/* reveals that the true threat is not some easily dispatched bogeyman, but something far more insidious: the expectation that Indigenous people be culturally and historically static. The film ends with a shadowy figure removing the painting from the wall and carrying it off—a gesture that can be read as either a final act of erasure, or (more optimistically) the removal of the colonial frame that encloses Ojibway existence. The interpretation, however, is left up to the viewer.

By ultimately deferring any sense of closure, the ending of *INAATE/SE/* self-consciously evokes the trickster tradition of Ojibway storytelling. According to the Khalils, *INAATE/SE/* was heavily inspired by the aadizookaanag, sacred stories about

Nanabozho—a figure "kind of like Jesus," according to Adam, "but... he's kind of a fuck-up." In the aadizookaanag, Nanabozho is both a community hero and a self-centered idiot, as likely to burn his own asshole out of spite as he is to fight off malevolent spirits. According to the critic Arnold Krupat, such trickster stories "do not operate according to the oppositional logic that has characterized the thought of the modern, literate West." Instead, they offer a more dialogical form of narrative, in which "we find not puzzling oppositions but complementarities... that force our minds to think creatively."[7] Like the aadizookaanag, *INAATE/SE/* uses a series of contradictions without easy resolution, demanding that we grapple with whatever unsettling feelings it may have provoked on our own.

To my mind, it is precisely *INAATE/SE/*'s puckish sense of irony and its resistance to closure that makes it a work of "inherently Ojibway cinema." An Ojibway worldview, if it can be said to exist at all, is defined by its dialogical outlook—the understanding that the world is in a constant state of change and renewal, and therefore must be approached with

7. Arnold Krupat, *All That Remains: Varieties of Indigenous Expression* (Lincoln: University of Nebraska Press, 2009), 24.

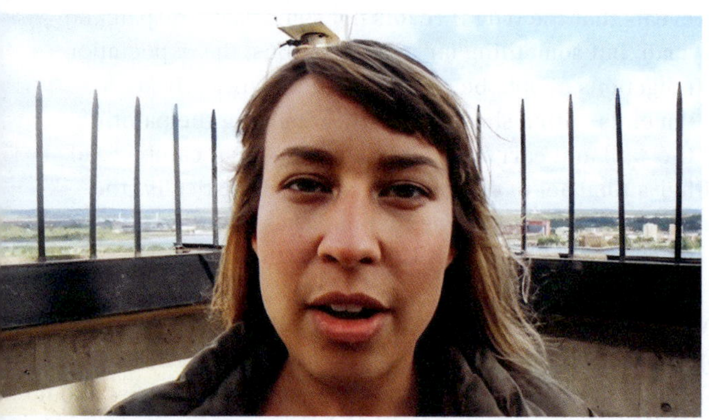

fig.4

intuition, pragmatism, and intellectual flexibility. Even something as seemingly precious as the Seven Fires prophecy is not sacrosanct but is a story that is reinterpreted and transformed by each generation of Ojibway to suit their own needs, as Adam explains: "In a hundred years, the different fires or chapters will be different. And two hundred years ago they were different. And it's meant to be this living document, as opposed to this thing that's codified and printed."[8]

Like the water of the St. Marys River that flows throughout *INAATE/SE/*, the constant flux of Ojibway culture can never really be captured on film. Instead, it exists only in the lived experience of a community, continually renewed through acts of collective imagination and memory. Ultimately, *INAATE/SE/* is just that: an expression of the Ojibway community at the Sault—not an artifact, but the ephemeral trace of a people defiantly making and remaking themselves every day.

8. Louisiana Channel. "Adam Khalil on Why Irony."

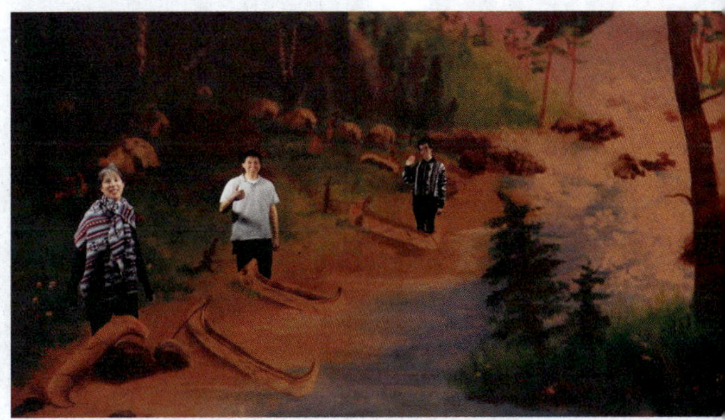

fig.5

Adam Spry

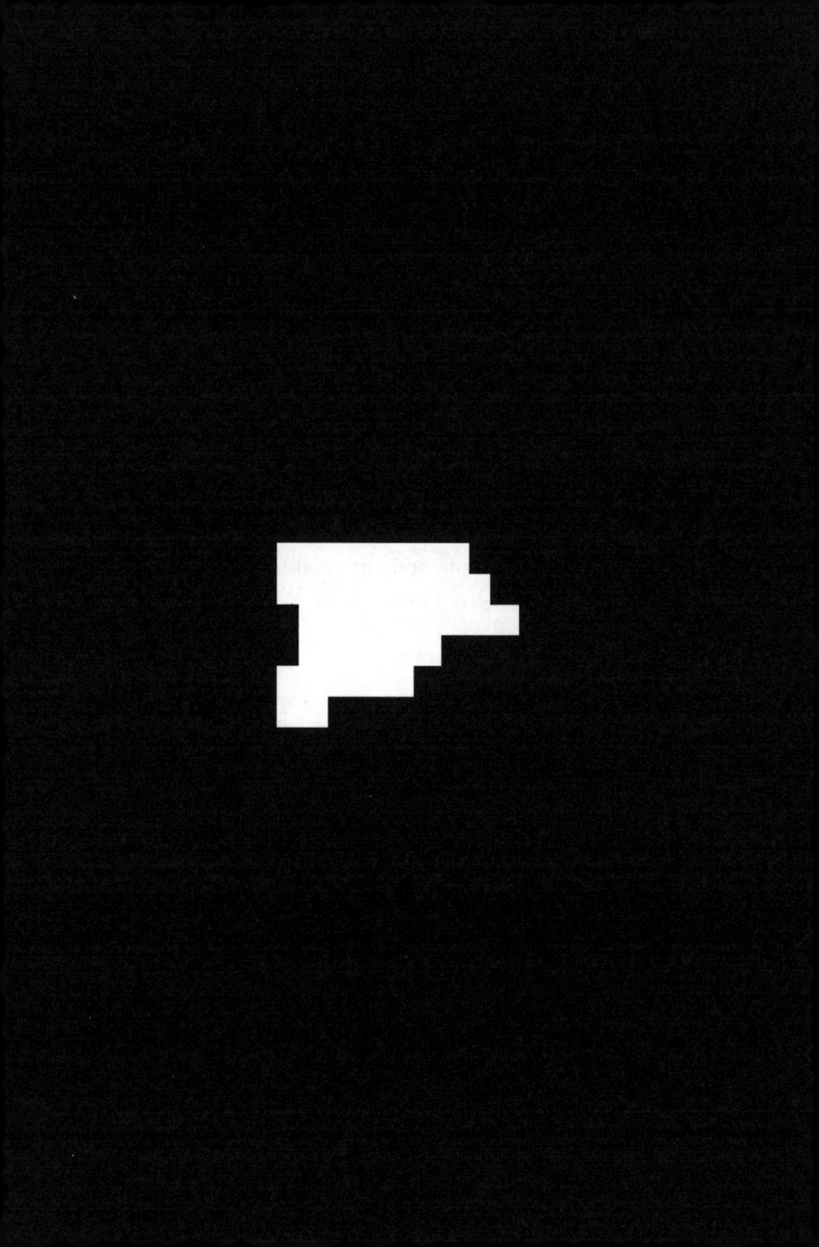

Desire Lines: Sky Hopinka's Undisciplining of Vision

Diana Flores Ruíz

Movement, memory, and imagination beget one another in the films of Sky Hopinka, a member of the Ho-Chunk Nation and descendant of the Pechanga Band of Luiseño Indians. Expressionistic and experimental in form, Hopinka's work concerns the vitality of contemporary Indigenous experiences. His films mediate scenes of land, kin, and community through in-camera and postproduction manipulations. Hopinka frames the dynamism of present-day Indigenous life with both extant cultural texts and the latest iterations of how Indigenous people use them to create new cultural productions. Historical documents and recordings take root in an unfolding present, which in turn produce new resonances for contemporary and future Indigenous audiences. Merging aesthetic inheritances of the essay film and the lyrical film, Hopinka's enunciated subjectivity keeps the scope of his works personal.

Across his moving-image practice—over a dozen short films, a recent feature-length film, and a growing number of installations, created across 16mm film, digital video, still photography, multiscreen works, calligrams, and poetry— Hopinka has re-routed the possibilities of audiovisual relationships to place and time on his own terms. Any medium-specific analysis of his individual projects, however, would diminish his larger contributions to a multisensory, multimedia approach that deliberately undisciplines vision.

Hopinka's visual poetics use conceptually robust editing techniques to create space, forge relations, and merge disparate temporalities. His films favor nonsync and layered sound designs, beguiling cross-fades, hypersaturations, extreme color inversions, and hypnotizing time-lapses, in addition to many other techniques. From film to film, strategies for poetic envisionings of Indigenous life develop alongside the particularities of subject matter and source materials.

While these rich editorial moments might solicit a reaction through their arresting impressions, Hopinka's refractions also operate in more concrete ways during his filming. For example, during infrequent scenes of Native groups or gatherings—in which audiences don't get to have a sense of their relationship with Hopinka—he works with their images generously and protectively. The camera might linger while pointing down, be kept at a distance, adjust the focus to blur, or intermittently turn away from a dance or ritual. Hopinka uses these simple cinematographic moves as well as mesmerizing, technically complex post-production effects to safeguard Indigenous peoples' images even while celebrating their presence.

Throughout Hopinka's films, variations of land inversions and superimpositions become novel ways to visually experience lands, skies, and waters in time. Hopinka's deft, rigorous attention to rhythm and pacing situates these seemingly simple formal moves in ways that allow viewers to linger briefly in these compositions, but not long enough to take them for granted.

Hopinka's films take up the anticolonial covenant of "shooting back," aesthetically and politically countering the historical terms and conditions through which cinema has represented Indigenous peoples and cultures.[1] Given a broad overview of his films, Hopinka's contributions to undoing the harms of dominant visual culture might be characterized by a nuanced double move. Through formal innovation, the films construct a poetic and expansive Native diegesis, a space where Indigenous presence, ways of thinking, and modes of relation do not have to account for settler legibility. Through this visual worldmaking, Hopinka's films critique cinema's historical complicity in settler colonial visual regimes, including ethnographic documentary and the accessorizing of landscapes in Westerns. Yet Hopinka displaces the centrality of whiteness in making such critiques.

Hopinka "shoots back" by creating new visual grammars and foreclosing ways of seeing that were historically promulgated by extractive tendencies in cinema, ethnography, and art history. Hopinka cultivates the political edge of abstraction in his poetic approaches to the present and futures of Indigenous cultures.

Transits of Survivance

"What it means to be in transit is to be in motion, to exist liminally in the ungrievable spaces of suspicion and unintelligibility. To be in transit is to be made to move."
—Jodi Byrd, The Transit of Empire: Indigenous Critiques
of Colonialism

In *The Transit of Empire*, Chickasaw scholar Jodi Byrd examines how material and ideological settler structures of extraction rely upon yet strategically obscure the role of Indigeneity. As she characterizes the reckoning of Indigenous dispossession and its wake, she notes "a difference between recovered and having never lost in the first place."[2] For Byrd, it is historical analysis that can make Indigenous peoples' dispossessions perceptible against perpetual systemic denial.

Indigenous storytelling forms a connective tissue between the affective states of living and creating in spite of settler violence. Chippewa scholar Gerald Vizenor characterizes this work as "survivance"—that is, something that "goes beyond mere survival to acknowledge the dynamic and creative nature of Indigenous rhetoric."[3] Survivance is an "active sense of presence, the continuance of native stories, not a mere reaction, or a survivable name. Native survivance stories are renunciations of dominance, tragedy and victimry."[4]

Hopinka's films enact just such a process of survivance. They operate beyond the spectacle of romanticized or trauma-centric pasts crystallized by popular cinema and histories of anthropological extraction. They do not shy away from the complexities of such histories' enduring reach into the present, but their focus remains on Native experiences and perspectives.

Moving through Language

Hopinka began making films around 2010, while he was studying Chinuk Wawa, a language from the lower Columbia River basin. As is the case with many Indigenous people, Hopinka didn't grow up speaking his heritage Ho-Chunk or Luiseño languages. Born in the state of Washington, physically distant from his tribal lands in Wisconsin and Southern California, Hopinka turned to Chinuk Wawa when he was living in Portland, Oregon. He learned through "Where Are Your Keys?"—a set of language-acquisition techniques that draw on embodied gestures to cultivate an inviting, intuitive approach to learning.[5] "Where Are Your Keys?" moves beyond orthodox language pedagogies, lessening the focus on correct grammar structures.

Now a teacher of Chinuk Wawa himself, Hopinka gives the endangered language a material longevity through the production and exhibition of his films. Language revitalization is an active process, one that Hopinka treats with nuance. His films tease out the complexities with which Indigenous languages are (and are not) passed down or revived through techniques that he devises to extend questions about cultural heritage into the very mode of communication itself. In his films, Chinuk Wawa terms and narrations might remain untranslated into English, for example, yet when filming with friends, Hopinka does not impose pressure or make any assumptions about their speaking Indigenous languages. His first feature-length film, *malni – towards the ocean, towards the shore* (2020), models a generous method of working across and between Chinuk Wawa and English without ascribing more value or emotional heft to either. With few Chinuk Wawa interlocutors, Hopinka's methods of cinematic language revitalization often use historical documents repurposed for the present. Hopinka expands the circle of speakers with whom he can talk through creative uses of archival texts and recordings.

In one of his first short films, *wawa* (2014), Hopinka devised a formal structure to bring a thirty-year-old (at that time) recorded conversation to bear on present-day language lessons. In the film, Hopinka shows a close-up talking head from an interview he conducted with the white linguist Henry Zenk. Zenk provides a window into his early lessons and practice in Chinuk Wawa with Wilson Bobb, a Grand Ronde and Yakima Nation elder fluent in the language. Hopinka cuts to a red screen and narrates the English translation of Bobb's dialogue in a 1983 recording. Zenk's side of the conversation with Bobb is presented in English text on-screen, without Hopinka's voice.

The excerpts chosen by Hopinka attest to the affection developed in the men's friendship. Often playful, Bobb is encouraging of Zenk's then-novice practice: "You know, if you don't know how to say it, later on you will learn how," Bobb assures him. The transcript does not just record a practicum, but enacts language pedagogy itself. Hopinka's recasting of the transcript enhances the significance of the film's other scenes depicting a group language lesson and expressing the labor of language acquisition. In the final shot, Hopinka translates the word "wawa" to "talk/discourse/dialogue/murmur," and the film takes up the full range of language study, as done both individually and socially. In extreme close-up, Hopinka flips through a Chinuk Wawa dual-language guide and sounds out particular pronunciations over and over again. The private tedium of learning a new language in these shots is offset by the pleasure of language in practice with others.

The film then cuts to a scene of a group of people (including Hopinka) speaking Chinuk Wawa in the corner of a conference room in New York City. They pass the camera around to one another in their seated circle, and are shown mostly in medium and medium close-up shots. Patient and supportive, they listen to each other speak, nodding, gesticulating, and nonverbally communicating as others talk or pause to think, searching for words. It's a calm, easygoing atmosphere of putting the "Where Are Your Keys?" techniques into practice. Their conversation is not subtitled, and the audio of their conversation is mostly removed in favor of the interview recordings that play instead. As the film progresses, texts from these off-screen interviews begin to appear over the image, stacking from the bottom to the top of the screen. Gradually, layers of text and sound surge into the scenes, as text overlaps and fills the image with multiple meanings of the interviews' translations.

Hopinka's phonetic practice escalates into a rapid, nearly exasperated overload. It's difficult if not impossible to read all of the crowded text or distinguish each of the sonic layers playing simultaneously. The audio from the filmed interview with Zenk continues to play as the pacing of the cuts increases, flashing between the group lesson and sped-up page-turning. Throughout Hopinka's films, a formal reciprocity between aural and written language plays out through the image's capacity to hold information and shape stories. Sometimes this reciprocity is treated with ample contemplative space, but at other times, as in the collaged climax in *wawa*, it accumulates to a point of overwhelming intensity.

Toward the end of the film, Hopinka pierces through the frenzied audiovisual crescendo to issue an urgent testament to keep the language alive. The film goes silent and a close-up of Zenk, looking wistful and straight into the camera, is synchronized with his written words from the archival transcript: "There's no one to speak chinuk wawa with." Hopinka cuts to red again, for a longer duration, reading Bobb's response: "Just you and me. But, with the two of us just going on talking away, later on you will learn. You should say everything that you want to say, even if it's completely wrong. Say it. That's the way you'll learn it. You certainly will know it really well."

Hopinka could have concluded the excerpt there with this rousing call to move past hurdles and put language into practice. But Hopinka keeps reading. Through Hopinka's audiovisual mediation, Bobb says to Zenk, "You'll speak it so very straight, you won't be at all white." The film flashes to the group lesson with Hopinka centered in a trio, all making eye contact with the low-angled camera. It is over this shot that Bobb tells Zenk, "You'll be Indian." Bobb's words finish out the film, sealing the complicated intersections of language, culture, and identity that the film has implicitly raised throughout. This conclusion shifts the film into a more circular pattern, one in which language as a social relationship and language as a historical vector circumnavigate one another.

Bobb's comments resonate with the debates over the history of Chinuk Wawa's formation, which the film introduces through Zenk's interviews with him: a linguistic shift from "proper" to "jargon" as a result of white fur traders and settlers simplifying the Chinook language into a pidgin language. Elsewhere, Zenk and others have written about the development and spread of Chinuk Wawa prior to settler arrival as a shared language produced by different Native tribes of the lower Columbia River to facilitate communication.[6] Unlike many debates over origin, the popular use of Chinuk Wawa in the mid-nineteenth century is uncontested. The Confederated Tribes of the Grand Ronde included over twenty-five dialects; they used Chinuk Wawa as a lingua franca—so much so that it became a first language for many growing up on Grand Ronde Community reservations.

As one of Hopinka's earliest films, *wawa* lays the groundwork for his practice of eschewing dominant forms of grammar in the service of immersive, lived uses of language. Hopinka constructs new schematics of cinematic and communicative grammars.

Spaces of Visual Sovereignty

My choice to introduce Hopinka's films with *wawa* stems less from auteurism or chronology than from a critical determination to emphasize some of the formal terrain that his films traverse. To be sure, there is much to be said about the legacies of experimental and documentary filmmaking practices that inform his works and that he, in turn, innovates. Similarly, Hopinka's films offer visual anthropologists and art historians critical texts through which to reframe the historical representation of Indigenous people and/in place. Yet, although my position is that of a film and media scholar trained in such analyses, I worry that those analytic approaches limit the stakes of Hopinka's work.

Instead, I want to resist the academic proclivity to read Hopinka's work in ways that might ultimately recenter historical approaches to visuality within disciplines that have and continue to benefit from Indigenous dispossession within field-defining origin stories. Today, these historical academic disciplines are no longer monoliths: committed scholars redefining their fields continue to make progress. Fidelity to the self-sustaining bounds of particular disciplines, though, can risk instrumentalizing Hopinka's practice, incorporating a sliver of his cultural production into debates too often rooted in self-justification. However, I don't want to claim these films as a teleological defense, nor do I want to uplift particular fields of knowledge production. I am more interested in how Hopinka undisciplines sound and image in ways that exceed settler colonial taxonomies and hierarchies of perception, time, and place.

In *Jáaji Approx.* (2015), Hopinka continues his work with archival recordings in innovative ways. This time, they're even more personal than in *wawa*. He draws from decades of recordings of his father, or Jáaji, which translates into English as the direct-address form of "father." Hopinka's father was a Ho-Chunk powwow singer and drummer. In *Jáaji Approx.*, his recordings are played alongside and merged with static, handheld, and fixed moving images of the places and passages traveled independently by father and son. The film's awe-inspiring use of scale and superimposition in depicting views from the road make it tempting to invoke art historical discourses on the concept of landscapes.[7] Perhaps, however, it is more generative to consider how the film opens up what Anishinaabe and Haudenosaunee scholar Vanessa Watts calls "Place-Thought," which she defines as the "non-distinctive space where place and thought were never separated because they never could nor can be separated. Place-Thought is based upon the premise that land is alive and thinking and that humans and non-humans derive agency through the extensions of these thoughts."[8]

"Place-Thoughts" are layered in time, sound, and image. In *Jáaji Approx.*, Hopinka's voice-over introductions to the recordings toy with a matter-of-fact delivery of information: whose recording it is, the date and time recorded. This narration sets up the expectation of consistency and measured distance in presenting recorded materials throughout the film. As soon as the recording machine first beeps, though, Hopinka inverts a shot taken from the dashboard of a car on the open road.

More than half the image is of a brilliant daytime sky above a cloud-covered mountain range in the far distance.

At the beep, his father begins to describe the intuitive interconnections and energetic choreography between a drumbeat, singers, dancers, audience, and travel. Fused into the center of the image are phonetic subtitles of his father's words, but after only a few, the film cuts to a handheld shot in which the pavement takes up about half of the frame. A series of short takes follows, showing the varied scale of routes that Hopinka walks and drives through: city and rural roads, trails along a vast river cliffside and within dense woods, even a still shot at the entrance to the Pala Indian Reservation. Speaking over these shots, his father reflects on movement and music in transit: "Just leaving the powwow, then you're cruising. Like you'll be starting to crash out and, you're driving the noise, the wheel, the sound of the road, it sounds like a song then."

By the second recording, Hopinka adds an endearing "my" to "Jáaji's recordings" and slightly delays the time of the recording, as if he almost forgot. The brief remarks at the top of the recording are subtitled phonetically on-screen, but then switch to English subtitles once his father begins to sing. The recording ends just as a large gasoline tanker truck zooms diagonally across the screen, narrowly avoiding the car on the shoulder of the road. The contemplative atmosphere of the film is interrupted by a reminder of the risks of the road.

The film stays in the car a while longer, parked in the next shot across from an illuminated gas station. Now Hopinka's off-screen introduction provides the date but scraps the verbal timestamp as he seems to get caught up in the recording, speaking simultaneously with his father in naming the "old song from 1977." His father's singing begins, but suddenly the audience hears Hopinka change his mind and stop the recording before his father completes the phonetic translation on-screen:

"No, uh, Ho-Chunk Song One instead, with a cross-fade into my accompaniment." Off-screen tapes click, materializing in the viewer's mind some of the selections Hopinka makes in the film. In *Jáaji Approx.*, Hopinka considers and toys with the anthropological impulse to standardize cataloging practices. With each recording, however, he strays further away from the clinical announcement of recording facts and becomes more engaged with what his father is saying or singing.

In the cross-faded accompaniment that follows, arguably the audiovisual high point of the film, the pair sing in a round, which impresses the sense of an echo into the composite sky-and-land compositions on screen. An inverted extreme long shot of distant mountains against a basin and rolling hills hovers above a silhouetted jagged edge of indeterminate scale in the distance at the base of the screen. The two shots' clear and hazy skies meld in the middle of the screen. Younger and elder Hopinkas create a vocal harmony across time, medium, and place. As the composite image is deconstructed, one layer at a time, Hopinka keeps the recorded audio intact. His father's comments about stopping on the road make him laugh—an act that briefly injects a sense of the quotidian into an otherwise transcendent moment created by matching the rounds of a song with the land and sky. The inclusion of the conversational aside reminds audiences that this is a father and son, that these songs and ways of being are part of the fabric of everyday life. Rather than detracting from an inspiring moment, their exchange grounds it, keeping it specific and unromanticized.

Hopinka cultivates defamiliarization with a limiting twist— challenging the viewer's expectations and contexts for when and how the land might shift from being "unremarkable" to being instead endowed with visual interest or potentially even made spectacular. Hopinka resists the latter by grounding inverted, collaged shots in his subjective relations. In doing so, his creative convenings of disparate times and places push back against the enduring settler demands to parcel territory and profit through landscape.

Since the nineteenth century, photographic technology has been an accelerant to settler mythologies of pure, uninhabited spaces. The boundaries of the frame, its perspectival address, and the duality of the physical formations of nature and the coherent landscape images as produced through an artist or camera all combined to establish an enduring system of representation that either evacuated Indigenous life entirely or made it ornamental. Patrick Wolfe's foundational formulation that settler colonialism is a structure rather than an event is borne out by how visual culture's historical propagation of landscapes has fostered a "logic of elimination" that methodically erases Indigenous people from their own lands.[9]

Hopinka's formal strategies reconfigure ways of seeing and being to break with landscape's commodification and utility for empire. By employing non-spectacular and poetic modes of presentation, his films repudiate the settler optics of land representation and possession. His sense of movement through and between places that are physically real and accessible, as well as composite or imagined, suggests alternative ways of moving through and perceiving place that can actively nurture memory and imagination.

Hopinka's audiovisual engagement with land functions within Cree writer Winona Wheeler's notion that "land is mnemonic," that "it has its own set of memories... it nudges or reminds."[10] In *Jáaji Approx.* and other films, Hopinka's interventions into landscape are engaged in a campaign to repurpose their historical inflections. Similarly, Byrd notes:

> For American Indians, who have lived for tens of
> thousands of years on the lands that became the

                                                    Diana Flores Ruíz

United States two hundred and thirty years ago, the land both remembers life and its loss and serves itself as a mnemonic device that triggers the ethics of relationality within the sacred geographies that constitute indigenous peoples' histories.[11]

Hopinka's intimate cinematography and inventive editing recalibrate the historical terms by which and for whom visibility operates in his films. As evidenced by *Jáaji Approx.*, his reworking of landscapes excises the "settler-scape" from Native lands and imagination.

Editorial Ethics and Refusals

In *I'll Remember You as You Were, Not as What You'll Become* (2016), Hopinka employs calligrams—defined as texts that take the form of a pictorial or ornamental design—at the beginning and toward the end of the film. The language in the calligrams is excerpted from early twentieth-century ethnographic texts written by anthropologist Paul Radin about the Ho-Chunk Nation.

For Hopinka and other Indigenous artists, working with archival materials sourced through anthropology brings up paradoxes of voice: many surviving texts and teachings were preserved through the lenses of white outsiders invested in a project to frame Indigenous ways of life in the past. One way artists have dealt with this issue is to pursue the named individuals, the "informants" consulted or conscripted by anthropologists.

In recognition of the contested ethical nature of such texts (written by outsiders culling privileged or sacred information), Hopinka refracts Radin's take on his tribe into new forms. The calligrams shape the excerpts into the figures of geographic

Ho-Chunk effigy mounds. In so doing, Hopinka brings out the "Native informant" as a mediator between lived and extracted knowledge. The calligrams' focus on key pieces of information, instead of on the anthropological frameworks that they originally served, turns the attention back to Ho-Chunk teachings. Hopinka reinvigorates archival materials in order to extend and adapt their meaning in the present.

Appearing first is a triangular, birdlike calligram using Radin's text that describes a "vision of a Road of Perfection… to be rewarded by a return to earth and to the vicissitudes of the living." It sets the stage for the tone and direction of the film, described by Hopinka as an elegy to the Anishinaabe and Chemehuevi poet Diane Burns. Hopinka juxtaposes these Ho-Chunk calligrams with a video of Burns's poetry reading, creating intergenerational connections of Indigenous knowledge. Next, Hopinka reworks a longer, traditional Ho-Chunk text sourced from Radin's fieldwork into a starlike shape:

> But they apparently do not insist that existence
> depends upon sense perceptions alone. He claims
> that what is thought of, what is felt, and what is
> spoken—in fact, anything that is brought before
> his consciousness—is a sufficient indication of its
> existence, and it is the question of the existence and
> reality of these spirits in which he is interested.

These calligrams link the spiritual and visual poetics of reincarnation. By working with an archival poetry performance, Hopinka creates a space for Burns's thoughts, feelings, and voice to permeate the present. Her poignant messages and dry wit solicit a spiritual sensorium that grounds the film throughout in "the vicissitudes of the living" noted in the first calligram.

Following the initial calligram, *I'll Remember You as You Were, Not as What You'll Become* presents a highly stylized long take from a dance credited as a Naimuma powwow. The editing transforms the footage through hypersaturation, photonegative inversion, blur, and vertically striated filtering. In conjunction with neon-bright colors, the effect of a lenticular veil of light beams produces a celestial quality. The editing is transformative, producing a poetic abstraction of the dance that offers something back to the dancers, while at the same time keeping settler demands for information and access to privileged Native spaces at bay. The dancers flicker in and out of focus, bestowing on viewers an impression of the vibrant, textured movement that can emerge from a collective Native experience when captured through non-extractive means.

Even with an ethics of care and a tool kit of editorial intervention at his disposal, Hopinka still faces quagmires in filming within Indigenous-centric and exclusive contexts. Of all of his films thus far, this situation is perhaps most pronounced in *Dislocation Blues* (2017). Using footage from multiple visits to the Standing Rock Sioux Reservation in North Dakota, Hopinka's film splinters the kind of resolution that might be expected from the front lines of a highly mediated protest. The constant presence of cameras and microphones indicates the copious media coverage, both that broadcast to audiences in the moment and that gathered for future documentaries, visual diaries, and other media about water protectors at Standing Rock.

In his book on Standing Rock, the Lower Brule Sioux writer Nick Estes explains that the Lakota phrase and rallying cry of the Standing Rock protests, "Mni Wiconi" (which translates to "water is life"), is "a future-oriented project... as much as it reaches into the past." The idea that water is life "forces some to confront their own unbelonging to the land and the river."[12]

In *Dislocation Blues*, Hopinka keeps non-Indigenous viewers on the hook to continue to do the work by offering more questions than answers about the movement. In typical fashion, he offers much but explains nothing, denying any expository entry to the work. Posting limits on what kinds of knowledge he will make accessible is a practice that engenders the kind of refusal that, as Mohawk scholar Audra Simpson attests, "makes some liberal thinkers uncomfortable, and may, to them, seem dangerous. When access to information, to knowledge, to the intellectual commons is controlled by the people who generate that information, it can be seen as a violation of shared standards of justice and truth."[13]

Rather than narrativize his experiences as a coherent or stable account of the protests, Hopinka instead registers the onerous process of accounting for such a momentous assembly. He relays an open-ended processing of the gathering alongside two water protectors, Terry Running Wild and Cleo Keahna. Running Wild's voice off-screen suggests a perspective from an unfolding present, while Keahna mulls over the same experience in a retrospective virtual interview.

Throughout, Hopinka's sketches of the atmosphere draw on alternative aesthetic techniques different from those in his previous films. In place of post-production additive superimpositions, hypersaturation, photonegative overlays, and the like, Hopinka chooses to shoot with angles, positions, compositions, movements, and durations that amplify the visual impressions of what is occurring in real time at Standing Rock camps. Long takes of sun flares, billows of steam and smoke, dusk light filtration, blankets of snow, mirrored reflections, and the wind's rustling touch, to name just a few visuals, ground the viewer in place as Running Wild and Keahna talk through their time there. Hopinka intercuts these still, observational takes with whirling and jostled shots of people conferring, dancing, watching out for one another. The film doesn't have any normative close-ups of people at Standing Rock, opting instead for stark silhouettes and low, sometimes canted angles.

Once again, Hopinka here punctuates the action with a solid-color screen, this time using black instead of red. The combination of these formal choices echoes the concerns of Running Wild and the recollections of Keahna. Speaking in the present tense, Running Wild's interview veers between personal reflections about the protest, observations about solidarity in the camps, and relaying on-the-ground information about events unfolding within the camps, such as the Dakota Access Pipeline surveillance. Appearing via a Skype call on a laptop, Keahna processes the experiences in the past tense, working through the monumentality and messiness of accounting for the time, especially in relation to Standing Rock as a media event. "My time there is now being cast into this magical, rose-colored nostalgia. But it was like this," he says, gesturing up and down.

Keahna's commentary alternates between personal and collective moments, between cross-coalitional solidarity and Native-led actions. He cites instances in which false information was spread about the camps, and expresses an ongoing caution about discussing the movement. He remarks that he would "be reluctant to talk about [Standing Rock] with anyone who's not Native, who's not been a part of resistance movements in their life." He expands the historical inflections of this point, saying, "All of media and all of representation... even the basis of this country's infrastructure is completely catering to the white world's rules. Everything for them is for them. Everything for all of us is with them in mind."

Keahna's astute insights about the visual persistence and materiality of settler colonialism elevate *Dislocation Blues* as a work that aids the formation of an incipient Indigenous visual sovereignty. Tuscarora artist and scholar Jolene Rickard coined the phrase "visual sovereignty" as part of the wider Indigenous-led project to create specific analyses and expressions of self-determination. She quotes Mohawk scholar Taiaiake Alfred's call to "challenge Indigenous peoples in building appropriate postcolonial governing systems to disconnect the notion of sovereignty from its Western, legal roots to transform it."[14]

For Rickard, visual sovereignty is a way to, in her words, protect, reimagine, and affirm Indigenous philosophies and cultural practices.[15] Visual sovereignty is not exclusive to *Dislocation Blues*, as its characterization is active in all of Hopinka's films. This idea of visual sovereignty is a helpful framework to make visible, even prismatic, the implications of the politically motivated rejection embedded in Hopinka's refusal to explain, Keahna's ambivalence, and Running Wild's request to end the interview.

Continuing Myths and Movements

Sto:lo poet, novelist, and scholar Lee Maracle writes, "Every time Native people form a circle they turn around. They move forward, not backward into history. We don't have to 'go back to the land.' We never left it.... One does not lose culture. It is not an object. Culture... is constantly changing and will do so as long as people busy themselves with living."[16]

Hopinka's forward-looking casting and recasting of myths enlivens them for present and future Indigenous audiences. His *Fainting Spells* (2018) generates a cinematic Ho-Chunk myth centered on a personified Xaˌwiˌska plant. In another short film from the same year, *When You're Lost in the Rain*, Hopinka poses a more critical approach to the embedded mythology of settler expansion.

Hopinka's recent feature *malni – towards the ocean, towards the shore* explores a Chinook myth recounting the origins of death and the possibilities of reincarnation. Filming in the Pacific Northwest, where he first learned Chinuk Wawa, Hopinka incorporates scenes from a canoe journey with interviews and footage of two of his friends, Jordan Mercier and Sweetwater Sahme. Hopinka filmed separately with Sahme and Mercier, though their conversations fold into his narration throughout the film. Sahme's pondering of life and death is particularly poignant, as she had just lost her grandmother and is in her third trimester of pregnancy in the film. In turn, Mercier's position in a growing family—as father to a toddler and a newborn—brings up reflections about passing on Indigenous traditions.

Although the two don't physically share scenes in the film, their sentiments often parallel, circle around, and echo one another. They both discuss breaking cycles in the hopes of a better future for their children. Ever attentive to the ways in which intimate knowledge is conveyed, Hopinka embeds their insights in scenes of everyday living. Hopinka spent time filming with each of them on hiking trails, around town, and inside their homes, resulting in quiet, revelatory moments that maintain his aesthetic commitment to non-spectacularizing modes of representation.

As with *Dislocation Blues*, Hopinka is relatively sparing with his use of postproduction transformations of the image, particularly as compared to his earlier work. Some outdoor scenes are highly saturated, but slow motion is applied intermittently, and in-camera decisions about framing, composition, and movement navigate the stakes of seeing and being seen. Throughout the canoe journey that Hopinka follows, gatherings of increasing size sing, drum, and dance at night. Hopinka doesn't rush to the front of the crowd to get the most direct or unobstructed shots of the participants. Instead, he foregrounds elements: the shoulder-to-shoulder excitement or the knee-to-knee child's perspective, a teeming sense of community fostered by the festivities. In a medium shot filled with drummers and singers, Hopinka's camera even stays respectfully behind the crowd's recording cell phones, keeping their videos in frame. As the song progresses and dancers begin to fill in the floor, Hopinka pivots the camera away without cutting, giving audiences the sound but no vision of what's happening on the floor.

The soundscape of the film mobilizes Hopinka's editorial ethics: nonsynced sound, silence, fades, and ethereal scoring produce a sonic atmosphere that prioritizes an address to Native audiences. In a separate, more spacious gathering on a football field that occurs earlier in the film, Hopinka follows Mercier closely, at his side, just behind his drum. The sound of collective drumming fades to a faint impression, as if hearing the song from a great distance. Hopinka narrates over the atmospheric rhythm: "People say, if you sing, if you drum, if you dance, you do so for those who can't."

Lee Maracle, thinking through the "mass and weight" of spirit in transformative moments between life and death, has written that "sound travels in waves. It is transmitted by electricity. The body possesses an electrical system on which it operates.... Sound waves do not leave the earth's atmosphere. They remain caught forever in the atmosphere. The living voices of the dead remain trapped in the air we breathe and travel on the wings of their own waves."[17] With *małni – towards the ocean, towards the shore*, Hopinka makes sure that questions about rebirth and the afterlife are posed, sustained, and hypothesized through sound.

About three-quarters of the way into the film, Hopinka reads from the Chinookan source text that was dictated by Mose B. Hudson in 1932 and here is narrated over a panning shot across a sunset shoreline, ending: "That's as much as there is now of this Indian myth. Perhaps it is not correct entirely as I have told it."[18]

With that statement, the contested possibilities of rebirth as they play out in the myth open back up a bit, giving the film space and encouragement to add to the creative interpretation of the myth. Cutting to the ten-yard line of the football field shown earlier, Hopinka begins a long take of the most visually abstracted scene in the film. In a steady wide shot, dancers make their way across the field in what is nearly stop-motion, their movements blurred and semi-frozen into gestural sweeps of light. Though the stop-motion-like effect keeps the field's goal lines intact, the dancers' stylized movements recalibrate focus within the image. The shimmering tones of the score match the lightened movement across the field, making the ninety-second scene feel both elongated and disproportionately short for the magnitude of its impact. Compared with many of the other locations depicted in *małni*, this spiritual high point takes place in a rather banal location. Yet, Hopinka cinematically captures the football field with the same kind of reverence as in Sahme's waterfall scenes or Mercier's shoreline shots. Hopinka's visual contribution to continuing myths and to recasting their relevance for Native people today meets Native people wherever he is and however his communities move.

Desire Lines

Through interconnections among language, placemaking, and movement, Hopinka's filmmaking produces a "desire line" that diverges from disciplinary ways of seeing. The "desire line" is a term used by landscape architects and urban planners to describe the visible trace formed by people moving away from official or paved paths.[19] Desire lines encompass a physical phenomenon in which new trails are formed that deliberately ignore pre-existing paths. With enough foot traffic across time, desire lines show a preferred collective route and insist on an alternative way to move. They might popularize a shortcut, indicate a need for wider sidewalks, or provide suggestions for vistas off a designated trail.

Seemingly innocuous, desire lines can index changing social needs or mark everyday resistance, creating new visual relations between communities and the land they traverse or inhabit. Although they form in diverse topological conditions and sociocultural contexts, desire lines embody contested relationships between demarcated restraints and the possibilities of people in a place. What may have once been the most effective or aesthetically pleasing route may no longer serve or appeal to people's needs.

Desire lines, by their very existence, raise larger questions about the design of infrastructure and the regulation of land use. Whose needs aren't being met by the routes currently set in place? Whose and what kinds of activities are permitted, encouraged, or curtailed by their limits? What are the risks and rewards of moving out of sync with a system that is in place? Within a wider historical and geographic view, desire lines must be contextualized back in time, too, within the infrastructures of movement and its policing as originally imposed by settler colonial incursions throughout Turtle Island (that is, North America).[20]

Physical infrastructures, such as roads and reservations, as well as systems of media representation in the United States were built to support the spread and protection of white supremacy. Recalling a moment midway through *Dislocation Blues*, Keahna comments on Native survivance in spite of material and mediated settler infrastructures. When Keahna says, "Everything for all of us is with them in mind," Hopinka

Diana Flores Ruíz

cuts from a shot of passing cars on a peripheral highway to a quiet moment on Flag Road at Standing Rock. This is not a contrasting cut between "modern" and "primitive," as some of the most enduring and racist paradigms of mass-mediated Indigenous representation would suggest. Philip Deloria (Standing Rock Sioux) analyzes such paradigms that have "explained and contained Indian actions."[21] Taking a long view of non-Indigenous cultural productions depicting Indigenous peoples, Deloria summarizes how "primitivism, technological incompetence, physical distance, and cultural difference have been the ways many Americans have imagined Indians," and how "such images remain familiar currency in contemporary dealings with Native people."[22] Hopinka's audiovisual economy bypasses the adjudication of where and how contemporary Indigenous life takes place. In creating desire lines away from the historical modes of seeing Indigenous life, Hopinka poetically envisions contemporary Indigenous politics of space and movement.

In applying the notion of desire lines to film history, Hopinka's work cleaves away from historical cinematic approaches toward Indigenous representation. Hopinka's filmmaking reflects an acute awareness of the visual infrastructures through which Indigenous (mis)representations have been cemented in visual culture. In "shooting back," Hopinka refuses the historical thoroughfares of Indigenous cinematic representation. He refuses such conventions and expectations, denying the audience full access to Indigenous knowledge, oversimplifications of Indigenous epistemologies, and extractive or didactic frames to assuage non-Indigenous viewers. Instead, Hopinka's films create a desire line that reroutes toward Indigenous audiences.

Poetic forms facilitate the desire line of Hopinka's filmmaking, shaping a track that leads away from institutional pressures to educate non-Natives. In the absence of didactic distillations or expository information, his films provide abundant audiovisual insights, raise powerful questions about culture, and grant viewers a space to experience select frames of his own perspective. In doing so, Hopinka dismisses the centrality of settlers in making and enlivening Indigenous cultural productions.

This kind of dismissal facilitates a primary address to Native audiences. As a non-Native viewer, I find it generative to follow the desire line posed by Hopinka's film practice. In doing so, viewers might see something else that Hopinka's works offer: a gift of "presentness," a gift of time spent being and thinking in place. This presentness, coming from an individual, subjective perspective, is deeply rooted in a hopeful curiosity toward the future, forged by active lessons and ongoing relations that span generations.

For Hopinka, however, the individual cannot be the boundary line to his visualizations. While continuing his own work, he has created space for other Indigenous artists and contributed to their visions, too. Since 2016, Hopinka has organized the Indigenous-centric film program What Was Always Yours and Never Lost. The Whitney Museum of American Art screened the 2019 iteration of the program for its biennial of the same year.

Concurrent with these efforts to show more works by other Indigenous artists, Hopinka formalized his collaborations in 2018, co-founding the COUSIN Collective with three other Indigenous filmmakers, Adam Khalil (Ojibway), Alexandra Lazarowich (Cree), and Adam Piron (Cáuigù and Kanien'kehá:ka), to assist in the production, development, and funding of Indigenous films and media. The COUSIN Collective materializes and multiplies desire lines of Indigenous visions. COUSIN lives out what Vizenor terms "transmotion... [a] sense of Native motion and an active presence [that constitute] *sui generis* sovereignty. Native transmotion is survivance...

Native stories of survivance are the creases of transmotion and sovereignty."[23] Whether figured as desire lines, transit, or transmotion, COUSIN is indisputably Indigenous movement. Make way and keep watching.

1. Within film and media studies, scholars such as Faye Ginsburg and Fatimah Tobing Rony have charted the political and visual stakes of Indigenous filmmakers reversing a (settler) colonial gaze historically used to capture and represent Indigenous peoples. More recently, historical projects by scholars such as Liza Black (Cherokee) have examined the forms of resistance employed by Native actors, extras, and set workers within Hollywood films. See Liza Black, *Picturing Indians: Native Americans in Film, 1941–1960* (Lincoln: University of Nebraska Press, 2020); Faye Ginsburg, "Shooting Back: From Ethnographic Film to Indigenous Production/Ethnography of Media," in *A Companion to Film Theory*, eds. Toby Miller and Robert Stam (Malden, MA: Blackwell, 1999); and Fatimah Tobing Rony, *The Third Eye: Race, Cinema, and Ethnographic Spectacle* (Durham: Duke University Press, 1996).

2. Jodi A. Byrd, *The Transit of Empire: Indigenous Critiques of Colonialism* (Minneapolis: University of Minnesota Press, 2011), xi.

3. Gerald Vizenor, "Aesthetics of Survivance: Literary Theory and Practice," in *Survivance: Narratives of Native Presence*, ed. Gerald Vizenor (Lincoln: University of Nebraska Press, 2008), 19.

4. Ibid., 20.

5. Evan Gardner and Susanna Ciotti, "An Overview of Where Are Your Keys? A Glimpse Inside the Technique Toolbox," in *The Routledge Handbook of Language Revitalization*, eds. Leanne Hinton, Leena Huss, and Gerald Roche (Milton, MA: Routledge, 2018), 139.

6. Henry Zenk, "Bringing 'Good Jargon' to Light." *Oregon Historical Quarterly* 113, no. 4 (Spring 2012), 560.

7. Almost thirty years ago, W. J. T. Mitchell set out to transform "landscape" from a designated art historical object to a culturally embedded process. Admittedly inspired by the ways in which cinema and photography put conceptual pressure on the supposed stability of "landscape" as a painted representational practice, Mitchell contended that "landscape might be seen more profitably as something like the dreamworks of imperialism." Mitchell argued that imperialism "conceives itself precisely (and simultaneously) as an expansion of landscape understood as an inevitable, progressive development in history, an expansion of

'culture' and 'civilization' into a 'natural' space in a progress that is itself narrated as 'natural.'" See his essay "Imperial Landscape" in *Landscape and Power*, ed. W. J. T. Mitchell (Chicago: University of Chicago Press, 1994), 5–34.

8. Vanessa Watts, "Indigenous Place-Thought and Agency amongst Humans and Non Humans (First Woman and Sky Woman Go on a European World Tour!)," *Decolonization: Indigeneity, Education & Society* 2, no. 1 (January 2013), 21.

9. Patrick Wolfe, "Settler Colonialism and the Elimination of the Native." *Journal of Genocide Research* 8, no. 4 (2006), 387–409.

10. Winona Wheeler, "Cree Intellectual Traditions in History," in *The West and Beyond: New Perspectives on an Imagined Region*, eds. Alvin Finkel, Sarah Carter, and Peter Fortna (Edmonton, AB: Athabasca University Press, 2010), 55.

11. Byrd, *Transit of Empire*, 118.

12. Nick Estes, *Our History Is the Future: Standing Rock versus the Dakota Access Pipeline and the Long Tradition of Indigenous Resistance* (New York: Verso Books, 2019), 256.

13. Audra Simpson, "On Ethnographic Refusal: Indigeneity, 'Voice' and Colonial Citizenship," *Junctures: The Journal of Thematic Dialogue*, no. 9 (2007), 74.

14. Jolene Rickard, "Diversifying Sovereignty and the Reception of Indigenous Art," *Art Journal* 76, no. 2 (Summer 2017), 82.

15. Ibid., 84.

16. Lee Maracle, *I Am Woman: A Native Perspective on Sociology and Feminism* (Vancouver, BC: Press Gang Publishers, 1988), 109–10.

17. Ibid., 114.

18. The Origin of Death Myth from the Confederated Tribes of Grand Ronde, as dictated by Mose B. Hudson to Melville Jacobs, 1932.

19. French philosopher Gaston Bachelard is credited with the germ of the idea of the desire line, as he described "pathways of desire" in *The Poetics of Space* (1958), though the concept is also closely linked with

Michel de Certeau's "rhetorics of walking" discussed in his *The Practice of Everyday Life* (1984).

20. South African writers Noëleen Murray, Nick Shepherd, and Martin Hall note how desire lines "indicate the space between the planned and the providential, the engineered and the 'lived,' and between official projects of capture and containment and the popular energies which subvert, bypass, supersede, and evade them." The authors stress that the phenomenon of desire lines has the capacity to be applied to other colonial contexts beyond South Africa in which "modernist planning coincided with forms of racialized population control." *Desire Lines: Space, Memory and Identity in the Post-Apartheid City*, eds. Noëleen Murray, Nick Shepherd, Martin Hall (New Brunswick, NJ: Routledge/Architext, 2007), 2.

21. Philip Deloria, *Indians in Unexpected Places* (Lawrence: University Press of Kansas, 2004), 7.

22. Ibid., 4.

23. Gerald Vizenor, *Fugitive Poses: Native American Indian Scenes of Absence and Presence* (Lincoln: University of Nebraska Press, 1998), 15–16.

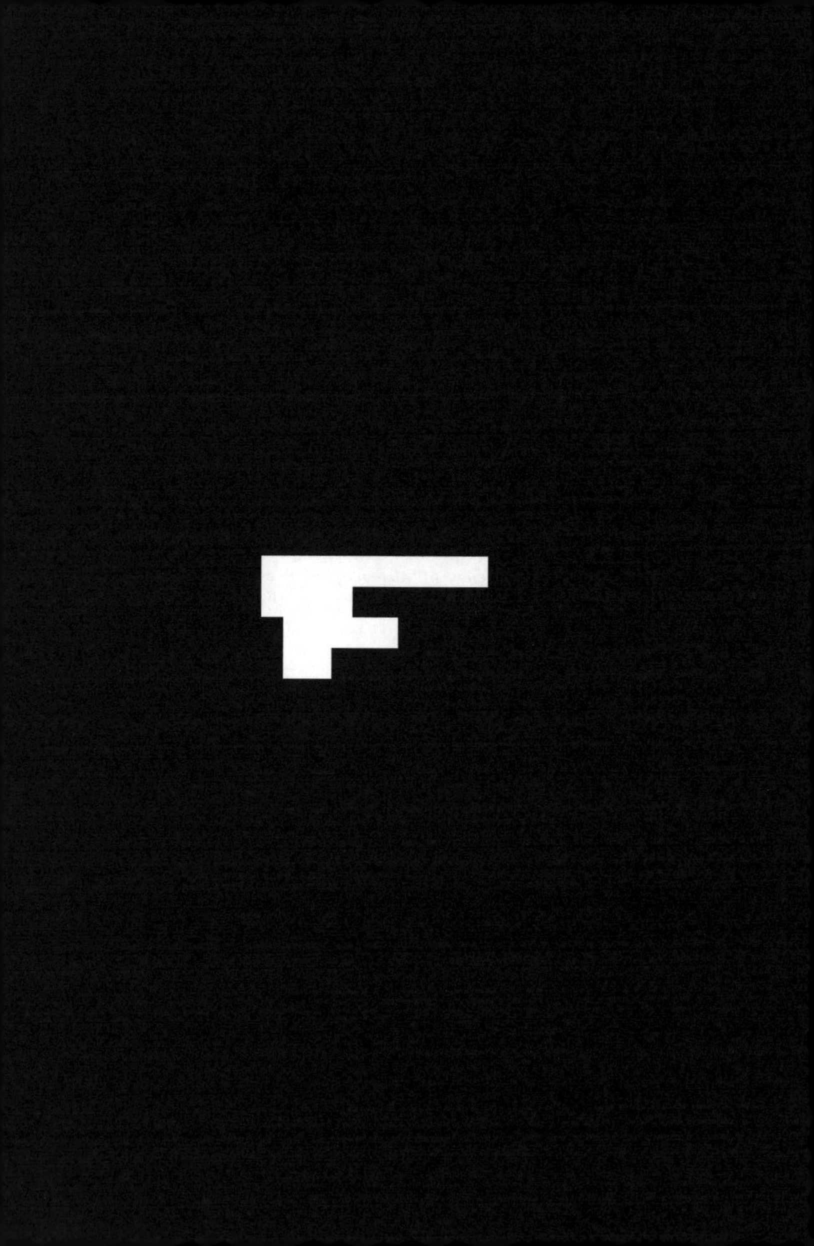

Winyan Yamni:
Three
Dreams

Kite

In 2020 I had three dreams. I am not one to have psychedelic or even interesting dreams, more often I am repeating a vague stress from my day or looking for lost items in my sleep. However, once in a while a dream emerges that is so strange or that feels so important, it cannot be ignored. *Winyan Yamni: Three Dreams* is an investigation of a possible Lakota filmic gaze, a proposal more than a finished thought, that dreams—be it the waking dream, the sleeping dream, or the instant realization—should be prioritized as a form of knowledge-making beyond positivism. In 2020, I heard a recording of Nellie Two Bulls sharing the Double Woman Song. Making this film, I wanted to explore how the creation of artworks could draw from dreaming methodologies of the stories of Double Woman, her ability to deliver inspiration or even complete artwork designs to the people. In this short film, I imagine the cord connecting Double Woman as the connection between dreams and creations, the camera and view, the body and its ghost. Sometimes we have to call our spirits back to our bodies or they can float away. All camerawork is done from 5'4" perspective.

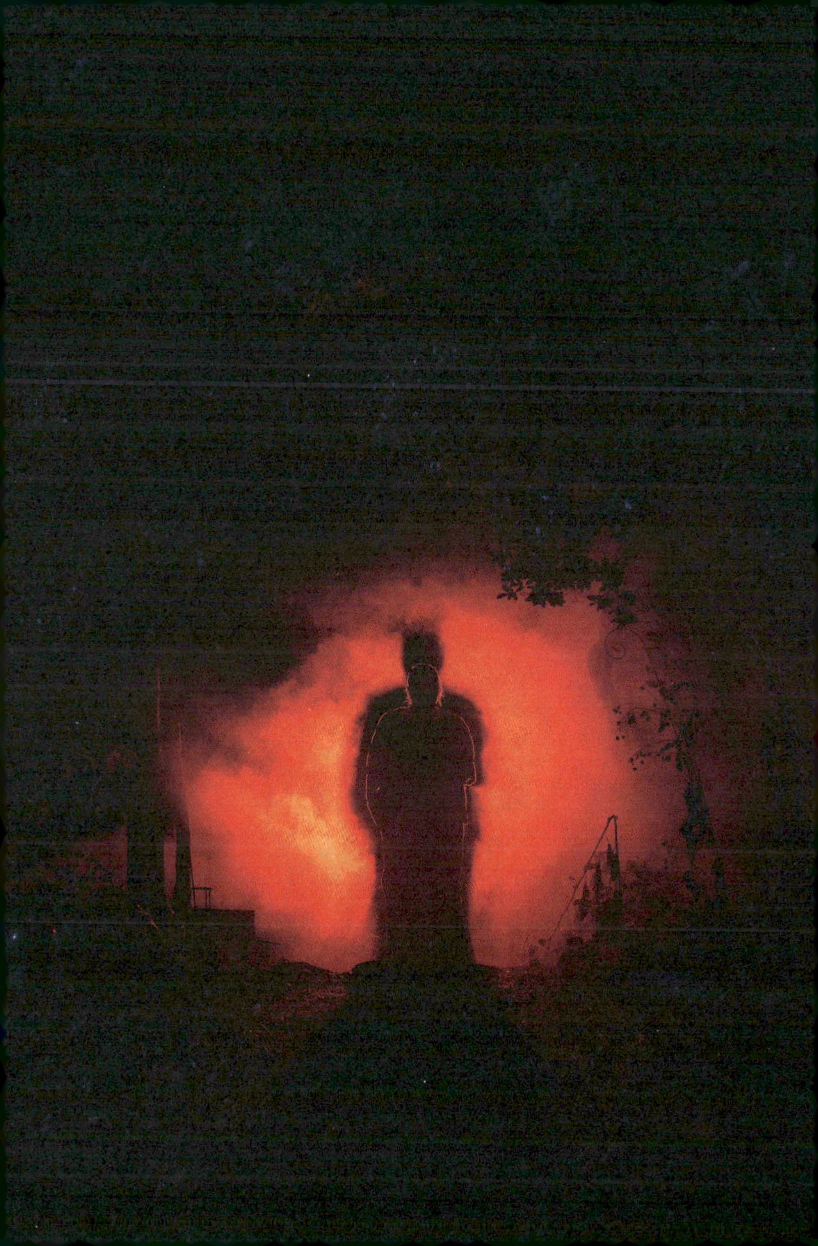

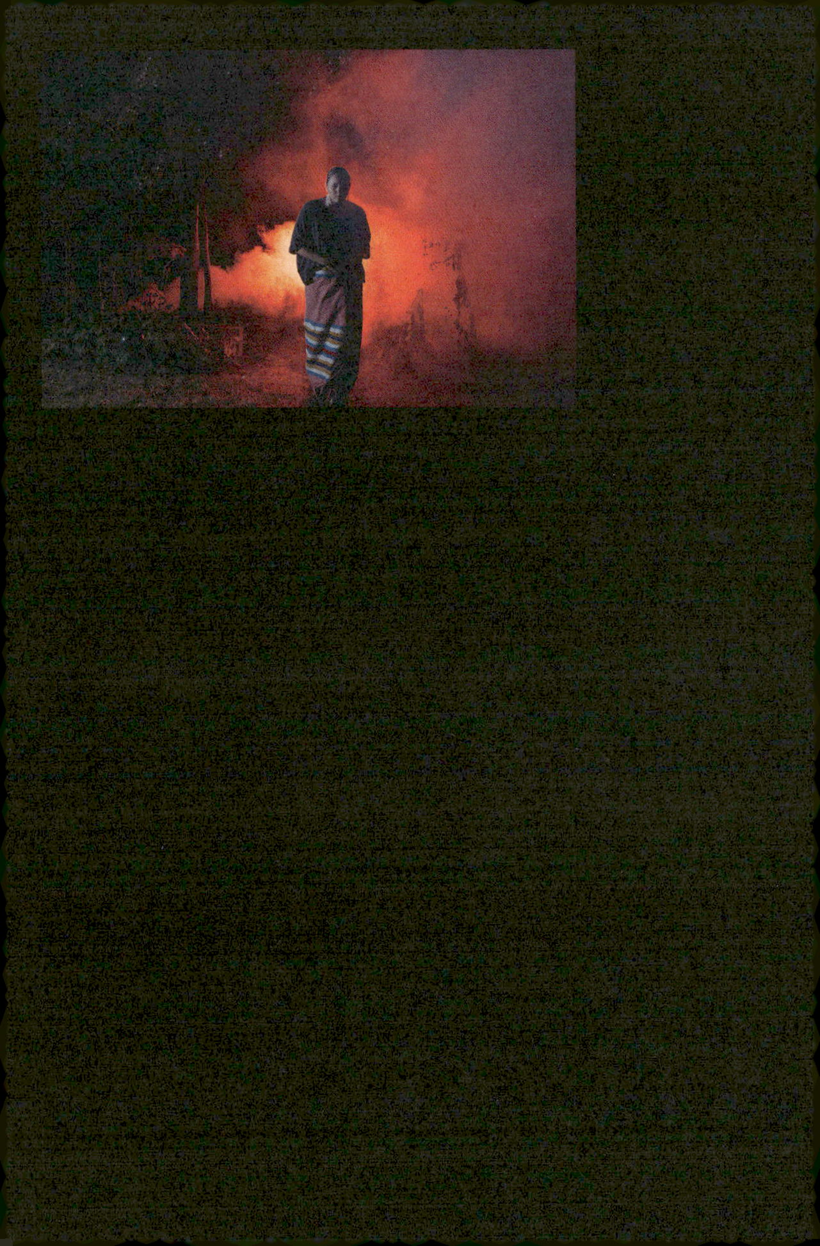

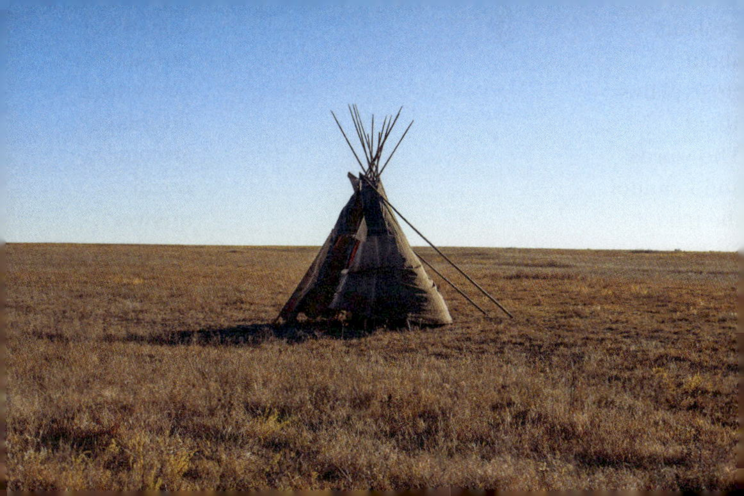

FIRST DREAM

I am walking through an older **school**[†] , it feels like a **prison**[†],
no windows.   I don't have a body,
just a **gaze**[‡] ; I   look to my left and there
is a full-   grown bear standing on
hind legs, **very**   **tall**[‡] ; he is talking and
slowly I tune into   what he is saying,
perhaps his mouth   is not moving,
slowly I realize   he is speaking
English, and I say,   "Oh, you can
speak English?" Still   walking down the
hallway, he looks   at me and says,
"Of course I can   speak English."
The hallway   goes on for a long
time. The bear   explains Leroy Little
Bear's theory of   Blackfoot **linguistics**[♦].
Our hands almost   brush. We get to the
cafeteria and sit   at a table, which actually
shifts between   cafeteria and classroom,
a place where   people meet, then he
explains   something
about   **language**[▽].
He explains   everything
about   **language**[♯].
The words   are blurry
and I cannot   recall
the true   **answer**[◈].
"Where   is your
wife?" I   ask the
bear. "Oh   she is
sleeping,"   he says. Our hands
brush.

† *buzzing fluorescents*
↓ *all my dreams have*
always felt like prisons
♮ *I can see my shoes*
‡ *He is too tall so*
I see his shoulder
♭ *"The aohtakaoistsi of*
Blackfoot, in contrast, or even
the bounded morpheme, suggest
only a potential to contribute
transitional meaning, the mark
a temporary aspect of a view,
quality, process, or essence
associated with an event not
yet delineated."
♉ *"Blackfoot experience*
does not incorporate
the temporal trinity of
the Indo-European time
artifact. In the latter,
time is something of
an imagined dimension,
conceptualized in the
usual way of things,
in terms of a body."
♈ *"Blackfoot language symbolizes an event becoming*
manifest from a wider reality of constant flux
and that it is the human life event that forms
the basis for anything that might be described
as a temporal reference point. By this notion,
distance can only be reasonably marked between
what has been passed and remembered, what has been
recently passed and maintains existing traces,
and what is evidently manifesting. What will
eventually become manifest is much more difficult
to speak of with any degree of certainty."
♁ *The language begins to blur and the*
high pitched tone of a bomb going
off drowns out the bear's voice.

All quotes from Little Bear, Leroy, and Ryan Heavy Head.
"A Conceptual Anatomy of the Blackfoot Word." *ReVision*
26, no. 3 (Winter 2004), 31–38.

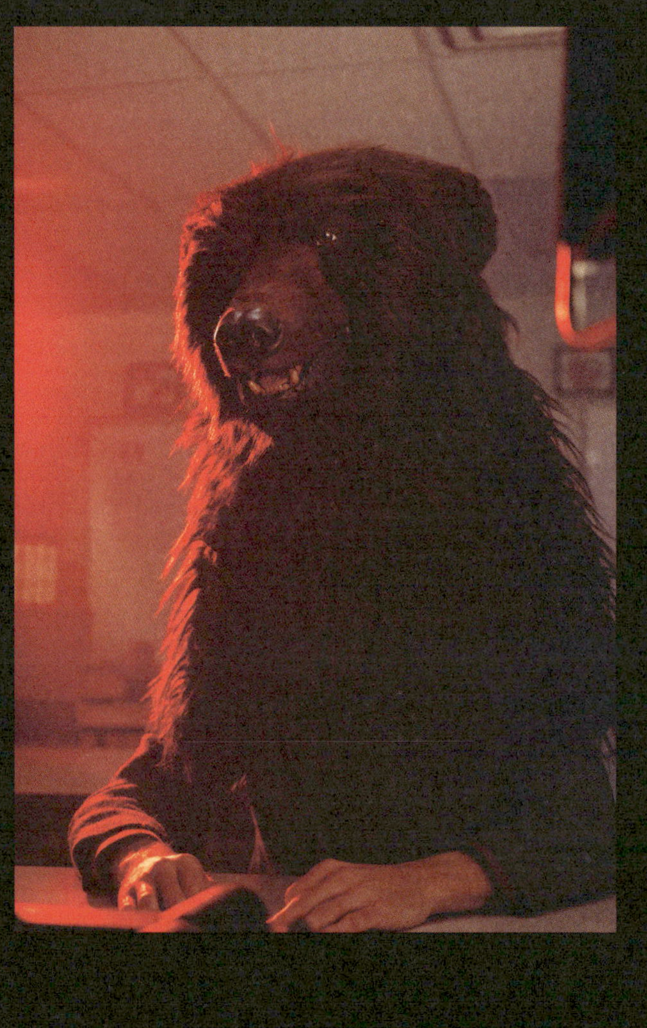

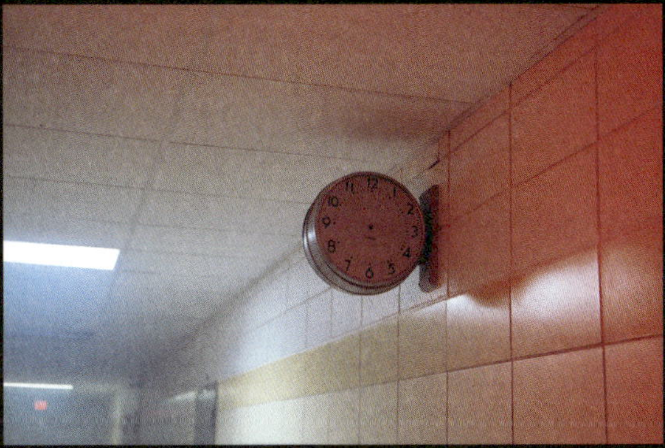

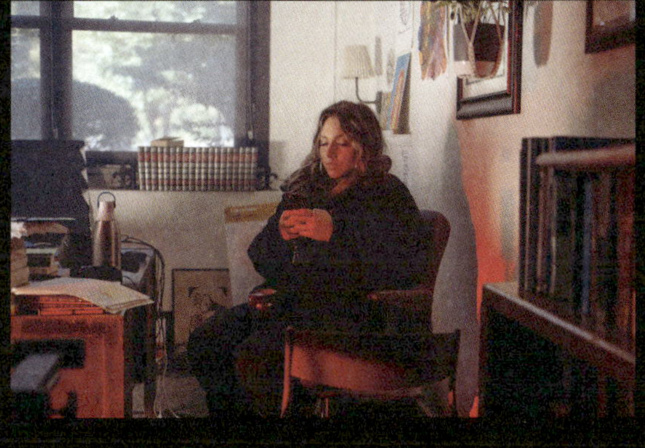

SECOND DREAM

I am at a film festival (it looks like the second floor of TIFF in
Toronto[†]) where I run into a filmmaker, and he says, "My film
is screening, you go see it," with a sly **grin**[↓]. In the theater, I
sit down in front of the screen. The movie begins. Now the
gaze slides into the screen and we are inside the scene. It's
the most beautiful dawn on the prairie, misty;
right in front of the camera there is a long
thin table covered in white rabbit fur, blocking
any pathway to the rest of the field. There
are tools resting on the rabbit fur, only the music alerts us that
something is deeply and terribly wrong. White horses graze
to the right. Slowly, extremely slowly, we gaze closer towards
a tipi in the back left background. There is a glow like there is
a fire inside. The scene is so beautiful, except for an intense,
unnerving feeling. Slowly there is an understanding that a
woman has just been murdered inside the tipi. Blood.

> [†] *perhaps   it   is*
> *ImagineNative*
> [↓] *He   then   rappels*
> *away   like   in   an*
> *action   movie*

THIRD DREAM

Again, I am just a gaze. I am on the back brick steps of my
house. I put out a bowl of tobacco for a friend who is dying in
the hospital. I **cry**[†] on the porch praying for my friend, a lot.
A woman whose   identity is not fully
perceivable[↓] walks   up and asks if she
can smoke the   tobacco out of
the small bowl,   the ceremonial
bowl, and I say,   **"Of course**[♮]**,"**
of course you   can smoke this
sacred not-meant-to-be-   smoked tobacco,
and she is very happy and   she goes away. I
wake up in the morning; it has rained. On the steps, the bowl
has filled up with water and the tobacco has overflowed out of
the bowl, washing out into the brickyard and into the grass,
totally dispersed. I get a **text**[‡], my friend has survived the
night, he will live.

[†] *"Wopila   tunkashila
for protecting him"*
[↓] *She swims in defocus
and   red   lights.*
[♮] *I've   had   people   ask   for
my   praying   tobacco   to
roll   joints   with   before.*
[‡] *"he   is   off
the   ventilator,
he   is   ok"*

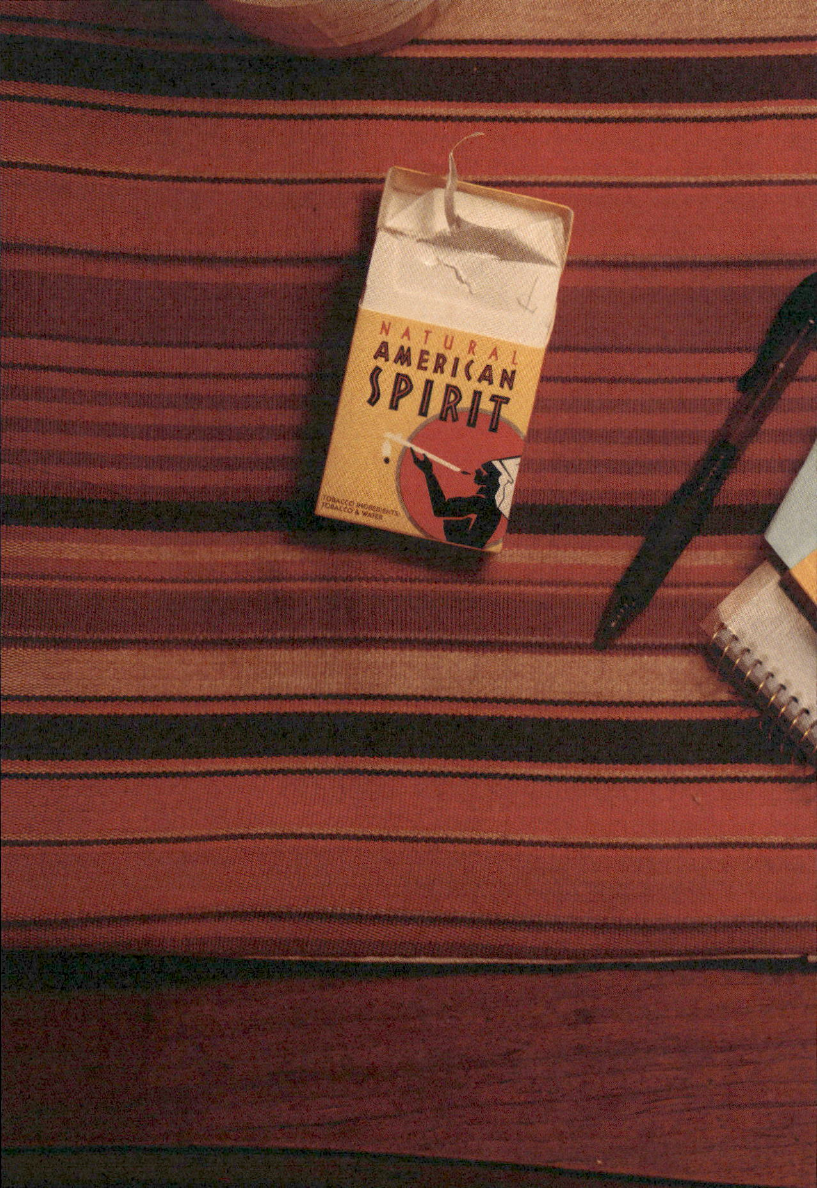

NATURAL
AMERICAN
SPIRIT
TOBACCO INGREDIENTS:
TOBACCO & WATER

VINE DELORIA JR.
NEW FOREWORDS BY
Leslie Marmon Silko and George E. Tinker
God
Is
Red
A NATIVE VIEW
OF RELIGION
30th Anniversary Edition

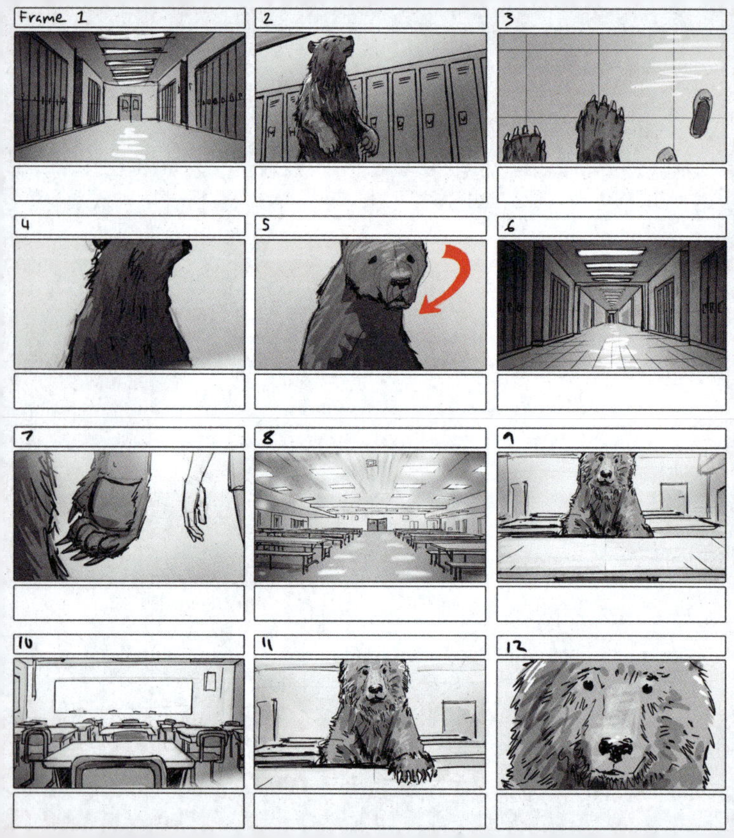

Frame 1
2
3
4
5
6
7
8
9
10
11
12

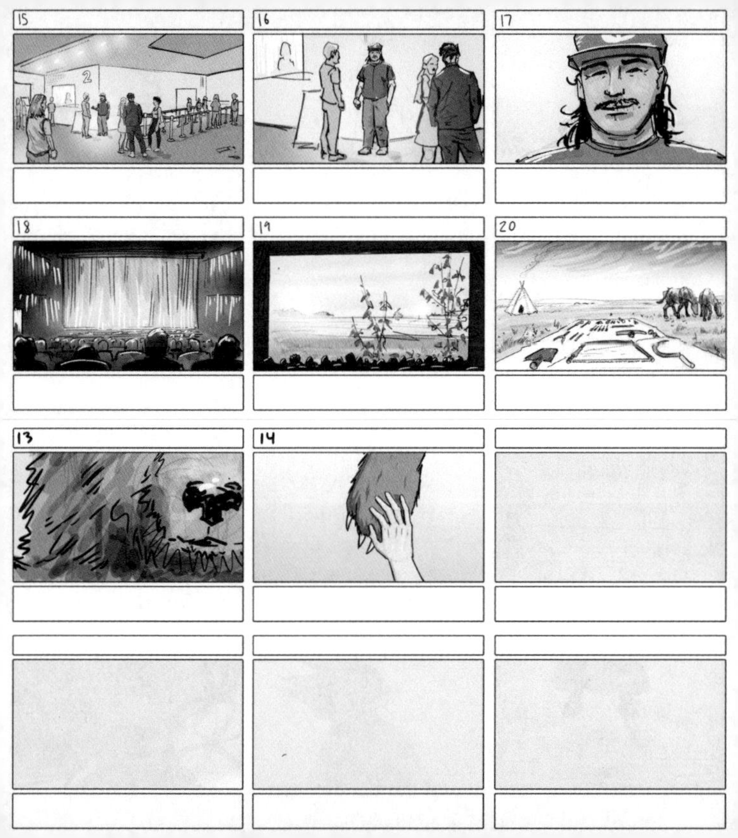

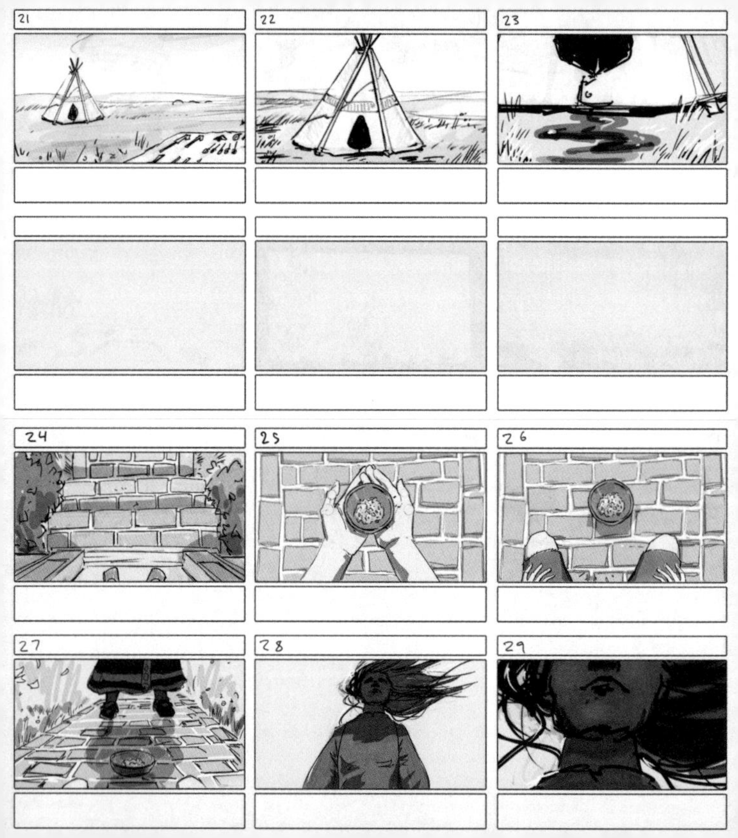

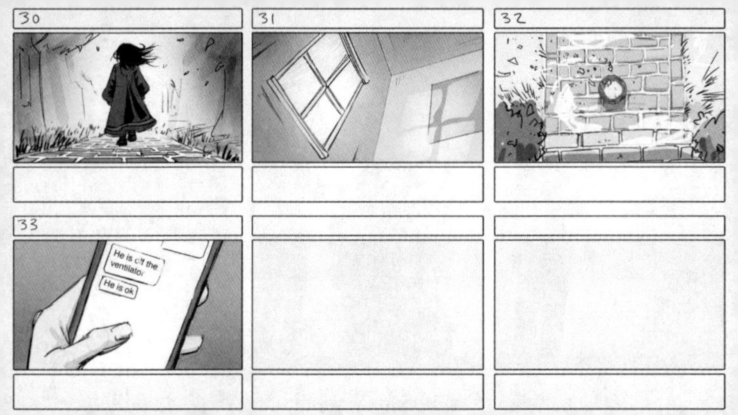

He is off the ventilator
He is ok

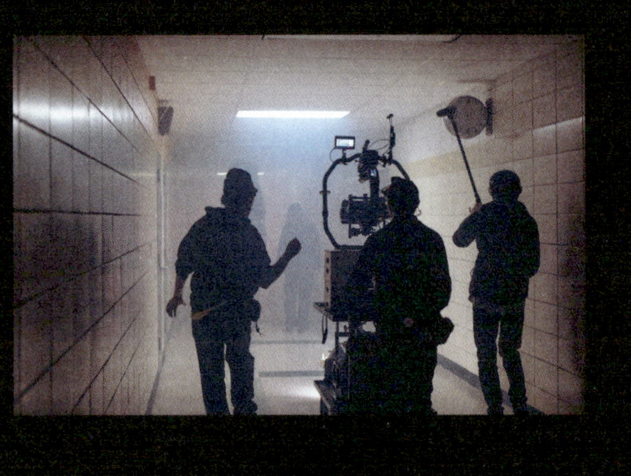

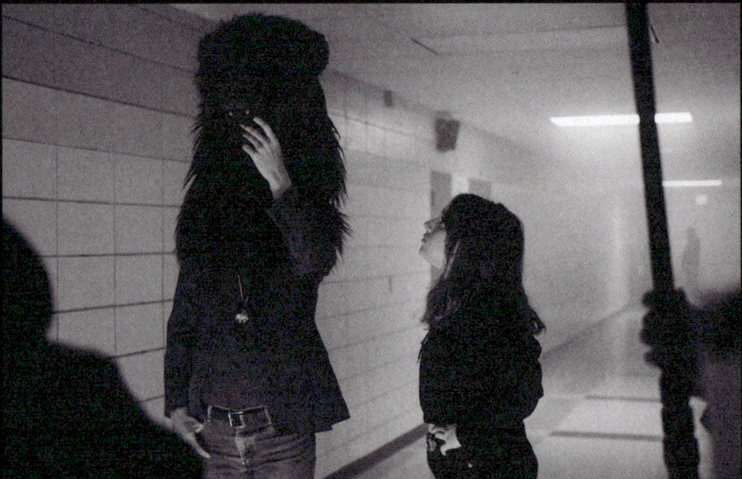

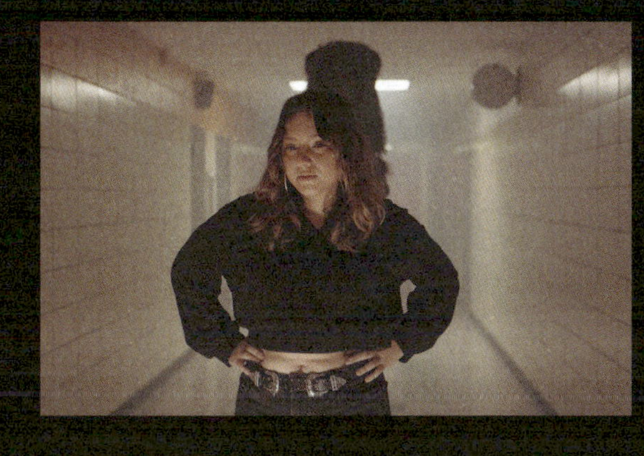

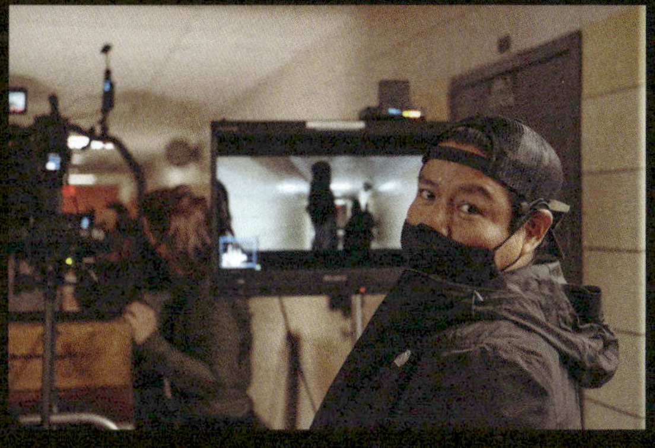

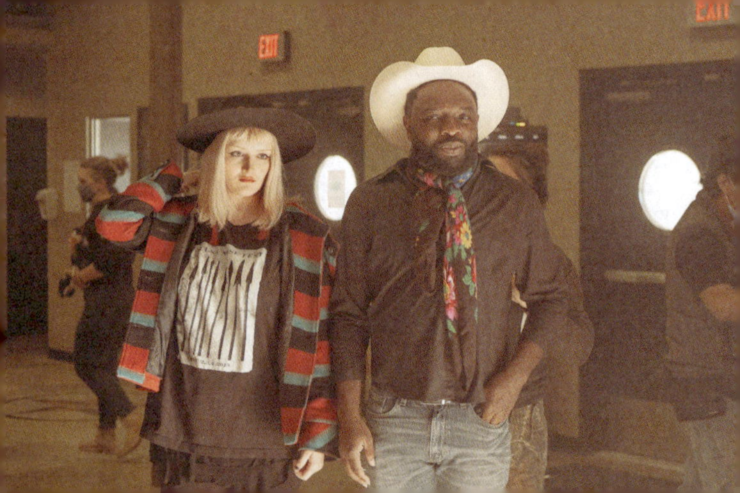

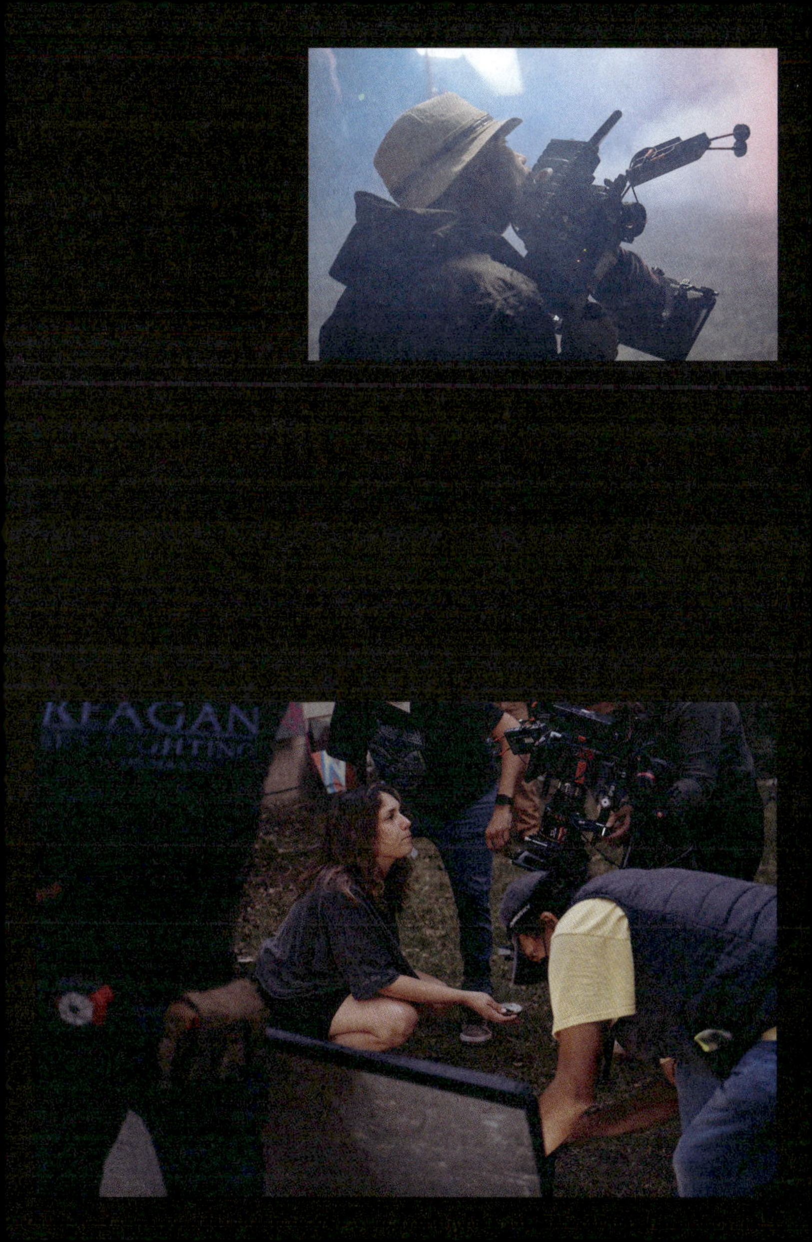
REAGAN
LIGHTING

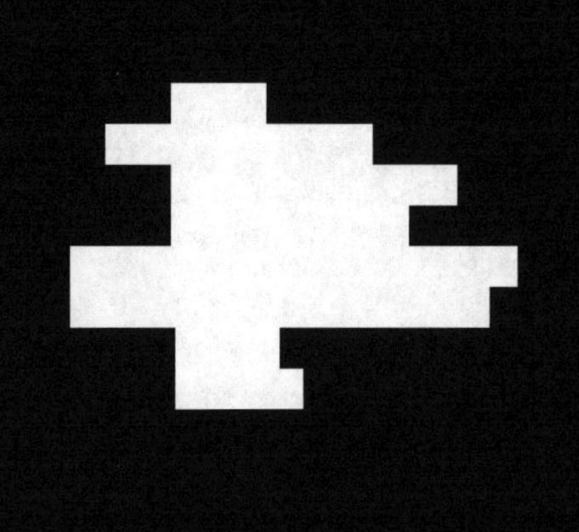

KIN:
**A Case Study
in Indigiqueer
Aesthetics,
Digital Co-authorship,
and Felt Governance**

Jas M.
Morgan

KIN is a dramatic comedy about a group of Indigenous queer and trans friends living in Toronto, Ontario, Canada. That's it. That's the concept. When my team pitched this concept to the country's Aboriginal Peoples Television Network (APTN) at the 2020 edition of the imagineNATIVE Film Festival, the program advisor told us that it wasn't a pitch. Our series was about "nothing." I wondered if they had ever seen a Justin Ducharme or TJ Cuthand film? I mention their names particularly because I'm a producer who, after years of commiserating with other Indigenous queer, trans, and Two-Spirit peoples about the lack of inclusion of our stories in media, decided to form Sewing Circle Productions, a Toronto-based production company devoted to telling the stories of Indigenous queer, trans, and Two-Spirit peoples. When founding the company, the first people who came to mind—those who had been telling these stories for years at small festivals and on screens in experimental formats—were Ducharme and Cuthand.

Though still in his twenties, Ducharme has already made a pronounced impact on film in Canada. He was born and raised in the small Métis community of St. Ambroise. In the early seventeenth century, the area consisted of Métis villages. Now St. Ambroise, which is located on the south-east tip of Lake Manitoba, hosts Métis events year-round. Ducharme has been jigging since the age of seven, performing with the St. Ambroise Youth Steppers and the Louis Riel Métis Dancers. After graduating from Vancouver Film School, he wrote, produced, and directed several short films—including *Positions* (2018), a short film about Aaron (MacKenzie Kingdon-Prouty), a queer sex worker living in Vancouver.

In *Positions*, the viewer is shakily taken in and out of Aaron's perspective, following him as he's giving head to a client, or when he walks down the street and calls his kokum on the phone. The interactions don't seamlessly fit together.

They are disjointed and unnerving—much like the brief interactions that make up most of Aaron's work. This depiction of sex work becomes absurd, but not so absurd as to lose sight of the character's humanity. Ducharme's films are inherently existential, like if Camus were queer and enjoyed chugging 40s of malt liquor with his friends; his characters move through the world with the sense that death is lurking in the shadows of every midnight encounter. But the viewer can still recognize his characters' connections to the material conditions of being an NDN, and how that position is grounded in Indigenous place, peoples, and objects. More than just a response to colonization or homophobia, a Ducharme film quietly reveals the ruptures in normative reality that can happen when a body runs into other bodies.

Belonging to an older generation, born in 1978, Cuthand is an experimental queer Indigenous filmmaker. Growing up in Saskatoon, Saskatchewan, Canada—a small prairie city with a population just over 200,000 in 1995, the year in which he started making films—Cuthand turned to cinema as a refuge from loneliness. Little did he know that these early films, alongside those by other queer Indigenous artists such as Clint Alberta, Zachery Longboy, and Terry Haines, would contribute to the development of an Indigiqueer aesthetics. Since the '90s, Cuthand's films have screened all over the world, and he even coined the term "Indigiqueer" in 2004 when he used it in the title of a film program that he curated for the Vancouver Queer Film Festival. He is now at work on his debut feature, based on his 2021 short *Kwêskosîw: She Whistles*.

With a style emblematic of the punk rock ethos of feminist creative communities, Cuthand's films are a freewheeling archive of DIY analog methods. His earliest shorts were shot on an old handheld camera, and today they remain some of his most iconic works. Narrative performance is at the core of all of his films.

Stream-of-consciousness dialogue is paired with campy point-of-view visuals, including self-shot sequences of Cuthand in vulnerable states, alongside members of his community, staged in "slice of life" scenes. There is an uninhibited immediacy to his style, which has helped make him a prolific artist, creating over thirty shorts in his three-decade career. You get the sense that each film is its own stand-alone thought; it lives as briefly as an experience that Cuthand tumbles through, before he moves onto the next.

In his book *The Freudian Body: Psychoanalysis and Art*, theorist Leo Bersani describes queer aesthetics as art that undoes a world of imaginary relations by pushing our sense of self into "The Real," an anti-identitarian and non-normative space that can be reached through pleasure. Of course, the queer analysts were all circle jerking around the idea of "The Other" at the expense of the material. Yet, queer aesthetics call to some of us NDNs. It was my exposure to Cuthand's films that introduced me to what we now often point to as Indigiqueer aesthetics. But, even though Ducharme is still only in the early stages of his career, his films have certainly sharpened my senses to the incredible potential of this realm.

Inspired by web series by other queer, trans, and women creators, and the work of queer NDN filmmakers like Cuthand and Ducharme, I founded Sewing Circle Productions in 2020. For years, I had spoken to both Cuthand and Ducharme about their struggles to have their films recognized among their peers. When I approached them with the idea of creating a consensus-based production collective so that we could finally tell our stories the way we wanted to, and conceiving of our series *KIN*, I had no idea just how much we'd learn over the next years.

In the following paragraphs, I will lay out our experience of making *KIN* from pitch to production. This is only one case study of a collective of Indigenous filmmakers, writers, and producers working with a small network. Of course, each series, film, and media project led by Indigenous peoples is its own process of negotiating relationships with corporations in fraught industries. We can only speak to our own experience. But I genuinely hope that more Indigenous producers, programmers, and directors will speak up about the culture in television and film industries—these industries can be tough for Indigenous peoples, and require us to make space for those who will come after us. Further, the few Indigenous producers and directors who are forging forward in inequitable production industries in Canada in this so-called era of diversity and reconciliation are fighting a lonely battle. We still need total industry transformation.

To start off, when deciding how I wanted to collaborate with filmmakers, it was important to define my company structure. How could I create a unilateral model that allowed me to make business decisions alongside a collective composed of creatives? Here, I found that my training as a community-based researcher was an asset. When I accepted my position as an Assistant Professor at Toronto Metropolitan University in 2020, I got to work alongside digital researchers such as Dr. Jason Boyd and Dr. Lorraine Jensen, and to witness first-hand Digital Humanities (DH) builds. DH builds are a unilateral and ethical model for digital community-based research. In arts-based research, the practitioners are filmmakers, artists, and other creators. Research funding can support industry growth, knowledge production, and canonization in the arts. For researchers, working alongside digital creators can allow new forms of research to occur that could not be facilitated through traditional thought production alone. Increasingly, researchers are turning to arts-based research as a space to create forms of cultural knowledge alongside community. In particular, I was interested in how digital media and film allowed for the co-authorship of digital knowledge, alongside Indigenous filmmakers. It's important to remember that research has been historically exploitative of Indigenous peoples, who have been the objects of study for centuries, often to their detriment. But then again, so too has cinema. What was important for our collective was to create mutually beneficial alliances that made it possible to share resources, and to make work that we cared about.

Serendipitously, my role as a facilitator of the Digital Wahkohtowin & Cultural Governance Lab at Toronto Metropolitan University allowed me to set up a partnership between the Lab and Sewing Circle Productions. Through this partnership, I could donate research funds from my Lab towards film production so that we could create films and observe that process to compile directives for collective organizing, reaching consensus, and screen governance. I had no idea how grateful I would be for this partnership when our relationship with APTN progressed; again and again, it allowed me to side with the directors in business choices because we always had the assurance of our own unique funding structure. This model allowed Sewing Circle Productions to partner with Toronto Metropolitan University, the Lab, to simultaneously create educational opportunities and support emerging Indigenous 2LGBTQ+ screen talent with a community-based business model that had cross-sector benefits.

We decided, as a collective, to take our project to the APTN pitch competition at the 2020 edition of imagineNATIVE. Of course, we came into this project knowing APTN had a reputation of not shooting or broadcasting Indigenous queer, trans, or Two-Spirit content—for example, APTN's erasure of Indigenous 2LGBTQ+ people had been discussed at a panel with Adrienne Huard, TJ Cuthand, Adam Garnet Jones, Kawennáhere Devery Jacobs, Anthony Johnson, Dr. James Makokis, and Fallon Simard during the 2019 edition of imagineNATIVE. Yet we trusted that, as advertised, this was a competition designed to elevate the voices of emerging creators, and we took our win as a sign that APTN was excited to represent these perspectives finally. As we developed *KIN*, we wondered if it would be the first time that a trans person would appear on APTN.

Dishearteningly, the process was riddled with conflict, inequity, and a lack of clarity on APTN's side. We jumped through administrative hoops for years, but the same care and respect was never reciprocated. Documented administrative and communication errors on APTN's side were constantly blamed on our team, and we received abusive communication from their non-Indigenous producers if this was ever pointed out. I don't believe that this is "just how production is." I was lucky enough to have a silent production advisor who consoled me throughout the process, saying meetings should never explode into screaming matches. APTN continued to blame our collective for traceable errors and grievances that we had brought to the attention of their producers and an executive director but were never addressed, at times to the detriment of the reputation of the creatives and production company involved with *KIN*. Most notably, documented communication errors on APTN's part resulted in production being delayed, with little notice on APTN's part, though we had already struck contracts with everyone working on set. This resulted in a huge loss of funds for our small, emerging production collective.

We get it, companies need to cover their assets, and we were dealing with the producers and executives who administer public funding on our behalf. This was a company that had me, the producer, sign a notarized statement of the Indigenous affiliation of my crew in order to place sole liability on me in the same week that they announced they had acquired *Inconvenient Indian* (2020) by Michelle Latimer—infamously, the subject of public scrutiny when journalists investigated her claims of Indigenous heritage, and she was labeled a potential "pretendian" by the Canadian media. While far too much happened in our interactions with APTN to outline here, the last blow was when they failed to meet their contractual obligations, despite the fact that we had filed the required agreed-upon documentation. Notably, after we delivered our scripts, they continued to send us an email every week or two saying they had not received them. I sent the scripts again and again, even attached in email threads that the producers replied to, and, yet, I still continued to receive emails, prompting me to send through the scripts if we wanted to move forward with the project. It was not lost on us that the content of our scripts were experimental, and that they dealt with controversial topics such as sexual abuse and abusive men in Native communities. We couldn't help but feel APTN were simply evading our scripts in order to put off our deal. Furthermore, though we had met all the obligations of our agreement, APTN came back mere weeks before we were supposed to move into production, asking for more documents before they would release our funds. This would have resulted in pushing the production *again*, delaying another payment to our writers, and further loss of funds.

The same smiling faces that were so proud to give us their prize publicly at imagineNATIVE made it near impossible to cash our "prize" in. In this way, the prize itself was innately mis-advertised. No licensing deal was awarded. Effectively, the prize was reduced to a series of meetings to attempt to negotiate a licensing deal with APTN, which any Indigenous production company can do at any time. Our final agreement was missing portions of the funding advertised as part of the prize during imagineNATIVE. This is an increasing trend in films: programming and prizes make it appear as if festivals and networks are "decolonizing" without actually changing the systems that make those spaces inequitable for Indigenous peoples. For film and television industries, sometimes it feels like they believe that publicity is enough, without any meaningful change. In light of this, we decided to break our agreement with APTN. The writers couldn't wait another year to be paid, which we felt represented inequities present in APTN's current production structure. As a new producer, my relationship to creators are ultimately far more important than my relationships to a network that ironically does not work equitably with Indigenous creators.

Despite our challenges, *KIN* went into production in summer 2022. Being on set felt like visualizing kinship: our director of photography, Métis filmmaker Conor McNally, is my friend and collaborator of many years. Working alongside the cast and crew felt like a community. This was my first time producing something, and I'm grateful to have such amazing creators around me who were willing to take that journey. We learned together what a unilateral model of governing production could look like, which will influence future policy resources discussing Indigenous-governed business processes and safe set practices. It was through this project that I finally understood my original research question: how can we use applied digital methods in research to visualize kinship as Indigenous sovereignties?

In response to my posed research question, I think about the NDN spacetime we created on the *KIN* set that broke from the inner workings of film and television that have been so oppressive to us, only a few of which I can name here: the time that Ducharme took to make transfeminine actress Aaylayna feel beautiful and safe on set for her first onscreen appearance, which went far beyond the traditional responsibility of the director; the fact that everyone behind the camera was Cree and Métis. Or the fact that our contracts were written alongside our core collective to ensure that the directors of each episode were treated fairly, particularly around issues of intellectual property and morality. I followed the lead of the directors when negotiating distribution so that they could be paid equitably and punctually. We made time for togetherness and building closeness. We never wavered on telling the stories that the writers wanted to tell, even if that meant receiving smaller distribution. We gave multiple credits to everyone on set to build capacity among community members. We even held community accountability processes to ensure that everyone felt safe working with other team members when a conflict emerged. Our set ran like a community, in a way that non-Indigenous production companies seem incapable of running because they can't think themselves out of the current models of production. (I'm sure many Indigenous production companies could likely say the same about their processes for working with community.)

I have never felt more lucky to witness a story unfold than the one that *KIN* tells. Our distribution model has certainly changed over this rollercoaster process, but at least now we get to conceive the future of *KIN* in ways that feel right to us. In my work over the past several years alongside policymakers, community activists, and creative knowledge producers, I've learned that simply being fearless, moving in the image of your people in exploitative industries, and telling the truth can challenge normative industry processes. These small forms of felt governance might not be the capital-G Governance that we think about when defining Indigenous politics, but they represent a space opened up for Indigenous ways of knowing and doing. We will be honored to premiere *KIN* at imagineNATIVE 2023, and we can't wait to see the response from the communities we intended to represent.

This was only our first challenge in negotiating what a collectively governed model for Indigenous film production could look like, from pitch to production. We still have so much work to do to determine the modes of governance that could be illuminated through this work. In collaboration with Yellowhead Institute, based on our experiences with *KIN*, we will release a report focusing on principles for collective-based film production that empowers Indigenous communities, and policy perspectives in publicly funded television and film in Canada. It's quiet work but, collectively, we want to find that place that we have all been searching for with our films and words: an Indigiqueer aesthetics.

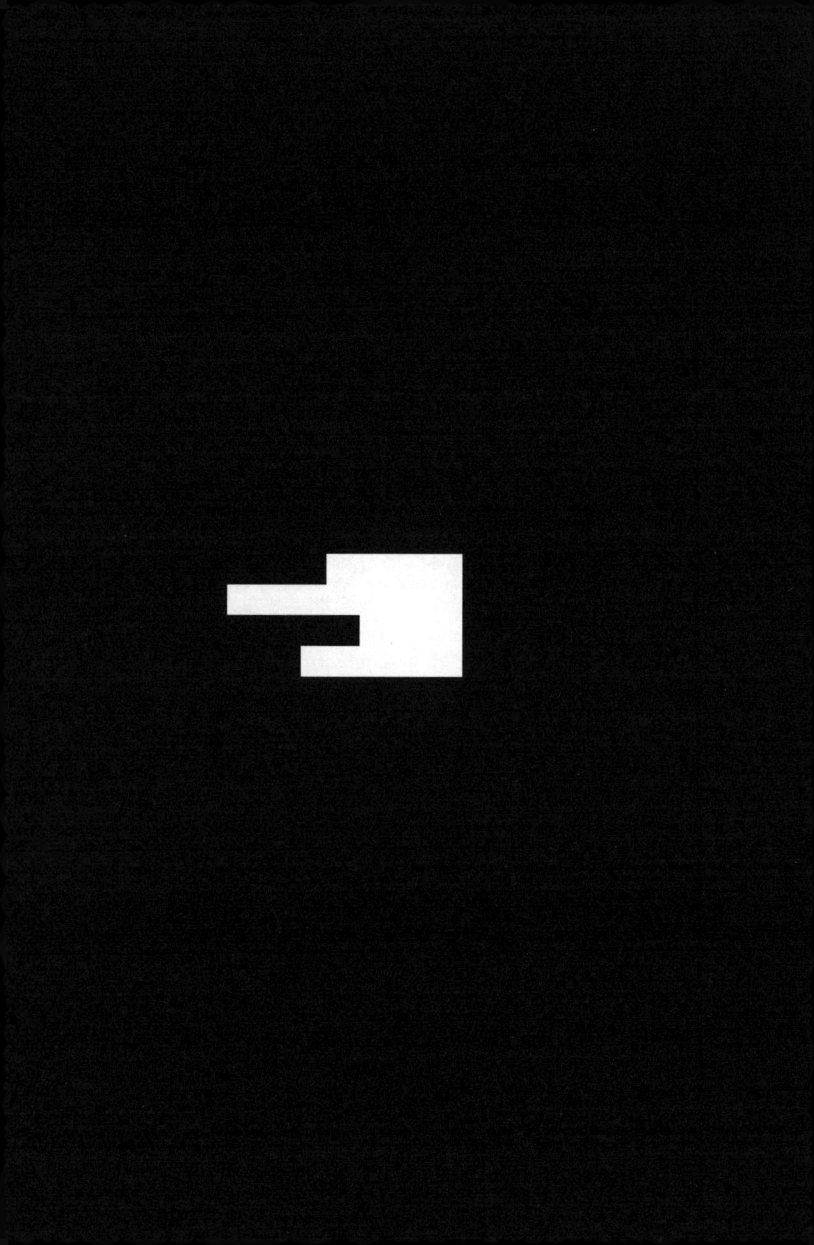

Thesis on the Audiovisual

Colectivo
Los Ingrávidos

THESIS 1: In political cinema of agitation there is a juxtaposition of the old and the new that entails an audiovisual practice in the form of aberration. In this cinema, agitation no longer emerges from new awareness nor calls for mass mobilization, but rather consists of putting everything in a trance, including the camera itself, relating the different instances of violence to each other, so that the trance, the crisis, or the aberration determines a constructivity that, intervened from the real, produces collective audiovisuals of the *Missing People.*

THESIS 2: A political cinema of agitation whose condition of possibility is the ravages of neoliberal capitalism and leads, in the audiovisual realm, to a double form of aberration: the sinister and estrangement.

THESIS 3: The exacerbation of the sinister leads to the intolerable. The vision, presence, and insistence of the intolerable opens up a horizon that enables the emergence and autonomy of the Missing People.

THESIS 4: In the political cinema of agitation there are three forms of the People: the Supposed People, the Missing People, and the Population.[1]

THESIS 5: The political cinema of agitation leads to an autonomy of images. Autonomy is not separatism—nor is it the taking over or occupation of the State, or the totalitarian productivity of images—but rather the creation and appropriation of parallel sensory, perceptual, poetic, and speculative structures within existing structures.

THESIS 6: One of the forms of the political cinema of agitation is the cinema of appropriation, which implies an aberrant sensory practice. The liturgical dimension of this aberration is burial (funerary trance).

THESIS 7: The burial of images and sounds is the kinetic trance of the appropriated audiovisual document.

THESIS 8: All such appropriation mobilizes and vindicates the opacity of the document.

THESIS 9: The opacity of the document is a sensory quality that activates the Burial-Exhumation dialectic.

1. The space of media representation that corporate governments have built around them excludes the People. What corporate governments presuppose as a correlate of their own unpopular image is a population, a mass that they can administer, quantify, manage. The consistency of this space of representation is completely homogeneous, overdetermined, quantified, and non-antagonistic. The determining dimension of the official discourse aims to model a total, coherent image that ends once and for all, replacing or transforming the Missing People and the Supposed People into a Population. What the image emporium of corporate governments presupposes is a spectator-population or an expectant-population, a mass of hallucinated people that responds out of the unison of a passive civility to the question: what is behind the governmental or corporate images and audiovisual productions? Or: to what expectant totality do the monstrous stagings such as those continually undertaken by world corporate governments and their tele-computerized allies against all possible construction and articulation of Missing Peoples refer? The quantified, subjugated mass—intimidated by these questions—answers without a voice, and, from the rostrum of its atomization, responds as a Population. Behind the sound-images that corporate-cinemas and government-cinemas disseminate, behind the hegemonic empowerment of the corporate-sovereign-mannequins, there is an ideal of a spectator: a regulated population without a clear political territory, in a desolate environment of insecurity, as well as in a vertiginous aesthetic-political uprooting.

THESIS 10: The Burial-Exhumation dialectic is the iconoclastic and materialist contradiction of appropriation cinema.

THESIS 11: Burial and Exhumation entail the testimonial dimension of appropriation.

THESIS 12: The sinister rapture of appropriation is shamanic possession, conversion, and bonding.[2]

THESIS 13: Shamanic *possession* is the sensory outburst of the political cinema of agitation.

THESIS 14: Shamanic *conversion* is the hyperkinetic stasis of the cinema of agitation.

THESIS 15: Shamanic *bonding* involves the vindication of the irrational character of testimony as well as its supernatural drift.

THESIS 16: The perception of a testimony as supernatural, dreamlike, messianic, excessive, irrational, and insane is what enables a sensorial appropriation and *connection* by the document.

THESIS 17: The sensory appropriation of the audiovisual document presupposes an Aesthetics of Trance as a condition.

2. The determination of these three shamanic procedures involves three specifications: perspectivist possession, transformational conversion, and speculative bonding.

THESIS 18: In the Aesthetics of Trance, the immediate data of sensation induces an agitation in the perception of the documents.

THESIS 19: The mediate states of perception mobilize an appropriation of the documents.

THESIS 20: Agitation, appropriation, and superstition are the impure practices of the Aesthetics of Trance.[3]

THESIS 21: The Aesthetics of Trance makes possible the semiotic collision and internality of materialism and shamanism.

THESIS 22: Materialism is the empirical, contingent, circumstantial, sensory, and concrete dimension of objects, documents, archives, remains, and elements.[4]

3. One of the non-impure and absolutive correlates of the Aesthetics of Trance is the funeral liturgy.

4. The materialistic part of shamanic materialism forces us to place all audiovisual materials in a horizon of radical contingency as a field of indiscernibility common to all the collective contents of the image; this mobilizes us to assume an autophagic principle of relationality between images and sounds that are absolutely contingent, which in turn enables us to unleash a rhythmic outburst dependent, on the one hand, on a radical non-commutativity in the order of a temporality fractured by iterative modules, and on the other, on a constant tension between the apparent impossibility of continuous commutation and the reality of an expansive recursion as a horizon of formal determinability of the collective contents of the image. This brings us to the shamanic aspect of shamanic materialism through which we can intervene, induce, and connect a trance as a rhythmic and bodily rapture on the determinability of audiovisual material according to an eidetic, archaic, ancestral, and mythical differentiality.

THESIS 23: Shamanism vindicates the suggestion, the omen, trance states, the spell, and the superstition on the basis of objects and testimonies.

THESIS 24: Shamanic Materialism proceeds by fragments, ruptures, loops, clusters, modules, drifts, ascents, descents, series, spirals, vortexes, pulses, rhythms, entropy, negentropy, hypostasis, collisions, linkages, aberrations, folds, burials, unearthings—and everything which reveals intermittent constellations and from whose magma figures, agitations, forms, structures, processes, relationships, perceptions, speculations, and sensations emerge. Shamanic Materialism is a Mesoamerican spell unleashed.[5]

THESIS 25: Shamanic Materialism makes simultaneous perception possible according to two incompatible, paradoxical, and irreconcilable perspectives.

THESIS 26: Incompatible perspectives are, at bottom, unreconciled perspectives.

THESIS 27: The historical a priori of Shamanic Materialism is non-reconciliation.

THESIS 28: Shamanic Materialism asserts an eventual perspectivism of History.

THESIS 29: Non-reconciliation is the transhistoric core of History.

THESIS 30: History is a grave for the eye. An overdetermination for the ear.

THESIS 31: The eye and the ear are attractors of contingencies.

THESIS 32: Materialism entails a prodigious accumulation of contingencies.

5. This unleashing deploys an intermittent and glowing interrogation that spans centuries through time, reaching us in an extremely current moment of danger and perplexity; the aforementioned Mesoamerican spell prompts us to ask: *What land is this?* The origin of the question lies in the astonishment that the mercenary and later chronicler Bernal Díaz del Castillo expressed when entering an "unknown" land; in the heart of an "unknown" and "unnamed" America, the European Díaz del Castillo made clear the crisis of his colonial somnambulism, fusing his astonished perception with the intermittent glow of a non-European reality— here what the Europeans really discovered was the perplexity of their own ignorance. His ecstatic question crossed the destructive centuries of colonialism and European barbarism to be taken up, among others, by the writer Juan Rulfo, who recovered it from abandonment in the wasteland and the devastated lands left behind by five centuries of civilizing excess. Now we can recover the question, not only from perplexity and wasteland but from trance and cinematic rapture. Thus, from an intermittent and glittering land, we also have the trance as "images of relation." We may recall that the "letters of relation" were the way that Hernan Cortés informed the Spanish Crown about the "progress" of his ominous conquest. Let us therefore recover the form of the "relation" as a report intended to *in-form*, but as the *un-formed* found in multiple "images of relation." Thus, through audiovisuals we seek to think, articulate, integrate, and connect the historical absence of reconciliation entailed by the arrival of Europeans to the land later known as America as well as the destruction of Tenochtitlan in 1521. Five centuries after these events, we assert the Aesthetics of Trance and Shamanic Materialism as forms of multinaturalist resistance that move us to re-appropriate, transfer, and transform the ominous corrosive process induced by that historical and asymmetric clash between radically different worldviews, and which brought about the birth and development of modern nation states in the Americas with their resulting violence and problems that have still not been reconciled today.

THESIS 33: Any contingency can be appropriated, organized, and reformulated as a multinaturalist circumstance.[6]

THESIS 34: Every multinaturalist circumstance is an immediately relational multiplicity.

THESIS 35: What exists in multinature[7] are not self-identical entities perceived differently, but immediately relational multiplicities.

THESIS 36: Shamanic possession is the sensory outburst of the political cinema of agitation in an environment of immediately relational multiplicities.

THESIS 37: Cinema-trance implies the ability to see simultaneously according to incompatible, paradoxical, and irreconcilable perspectives.

6. *The circumstance* is the point of radical connection between contingency and facticity from which reason emerges. It is this situational sense of the circumstance in which reason acquires a possible determinability at the same time that it appears as a larval dimension that accompanies every entity, process, and becoming (it should also be noted that the situational sense of the circumstance determines *place*, *position*, and *perspective*). This perspective of nesting and infestation of reason supposes the nihilation of something given. Reason, therefore, is, in principle, a lack of being with respect to a given being and not the emergence of a full being, this parasitic dimension of reason constitutes its expansive infra-being, that nothing of being, nothing of History in which contingency and facticity are *linked*.

7. *Multinature* is a field of shamanic intersection between a constant epistemology and variable ontologies.

THESIS 38: The cinema-trance of agitation induces a superposition of heterogeneous states as well as the explosion in the beings of qualitative multiplicity typical of myth.

THESIS 39: Myth consists of a record of the movement of updating the present state of things from a precosmological, prehistoric, and ancestral condition.

THESIS 40: Every mythical metamorphosis entails an eventual trance of contingencies.

THESIS 41: Myth is a multinaturalist hyperimage in motion.

THESIS 42: The determination and dialectical organization of the collective contents of contingent images constitutes and displays a hyperimage.

THESIS 43: Every hyperimage expresses an epoch of the image of the world as well as a system of current relational images.

THESIS 44: Cinema is a dialectical hyperimage of motion.[8]

THESIS 45: TV is a media-relational hyperimage of culture.

---

8. Currently, cinema lies between the zombie fetishism of the film, the instrumental tourism of museum finiteness, the tyranny of digital high definition of the industry, the simulation and forensic immersion of reality, and the viral realm of low definition. By failing to take into account the eidetic chiasm produced by the arrival of Television for Cinema, the Internet for Television, and the Pandemic for the Internet, cinema is shipwrecked between a unilateral ideological drift and a neoliberal disengagement.

THESIS 46: The Internet is a relational hyperimage of control devices.

THESIS 47: The pandemic is a metabolic overdetermination of systems of images.

THESIS 48: All metabolic overdetermination implies cognitive[9] fracking[10] as a practice of digital reason.

THESIS 49: Cognitive fracking is a productivist overdetermination that integrates and enables the relational hyperimage of control devices.

THESIS 50: Advertising, digital interaction, and algorithmic processing of data instrumentalize the productivity of contingent reason.

THESIS 51: Every contingent reason enables and supports the factual, productivist, and digital vector of reason.

9. The cognitive and ontological catastrophe that neoliberal capitalism supposes and implements subtracts from the nature of experience, thus revealing the objectifying emptiness of being, while in the audiovisual this subtraction leads to the double form of aberration: the sinister and estrangement.

10. Against the grain of *cognitive fracking* as a productivist activity of corporate control, we would like to point out and assert a series of audiovisual strategies (which are continually in danger of being exploited by neoliberal fracking itself) that come from three filmic (un)forms of industrial cinema: 1) 1988's *The Blob* by Chuck Russell: absorption, assimilation, and expansion. 2) 1979's *Alien* by Ridley Scott: accumulation, nesting, and infestation. 3) 1987's *Predator* by John McTiernan: strategy, camouflage, and ritual.

THESIS 52: Productivist Reason implies an autophagic
energy automatism.

THESIS 53: rEason is the productivist and autophagic nucleus
of systems of images.

THESIS 54: reAson is the radical and progressive affirmation
of the evidence of its reality.

THESIS 55: reaSon in the Anthropocene develops and affirms
an energetic hyperimage of the world.[11]

THESIS 56: reasOn has only one way of explaining what does
not emerge from it, and that is to reduce it to nothing.

THESIS 57: The reduction to nothingness, as a practice of
reasoN, implies an eidetic contraction and dispersion of beings.

THESIS 58: Every eidetic reduction opens paths to extinction.

THESIS 59: The instrumentalization of eidetic reduction leads
to precariousness as an existential condition in the epoch of
reason in the Anthropocene.

11. The retroactive affirmation of planetary geological and
atmospheric effects as clear causes of the corrosive effectiveness of the Anthropocene-Capitalocene determines the expansive
scope of the linking and relational activity of Reason as an
objectifying activity, as a faculty of the unconditioned, as
expansion, generation, and linking of categorical fields in the
direction of the conformation of object inlays, eidetic retrac-
tions, intentional permutations, as well as cognitive catas-
trophes and ecological extinctions. All of this is articulated
by Reason in the midst of a clear and continual contraction of
hydrocarbons and energy that is increasingly radical.

THESIS 60: The precariousness of the image is a condition of possibility of audiovisual appropriation.[12]

THESIS 61: Extinction, exhaustion, entropy, wear, fatigue, and destruction make up a possible ecological correlate of the directive images of contingent reason.

THESIS 62: The directive images of contingent reason imply three relational systems and processes of organizational internality: *the world* that *produces* reason in the Anthropocene, *the limits postulated* by critical reason, and *the nature* that *links* speculative reason.

THESIS 63: *The world*, *limits*, and *nature* constitute the guiding images of contingent reason.

THESIS 64: The constructivist differentiality of contingent reason according to its *connection* with each of these guiding images generates "three things": a productivist and objectifying reason in relation to the *world* (capitalist realism); a critical and reflective reason in relation to *the limits* (ecological realism); a speculative reason in relation to *nature* (speculative realism).

12. Precariousness implies a qualitative and eidetic retraction of objects, which enables an intermediate and connecting constructivity between relational qualities that objects emit and absorb, and that allows us to experience the shamanic constructivism of the audiovisual process from a synthetic point of view as additive and subtractive facets of qualitative and objectual incrustations, clearing a whole field of audiovisual entities and cinematic appropriations (dis)oriented towards objects.

THESIS 65: The first relational process of organizational internality (objectifying reason) implies a deterministic, scientistic, objectual, realistic, cognitive, epistemic production, as well as the assertion of the ontological one-sidedness of the world.

THESIS 66: The objectifying perspective of reason in the Anthropocene, in its productivist relationship with the world, presupposes a pre-existing and inherent structure to nature that enables the objectivity of the world.[13]

THESIS 67: Contrary to objectifying reason, the relational process of critical reason (ecological realism) presupposes the radical and irreducible exteriority and objectivity of nature on which basis the necessary limits for the destructive activity of reason in the Anthropocene will be determined.

13. This objectifying perspective also supposes and considers work as an anthropological invariant as a practical principle of transformation and effective production of the world. Would work as an anthropological invariant not suppose, in turn, and as a correlate of its apparent invariance, a speculative invariant (perhaps more metaphysical than speculative) as a horizon of telematic determination present in multiple layers of human and posthuman history? Wouldn't Reason, as a faculty of the unconditioned, be precisely the aberrant retroactivity of a radical affirmation that determines the conditions of real experience? It is no coincidence that, in the anti-ecological model of modernity, the pyramid is the figure that determines the representation of the food chain, symptomatically establishing a pharaonic condition of transcendent illusion for the current civil disassociation of the Capitalocene, thus producing not only pharaonic resurrection machines (corporate pyramids) but the objectifying assemblages of the sinister machine of capitalist precarization, devastation, and annihilation.

THESIS 68: The reflective perspective of critical reason, in its ecological relationship with the world, implies the establishment of limits for the productivism of reason in the Anthropocene.

THESIS 69: Finally, the relational process of speculative reason links the world as a perspectival hyperimage in motion from which nature is conceived as multinaturalist circumstance from its immediately relational multiplicity.

THESIS 70: The perspectivism of speculative reason, in its multinaturalist link with the world, enables the capacity of simultaneous perception according to incompatible, paradoxical, and irreconcilable perspectives.

THESIS 71: Speculative reason is the relational, anthropophagic, and autophagic perspective of Shamanic Materialism.

THESIS 72: Shamanic Materialism links ancestrality, extinction, and trance as speculative and multinaturalist perspectives of the dialectical hyperimage of movement.

THESIS 73: Incompatible, paradoxical, and irreconcilable perspectives constitute the relational correlate of the dialectical hyperimage of movement.

THESIS 74: What exists in multinature involves a turbulent mythical flow that continues to pulse and to extinguish; it is the powerful volcanic life of beings and things, a life that, through the cinematic and audiovisual process, expresses them not as differently perceived self-identical entities but as immediately relational multiplicities.

THESIS 75: The radical nature of the contingency asserted
by materialism implies recovering the idea that destruction
and annihilation can exist without any counterpart, without
any compensation; it is about recognizing that there
are absolute losses that will never be recovered, events
without any consequences, civilizations and entire peoples
annihilated and lost in the nothingness of History without
leaving any trace, like those great rivers that disappear in
the sands of a planetary desert. The idea that in the world
there are a number of things, objects, subjects, events, flows,
lives, and events that will be absolutely annihilated and
not recovered, the reality of that idea, we say, manifests
the abrasiveness of the vast machinery of annihilation that
inhabits the desert of the real.

THESIS 76: The perspectivism, the conversion, and the
mythical connection of the dialectical hyperimage open an
eventual field in History.

THESIS 77: Shamanic materialism as a cinematic and
audiovisual process leads to and entails a political film-trance
of agitation in which the agitation would no longer emanate
from a coming to awareness or call for mass mobilization, but
would consist of placing contingencies and circumstances in
a trance, including, in the first place, Reason itself, relating
violence and contingencies to each other, so that through
trance, violence, myth, ancestry, precariousness, and
extinction, a new cosmological and cosmopolitical perception
of the Missing People is formed.

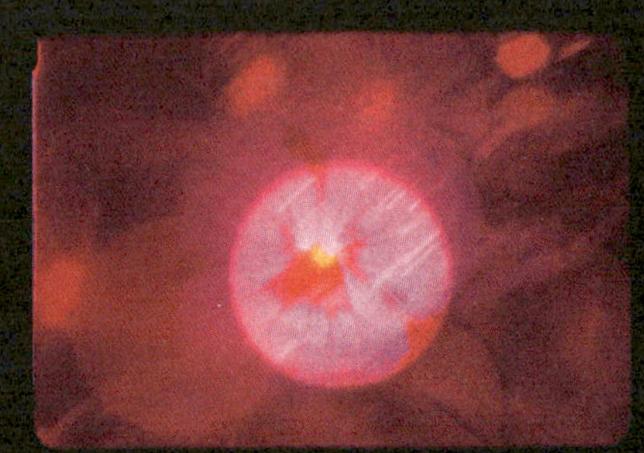

Tonalli, Colectivo Los Ingrávidos, 2022

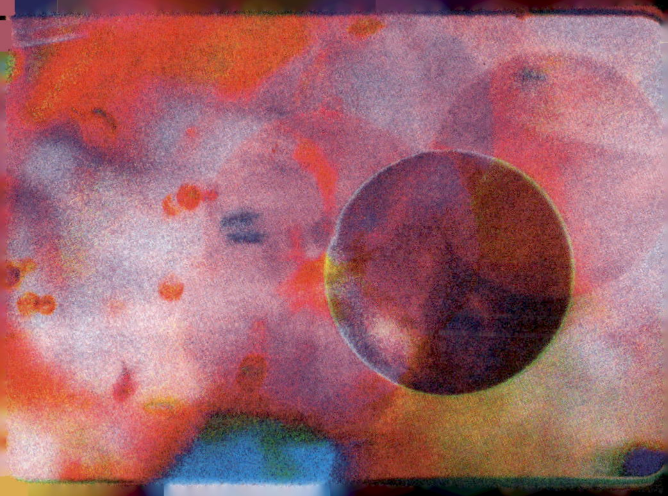

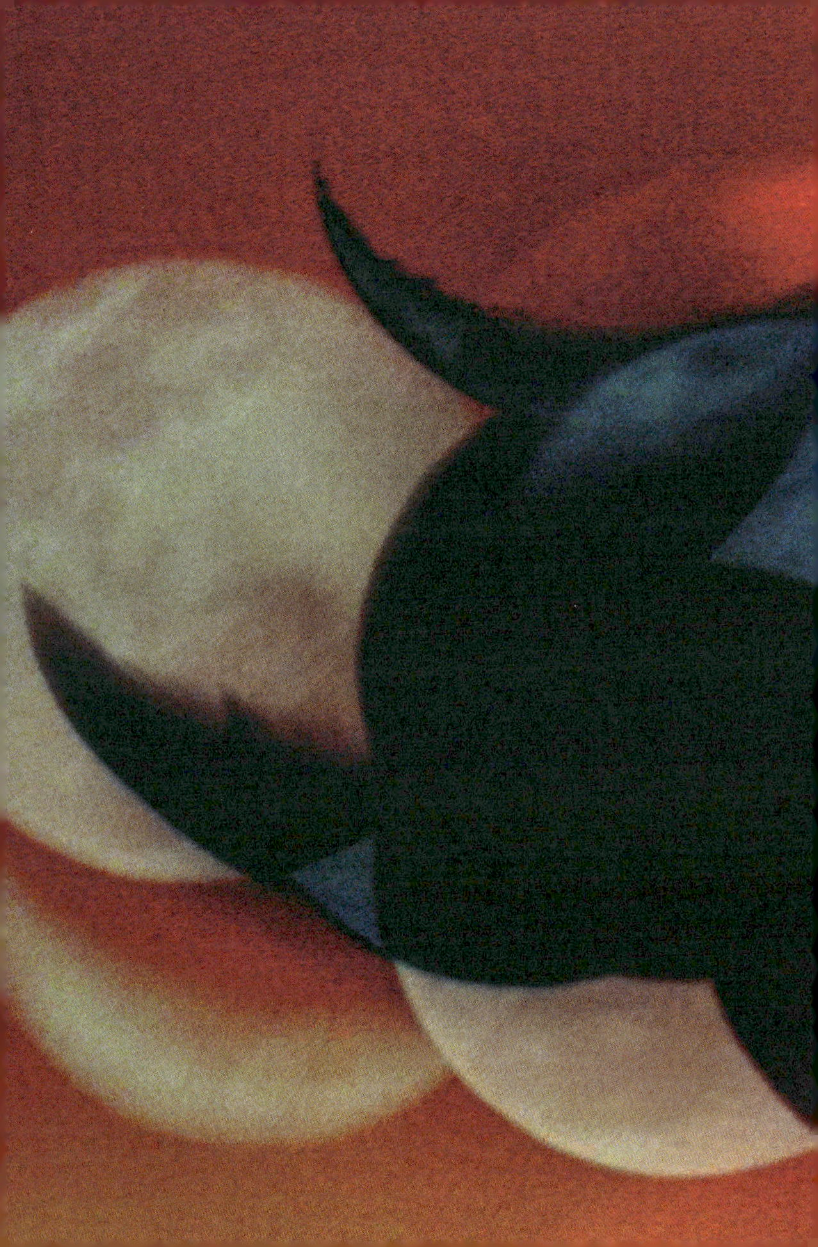

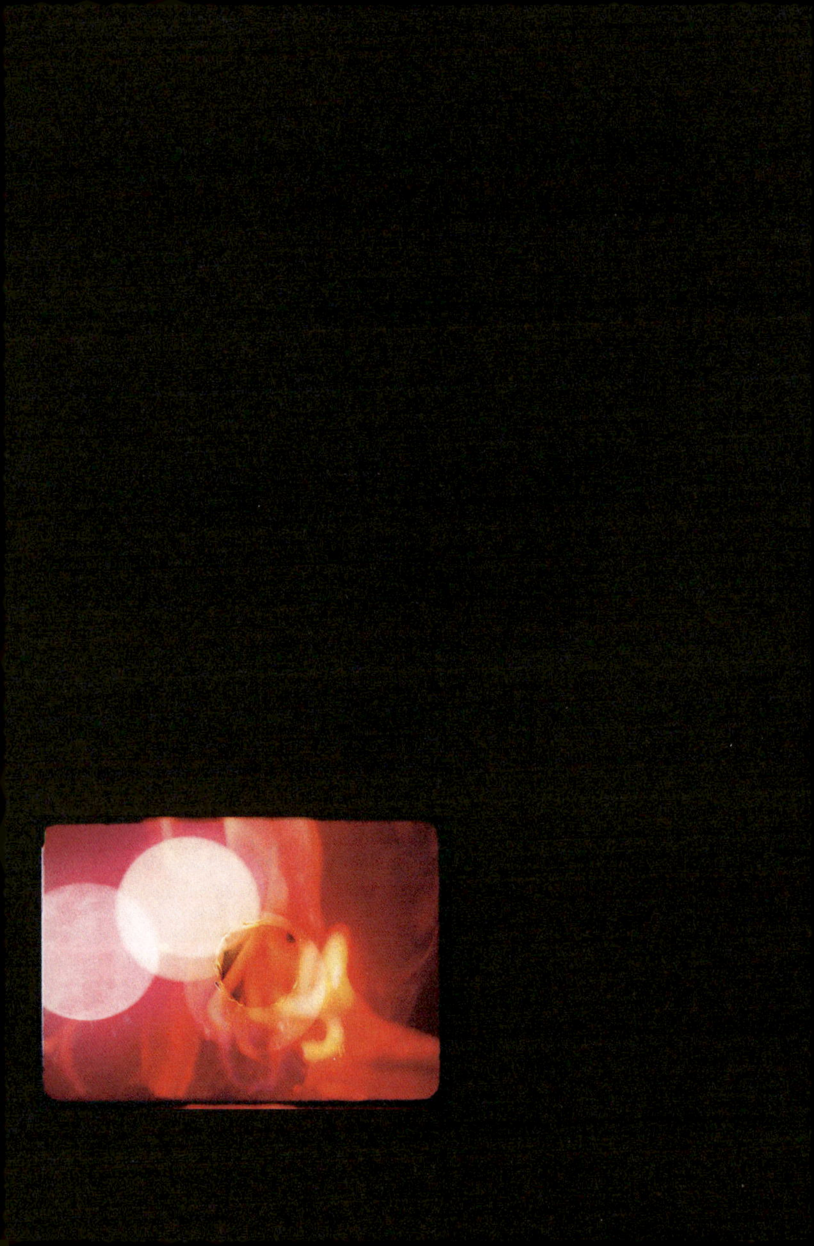

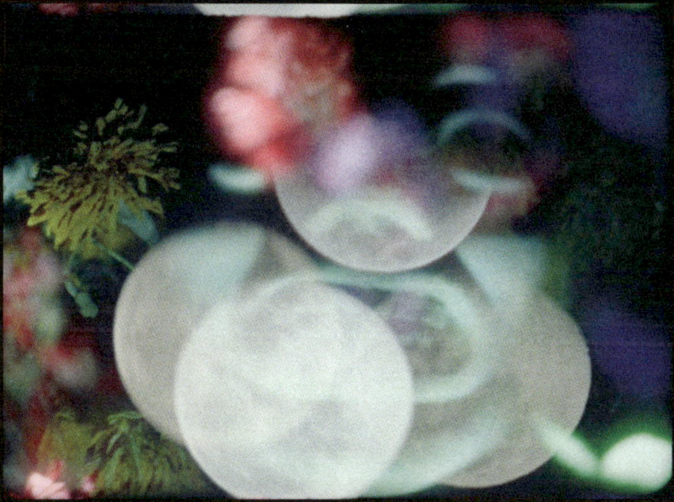

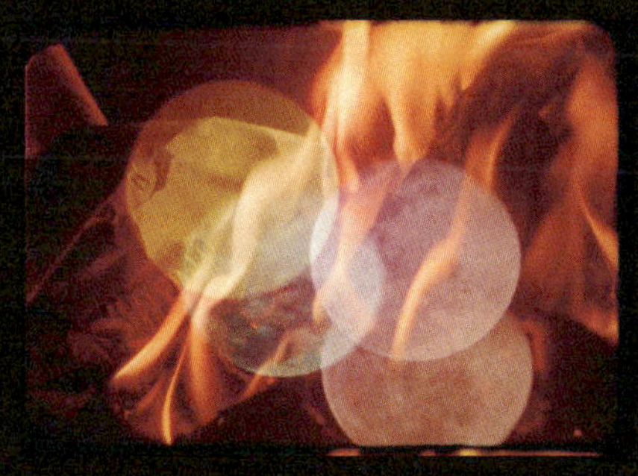

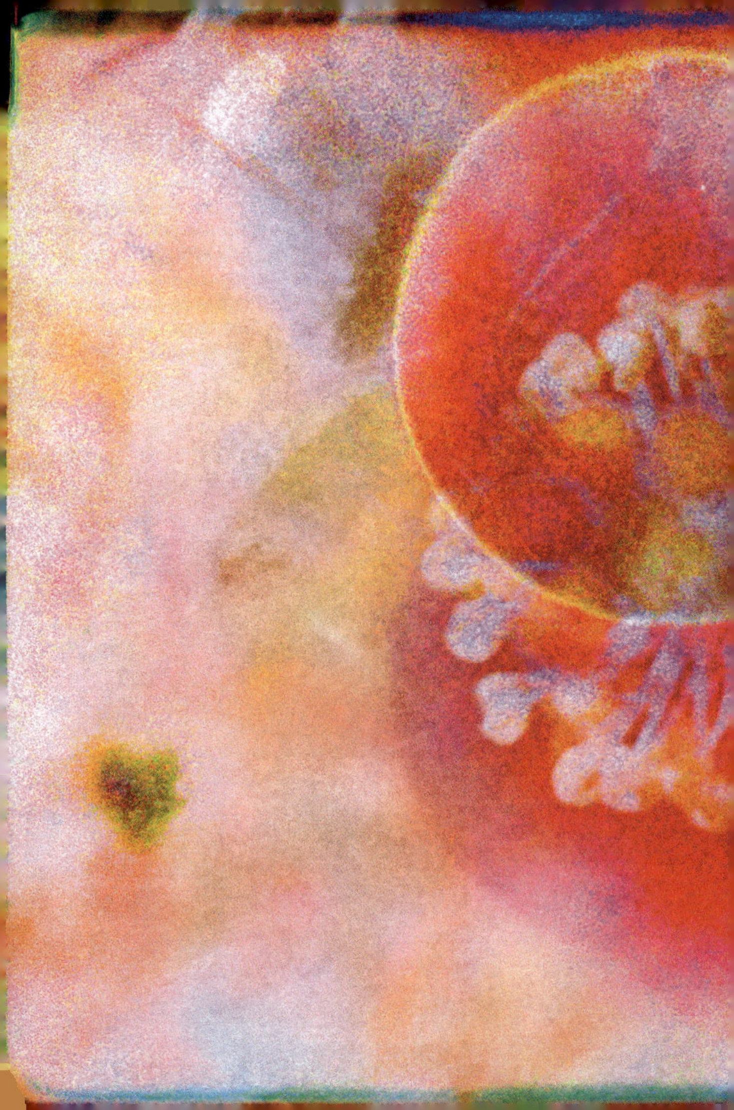

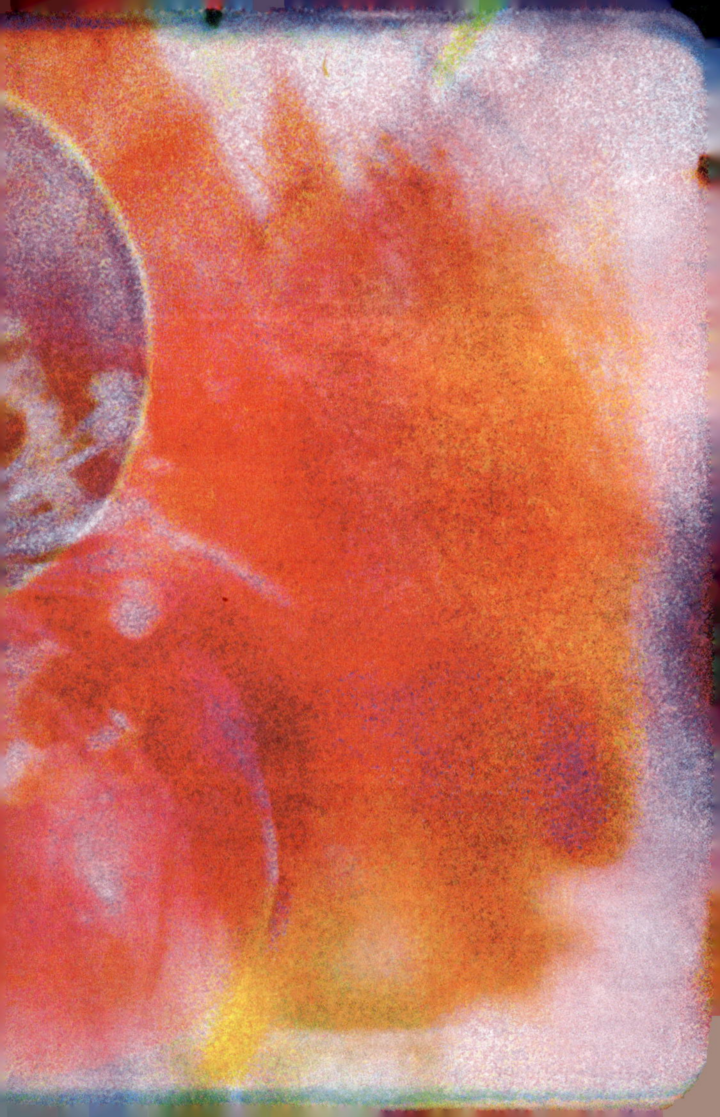

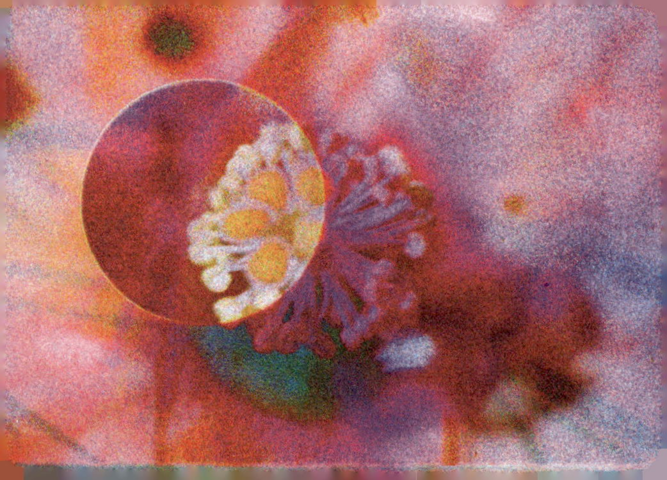

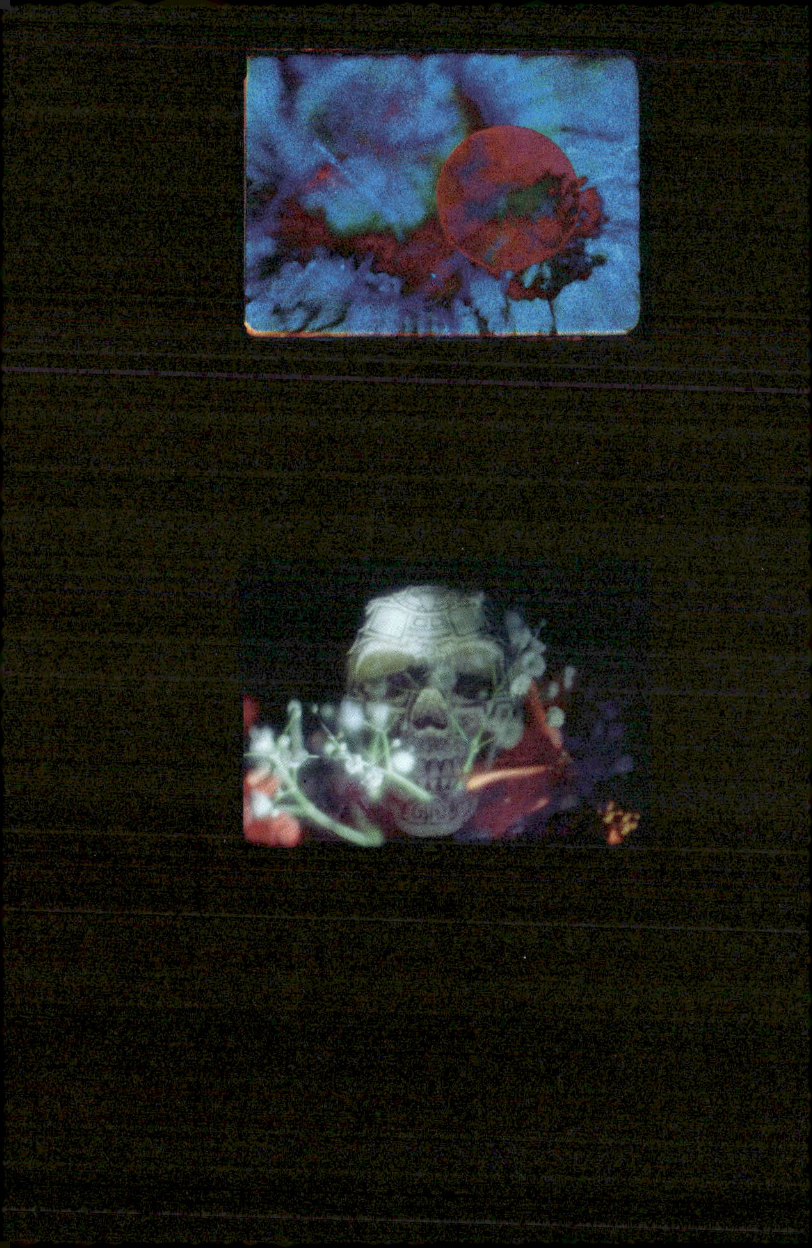

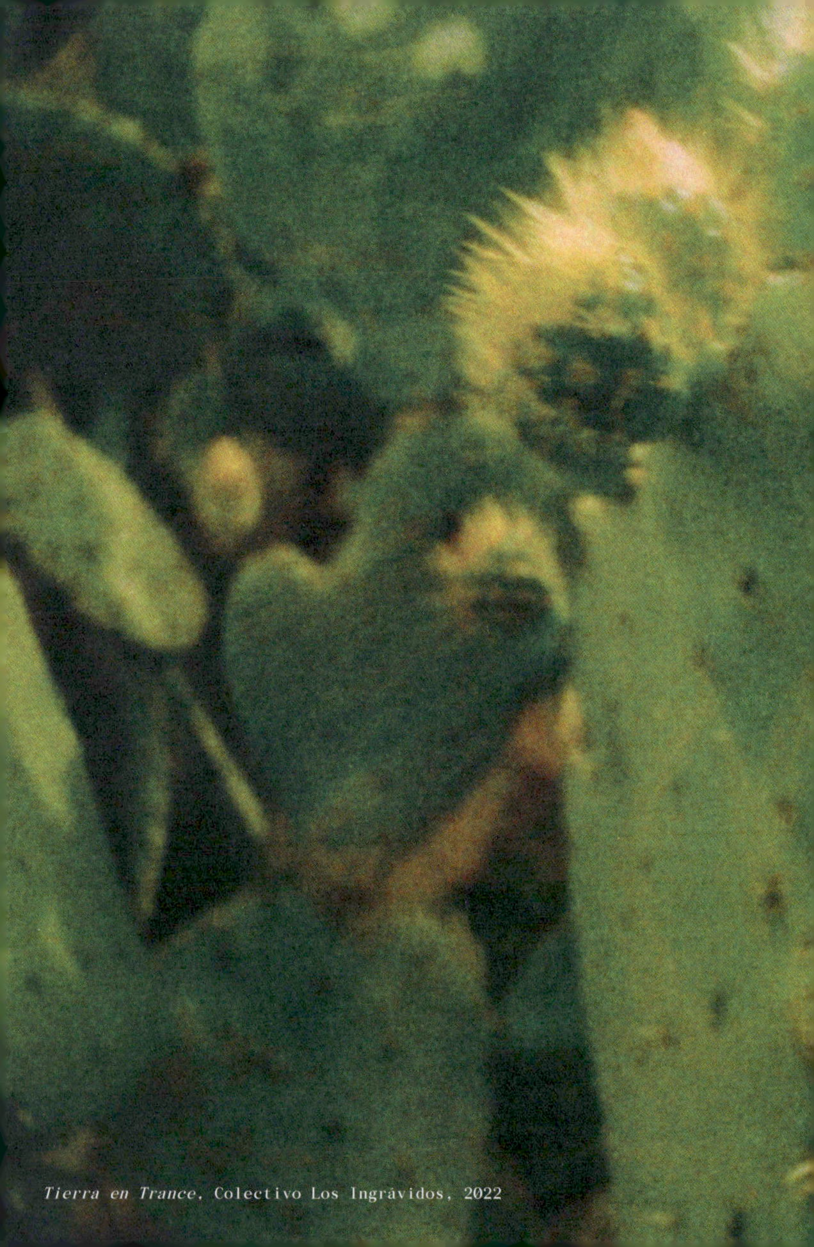

Tierra en Trance, Colectivo Los Ingrávidos, 2022

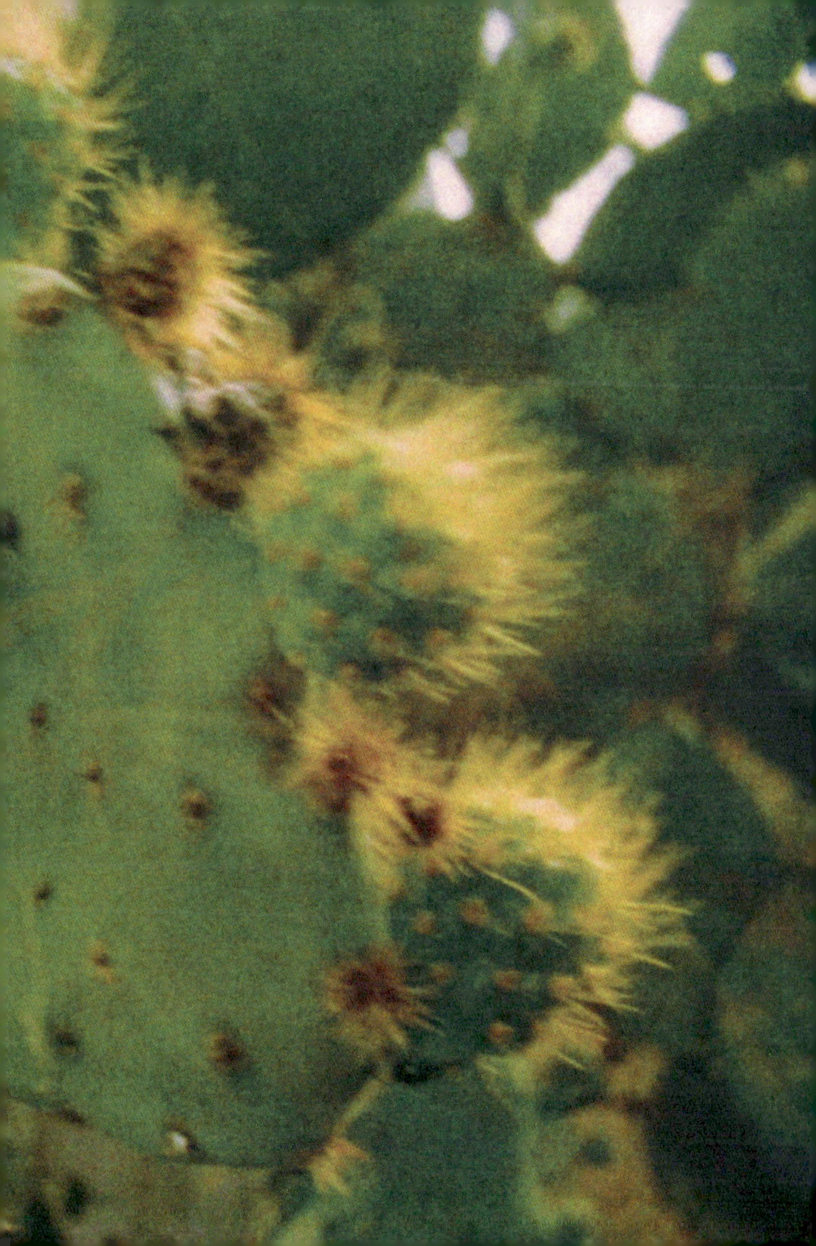

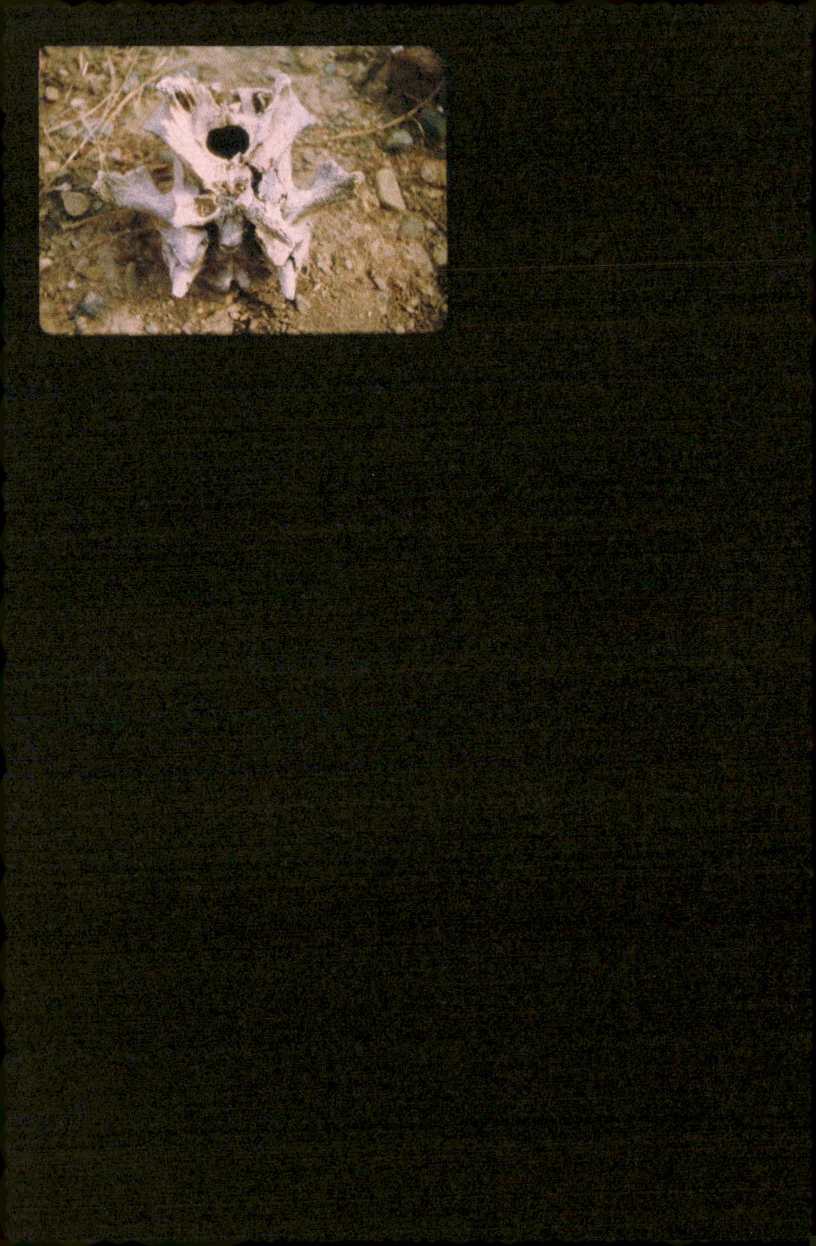

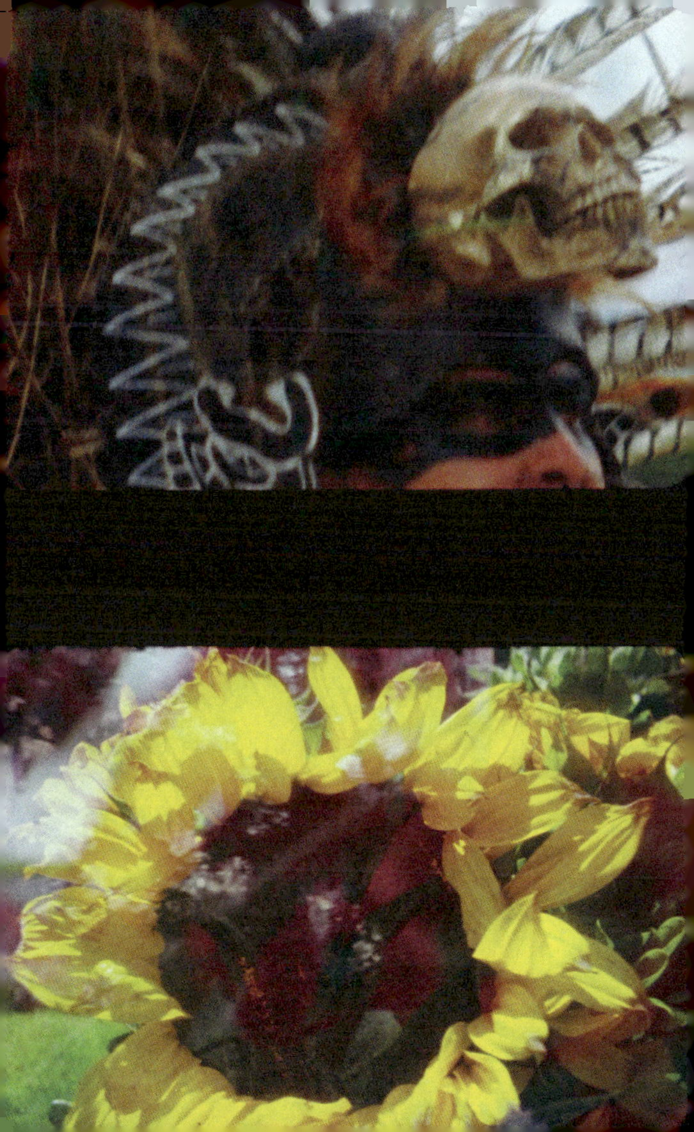

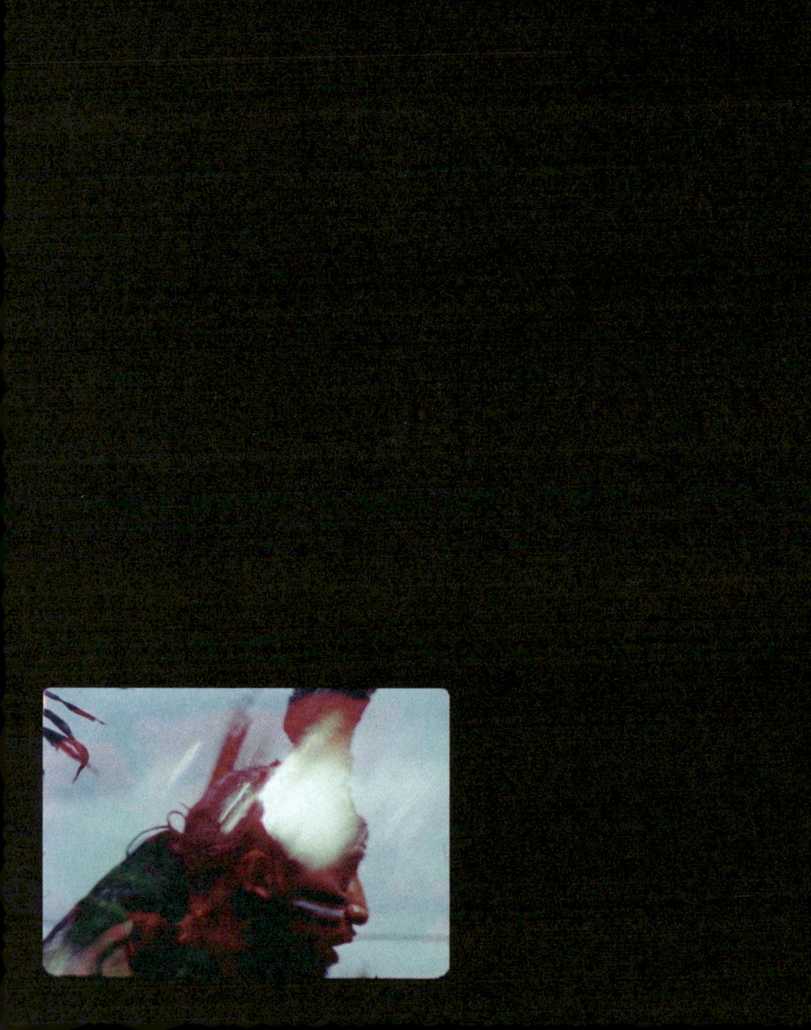

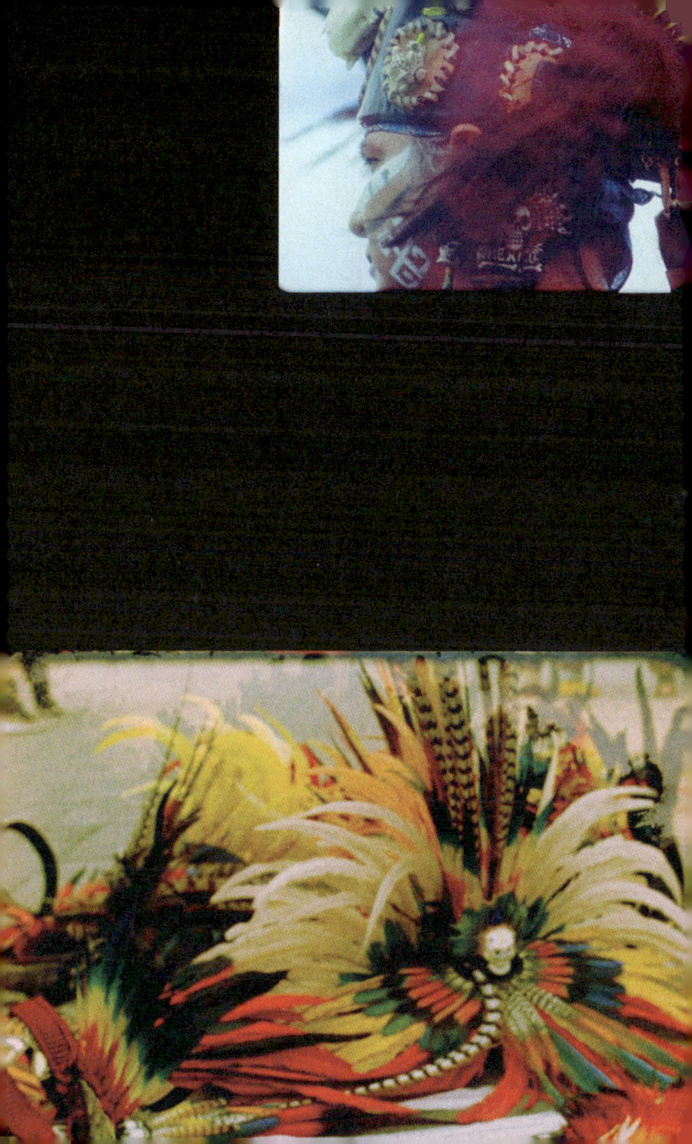

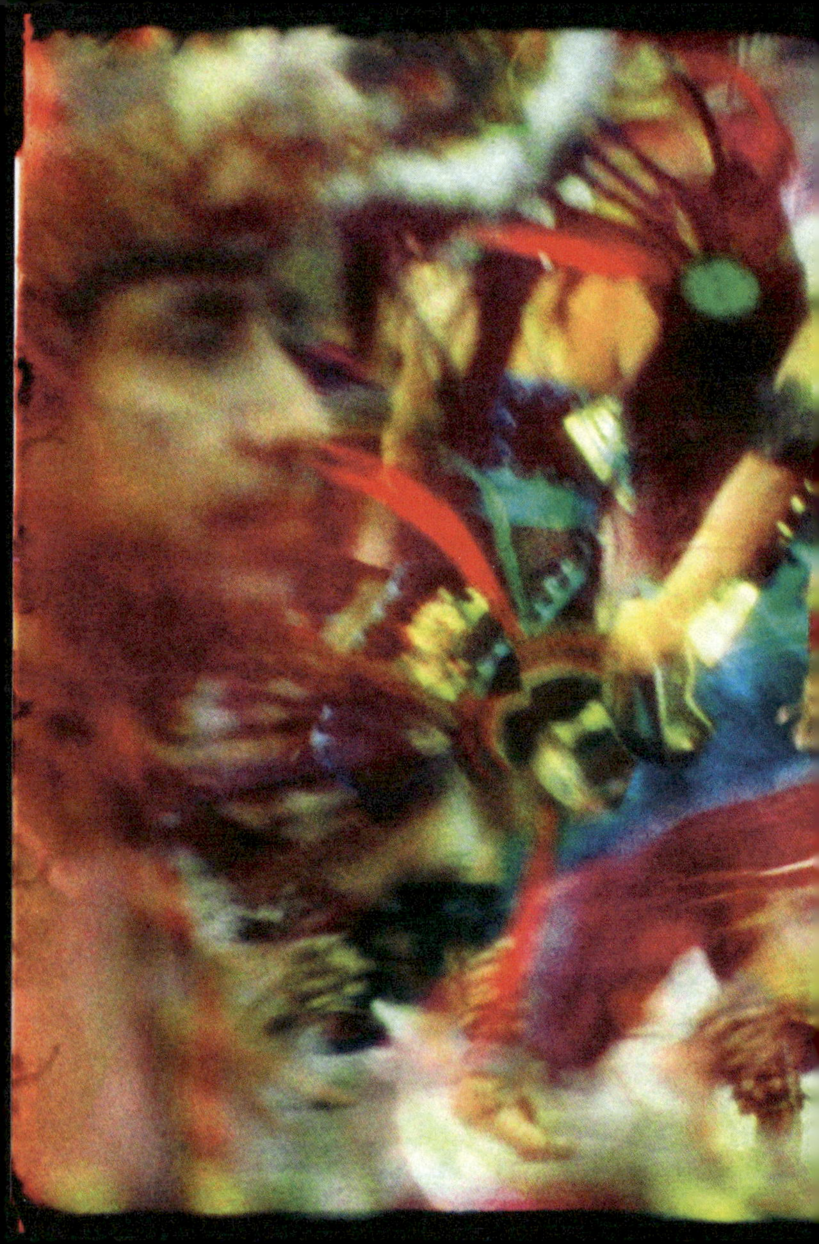

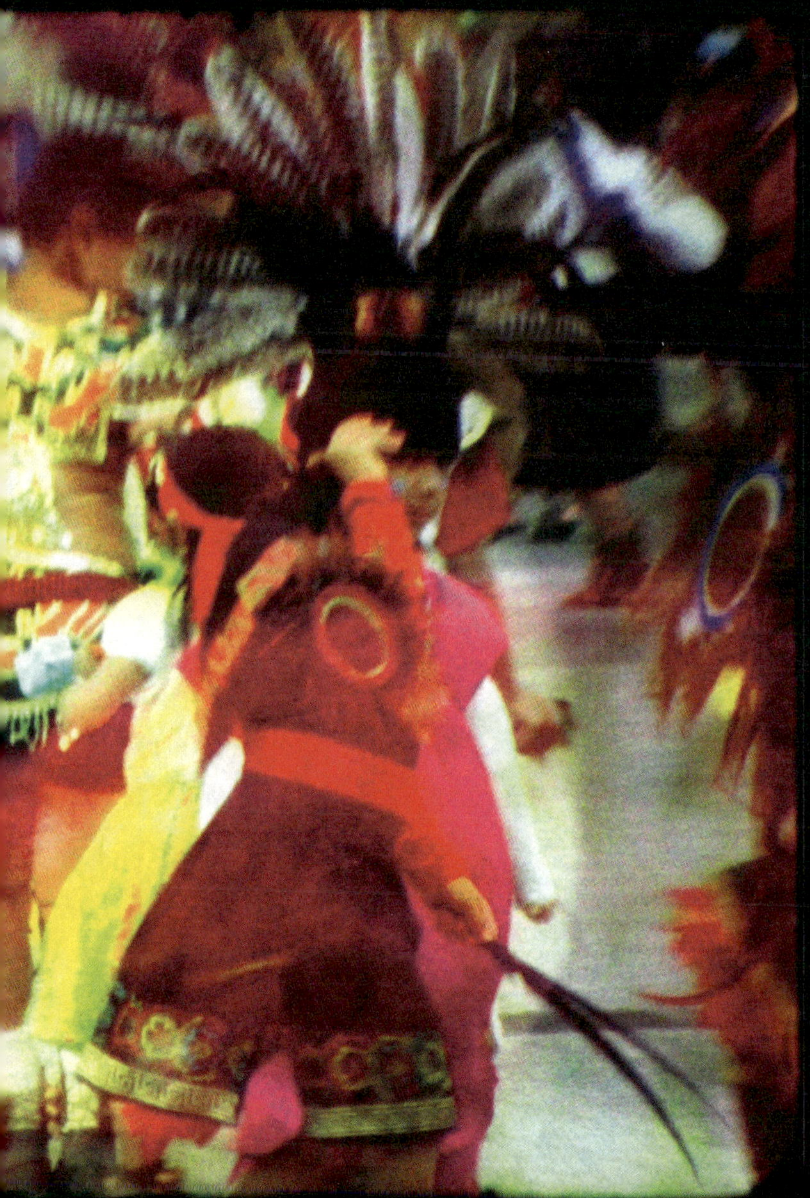

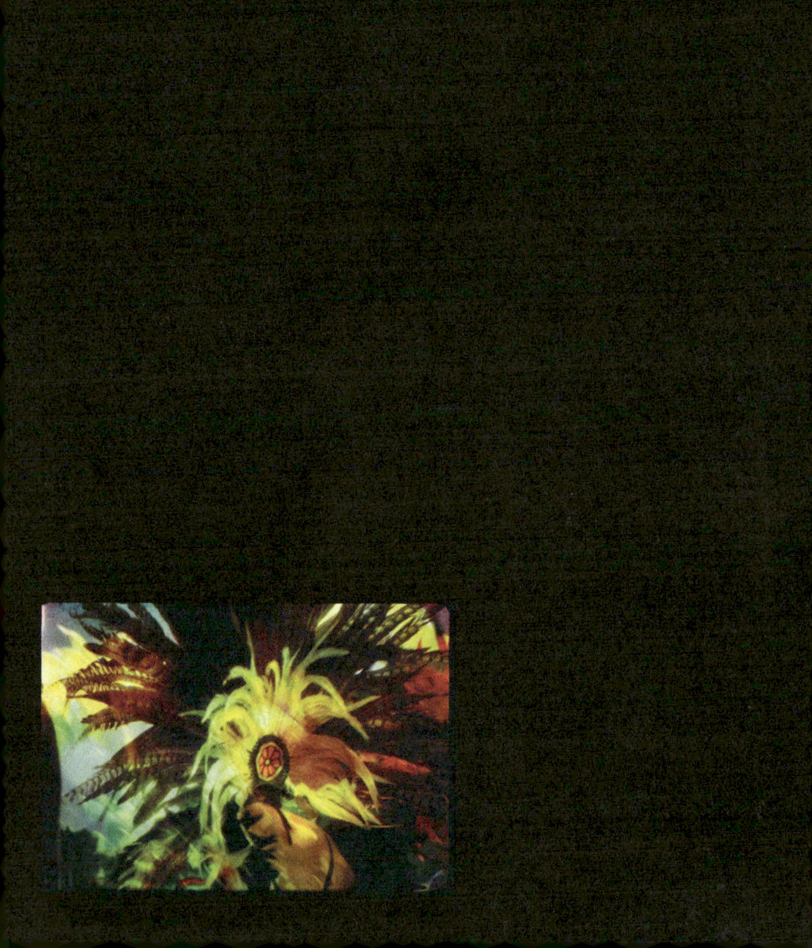

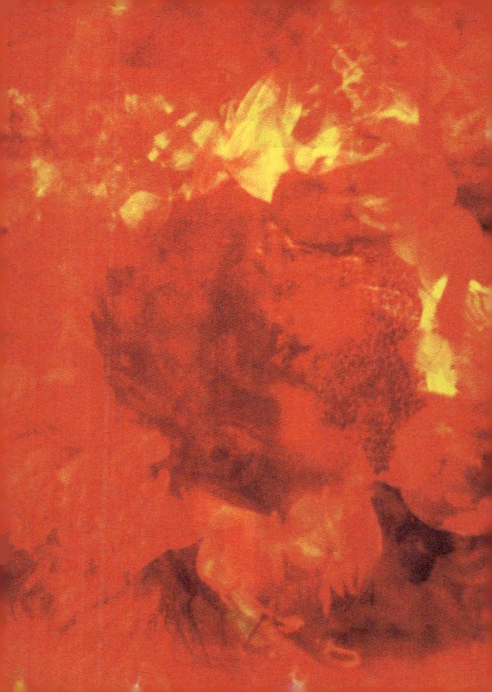

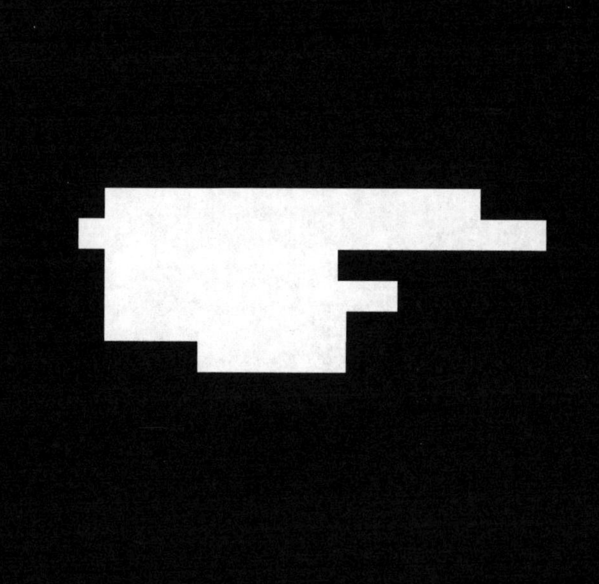

Reflections on Language Based on the All-Encompassing Sequence Shot: Formal Processes in Bolivian Cinema

Miguel Hilari

There are many metaphors in this language, but it should be noted that those who will speak it better, and with more profit, will accommodate themselves to the common and ordinary language. v.g. Inti halsu is more ordinary than Inti phallusu: Inti halanti is clearer than not saying Inti thalakhranti. In these metaphorical and exquisite ways, it will suffice to go from time to time, to give some salt and luster to the sentence.[1]

—*Ludovico Bertonio*

The *Dictionary of the Aymara Language* by Ludovico Bertonio was published in 1612, and is considered the first work on the subject. In "Annotation III, of some small things," Bertonio gives advice for beginners: he encourages the use of common and ordinary language, and recommends caution in the use of metaphors. As scholars Thérèse Bouysse-Cassagne and Olivia Harris state three and a half centuries later, a metaphor "evokes multiple contexts and its translation into another conceptual system is difficult and risky."[2] Referring to the translation of literary texts into foreign languages, Walter Benjamin makes a rather drastic comparison: he equates the relationship between the original work and its translation to a circle and a tangent that only slightly brush into each other at one point. The connection between both bodies, he writes, is equivalent to the "infinitely small point of

1. Ludovico Bertonio, *Vocabulario de la lengua Aymara* (Juli: Francisco del Canto, 1612), Annotation 3, paragraph 4. Translated for this essay by Almudena Escobar López.

2. Thérèse Bouysse-Cassagne and Olivia Harris, "Pacha: En torno al pensamiento aymara," in *Tres reflexiones sobre el pensamiento andino* (La Paz: Hisbol, 1987), 12. Translated for this essay by Almudena Escobar López.

3. Walter Benjamin, "The Task of the Translator," in *Angelus Novus* (Barcelona: Edhasa, 1971), 127-143.

4. As the opposition between collective and individual was a central concern in the cinema of Sanjinés and the Ukamau Group, the attribution of authorship was not without tensions and rhetoric. In this article I refer to the Ukamau Group as the author of the films and Jorge Sanjinés as the author of the texts, respecting their will.

sense." The translation, like the tangent, follows its trajectory to infinity, with the possibility of being contaminated by the original and thus expanding the borders of its own language.[3] The act of translating then is a friction, a brief encounter between two dissimilar bodies. Our objective today: to reflect on the all-encompassing sequence shot, a formal procedure developed in the 1989 film *La nación clandestina* (The Secret Nation) by Jorge Sanjinés and the Ukamau Group,[4] conceived by the filmmakers and read by critics as a translation between two conceptual systems: cinematographic language and the conception of time in Andean culture. By analyzing the development of the all-encompassing sequence shot, I want to question the idea of a radical opposition between "Andean circular time" and "Western linear time." More and better pages than these have been written about the beauty and importance of the films of the Ukamau Group. What interests me, rather, is to problematize the way in which the Andean cosmovision has been presented and read, affirming a series of conceptual foundations that we need to review critically.

The Translations

From its beginnings, cinema was conceived as a possibility of "translation" between the material world and human expression. The Soviet filmmaker and theorist Dziga Vertov dreamed of cinema as an energetic flow capable of connecting people from all over the world, overcoming space-time barriers to become matter in constant motion, a vehicle for translating lived experience into a universal language of images:

> The kino-eye means the conquest of space, the visual linkage of people throughout the entire world based on the continuous exchange of visible fact, of film-

documents as opposed to the exchange of cinematic or theatrical presentations.

Kino-eye means the conquest of time (the visual linkage of phenomena separated in time). Kino-eye is the possibility of seeing life processes in any temporal order or at any speed inaccessible to the human eye.[5]

In "On Language as Such and on the Language of Man,"[6] Benjamin affirms that objects emanate energy that can be interpreted by humans through language. The faculties of naming and judging are the central characteristics of language, which in turn would be reminiscent of Genesis, in which God creates the world through the word. Thus, language belongs to a spiritual sphere with the ability to create and give meaning to reality: language is, in itself, the translation of the living energy of matter into a humanly communicable form. Language is the way in which we relate to the world and the world is the organization of reality, trimmed, categorized, and named through language. In this text, Benjamin ignores the differences between languages and cultures to anchor language in his practice: he speaks of the language of technique, art, justice, poetry, and religion. The energy is emanated by matter and carried into a specific human language. Cinema would be one of several possible translations. This vision complements Vertov's, for whom cinema contains the possibility of a primal translation of reality, without the mediation of the spoken word: an ideal way of translating the language of objects directly into human consciousness. According to Vertov, cinema

5. Dziga Vertov, "Kino-Eye to Radio-Eye," ed. Annette Michelson, *Kino-Eye: The Writings of Dziga Vertov* (Berkeley: University of California Press, 1984), 87.

6. Walter Benjamin, "Über Sprache überhaupt und über die Sprache des Menschen" (On Language as Such and on the Language of Man), *Medienästhetische Schriften* (Frankfurt: Suhrkamp, 2002), 67-82.

should become a universal audiovisual language and would mean the definitive overcoming of linguistic and cultural borders between humans.

In Bolivia, it seems that Vertov's universalist vision failed miserably. In the 1960s, Jorge Sanjinés and the Ukamau Group began a long process of developing a revolutionary cinema, "at the service of the interests of the people, which becomes an instrument of denunciation and clarification, which evolves integrating the participation of the people and intends to reach them."[7] However, it is precisely this arrival of the movies to the people that is not satisfactory. In his 1970 essay "Sobre *¡Fuera de aquí!*" (About *Get Out of Here!*), Sanjinés mentions inconsistencies between form and content in films as the main obstacle to reaching the masses:

> Our first films had the intention of delivering liberating content, but they are films that, although from the point of view of the content are coherent with the recipients, they are not from a formal perspective, and this deficiency nullified their effectiveness to a great extent.[8]

In an interview from 1977, Sanjinés and the Ukamau Group mentioned the differences in the reception of the works according to the social stratum to which the public belonged. Cultural differences are identified as the cause of poor acceptance by the target audience, and some formal strategies are marked to be developed in the future:

> Peasants resist a film like *Yawar Mallku* because of its formal

7. Jorge Sanjinés and Ukamau Group, "Elementos para una teoría y práctica del cine revolucionario," *Teoría y práctica de un cine junto al pueblo* (México: Siglo XXI, 1979), 38. Translated for this essay by Almudena Escobar López.

8. Jorge Sanjinés, "Sobre *¡Fuera de Aquí!*," *Cine boliviano del realizador al crítico* (La Paz: Gisbert, 1979), 158. Translated for this essay by Almudena Escobar López.

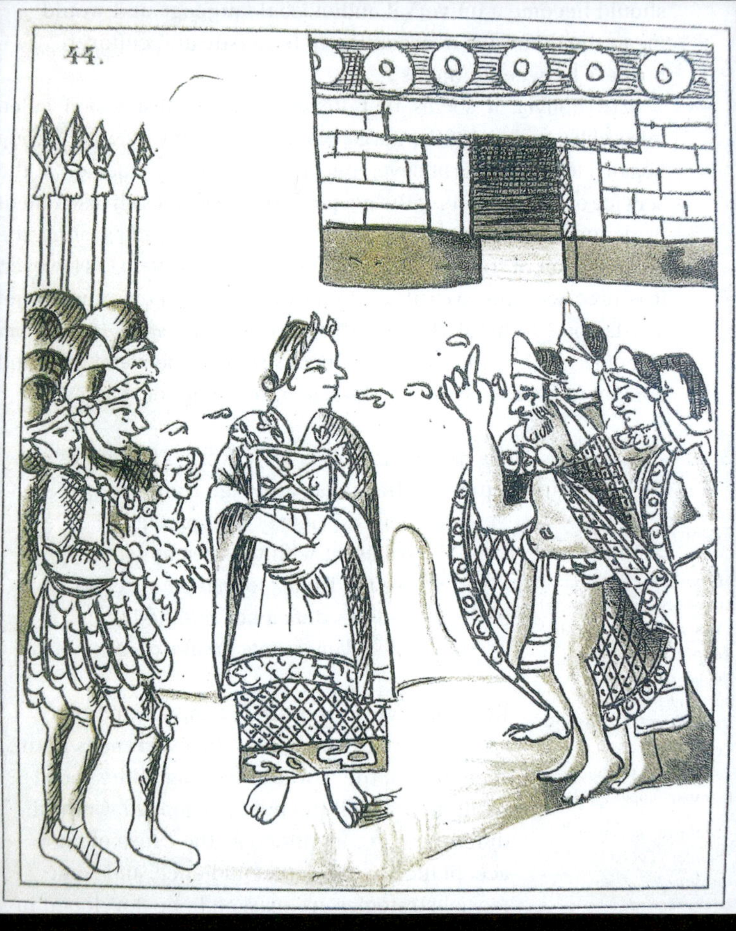

1. Malinche translating the meeting between Moctezuma and Cortés.
*Bernardino de Sahagún, Historia general de las cosas de Nueva España.
Libro XII: la conquista de México* (México, 1577)

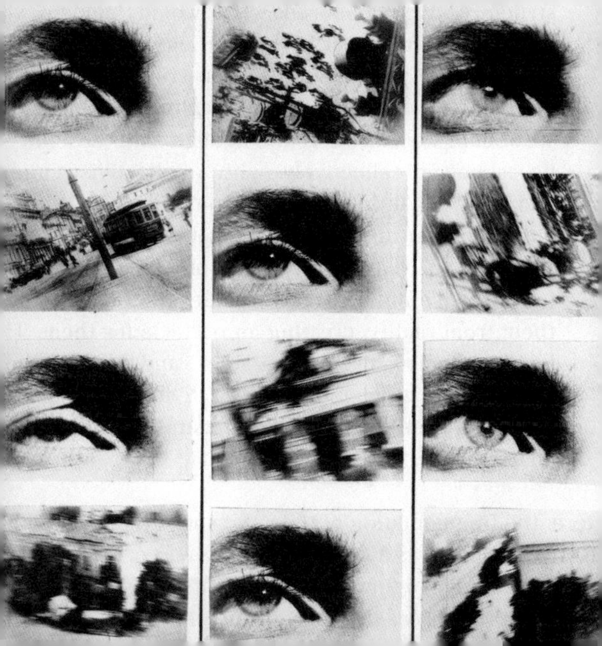

structure. We wondered what would happen, why that film didn't work in a peasant environment as it did in a petty-bourgeois environment, and we discovered that it was simply a cultural problem, that we should seek a coherent language with the ability to be conceived collectively, with a collectivist culture; and little by little we found solutions... In this way we also began to feel, for example, that the close-up was also an obstacle to a good understanding of our purpose. We noticed that formally the film distanced them from reality, creating an obstacle for them. This is why we now use longer shots, and general shots, which allow greater freedom of action for actors and prevent the authoritarian manipulation of the montage, characteristic of bourgeois cinema.[9]

Here, the fragmentation of time and space typical of film montage appears as an obstacle to the understanding of a film among peasants. This statement resembles the story of the girl from Siberia told by the Hungarian film critic Béla Balázs. The girl, who migrated from the Siberian countryside to work as a domestic worker in Moscow, went to the cinema for the first time and was shocked by the film. She was horrified by the division of the bodies into shots of hands, arms and heads that lost connection with the rest of the body, and assumed that the film was a butchery of human bodies.[10] The veracity of this story is doubtful,[11] but it is clear that for Balázs, the anecdote symbolizes the importance of socialization and learning that the language of montage needs.

9. Jorge Sanjinés and Ukamau Group, "El cine político no debe abandonar jamás su preocupación por la belleza," interview with Ignacio Ramonet, *Teoría y práctica de un cine junto al pueblo* (México: Siglo XXI, 1979), 155. Translated for this essay by Almudena Escobar López.

10. Béla Balázs, *Der Film. Werden und Wesen einer neuen Kunst* (Vienna: Globus, 1972), 24.

Subsequently, the fragmentation of time and space was identified by Sanjinés not only as an obstacle to the understanding of the films by the peasant public, but as the expression of an ideology:

> But it is interesting to note that fragmentation also interpreted a way of understanding reality consistent with an individualistic vision of society and life. Non-integrated society, resolved in permanent ruptures both in human relations and in its organic composition. By breaking the space we will frequently be painting a social universe of fragmentations, jumps, psychological violence. Society of individual spaces, of demarcated territories, of «own» places; society of ranks, of social differences, of privileges, of classes finally. There is no continuity, there is no harmony in Western society.[12]

In the '70s, there were several formal resources that the Ukamau Group implemented in its films to bring them closer to their target audience. Sanjinés mentions the change of an individual protagonist for a collective protagonist,

11. In the paper "Béla Balázs und sein Beitrag zur formästhetischen Filmtheorie," Helmut H. Diederichs mentions the nationality changes suffered by a provincial protagonist in Balázs's writings, depending on the country in which the theorist's books were published, Germany, Russia and Hungary. The provincial who does not understand the plot of a film in *Geist des Films* (Germany, 1930) is the administrator of a Russian estate who has not set foot in a city in fifteen years and therefore does not understand the language of cinema. In *Iskusstwo Kino* (Russia, 1945), the protagonist of the same story becomes an English colonial employee who was in Central Africa for many years, it is intuited in order not to hurt feelings in Russia, where Balázs lived temporarily. In *Filmkultúra* (Hungary, 1948), the provincial remains English, but the story of the girl from Siberia is added, perhaps in an attempt to balance things out.

the recreation of true events with the same protagonists, the inclusion of a narrator who anticipates the events destroying the intrigue, and the overcoming of fragmentation and close-ups through the sequence shot.[13] The intention was to demand an active participation of the viewer while also opening a greater possibility of reflection on reality. The closeness of these processes to the theories of Bertolt Brecht and André Bazin is evident,[14] but it is noteworthy that in "Sobre *¡Fuera de Aquí!*" there is no reference to European influences. Sanjinés attributes the formal development of his cinema exclusively to a series of observations that originated in "the daily practice of living with that culture that is truly ours."[15] From these processes, the most extensively developed is the all-encompassing sequence shot. It occupies a central place in *La nación clandestina*, which is considered by many critics to be the masterpiece of the Ukamau Group. Sometimes, the camera oscillates between different spaces and temporalities. The film tells the story of Sebastián Mamani, a rural Aymara migrant who arrives as a child to the city of La Paz where he is morally corrupted and betrays his people. Finally, he decides to return to his community to reconcile through an ancestral dance that culminates in his death. While the film was in production, Sanjinés published the essay "El Plano Secuencia Integral" (The All-Encompassing Sequence Shot), in which he emphasized the need to create an appropriate narrative technique to reflect the

12. Jorge Sanjinés, "El plano secuencia integral" *Cine cubano*, no. 125 (1989), 68. Trans. Dennis Hanlon and Cecilia Cornejo, "The all-encompassing sequence shot," *Jump Cut*, no. 54 (Fall 2012).

13. Sanjinés, "Sobre *¡Fuera de Aquí!*," 160-163.

14. Dennis Hanlon extensively explores the relationship between the Ukamau Group and European film theory: *Moving Cinema: Bolivia's Ukamau and European Political Film, 1966-1989* (Ph.D. Thesis, University of Iowa: 2009), 187-227.

15. Sanjinés, "Sobre *¡Fuera de Aquí!*," 159.

16. Cristina Alvares Beskow, "Un cine de combate junto al pueblo. Entrevista con el cineasta boliviano Jorge Sanjinés," *Cinema Comparat/ive Cinema* 4, no. 9 (2016), 22-30. Translated for this essay by Almudena Escobar López.

Andean worldview. In the past thirty years, both the filmmaker and the majority of film critics have agreed on the importance of this process as a mechanism for translating the Andean system of thought into film language. In a 2013 interview, Sanjinés explains the development of the all-encompassing sequence shot:

> We understood that this cinema that had the objective of reaching the largest number of Bolivian spectators had to be built under principles inspired by the internal mechanisms of another vision of the world, the vision of the majority, the vision of Indigenous cultures. And we were developing our own aesthetics, a language, a narrative that will later culminate in *La nación clandestina*, where we already built the all-encompassing sequence shot, which is a way of narrating that interprets the sense of circular time in the Andean world. Among the Aymara and Quechua, time is not linear, as it is for the Europeans, it does not respond to Cartesian logic. A space in which time turns and everything returns, which is what the camera does when narrating each sequence.[16]

The critic Pedro Susz also points to the importance of the all-encompassing sequence shot "as the most appropriate narrative resource for the visual translation of the Aymara circular conception of time, as well as the indestructible bond of the individual from this culture with his natural and social environments."[17] These words are quoted by many film critics,[18] and some scholars use similar points.[19]

17. Pedro Susz, *Filmo-videografía boliviana básica (1904-1990)* (La Paz: Cinemateca Boliviana, 1991), 169. Translated for this essay by Almudena Escobar López.

18. Leonardo García Pabón, *La patria íntima* (La Paz: Plural, 1998), 261. Santiago Espinoza and Andrés Laguna, *El cine de la nación clandestina* (La Paz: Gente Común, 2009), 166.

The all-encompassing sequence shot, then, was initially conceived as a translation of the Andean culture to the cinematographic language. The idea was to eliminate the obstacles that made it difficult for Indigenous peasant communities to understand cinema. The interesting thing is that for the intellectuals the translation worked in reverse. Susz was not a peasant who understood the film, but a scholar who saw the foundations of the Andean worldview revealed for him. After seeing the film, Bolivian intellectuals seem to be very sure that circular time is intrinsic to the Altiplano and that the Aymara live in it.

Sanjinés also thought of the intellectuals. Unlike his previous writings, in "El Plano Secuencia Integral" he mentions that now his films are also addressed to scholars who, despite the racism inherent to their social class, carry the internal Andean rhythms deep inside.[20]

Thus, with one camera movement the cultural differences between Bolivians are suspended. Scholars understand the peasants and the peasants understand the film. The all-encompassing sequence shot seems to be an impressive knowledge transmission vehicle, and one wonders: why has there been no continuity in its use? Shouldn't the entire nation have adopted this invention? From Unitel to RTP,[21] advertisers and journalists, scholars and peasants, individualists and collectivists: shouldn't the all-encompassing sequence shot be the basis of communication between Bolivians? If the fragmented montage is what hinders our

19. "The use of the all-encompassing sequence shot is the narrative resource that allows Sanjinés to structure the cinematographic story based on the circular conception of Andean time. It reflects, therefore, the visual perception that Indigenous cultures have of the world." Alber Quispe Escobar: "La imposibilidad mestiza en *La nación clandestina*. Construcciones emblemáticas en el cine de Jorge Sanjinés" (*Punto Cero*, Vol. 12, no. 15, 2007), 56.

20. Sanjinés, "El plano secuencia integral," 65.

audiovisual integration, why not transmit football matches in all-encompassing sequence shots and thus preserve the space-time unity of the match?

Perhaps the confusions between different levels and directions of this translation are expressions of the paradox of proposing a decolonizing cinema. Moving images were and are a privileged vehicle for the expansion of modernity. The scholar Valeria Canelas warns that it is not possible to separate the language of cinema from the processes of modernization and the violence that these bring with them, especially for rural populations in traditional societies: "How to articulate a cinematic discourse of empowerment and defense of the non-hegemonic identities? Isn't it contradictory to cinematographically represent realities that modernity, from which cinema is inseparable, has contributed to violate?"[22]

We can conclude that the translation of material reality into cinematographic language is a concern that has been present in cinema since its inception. Vertov dreamed of creating a universal language that connects everyone through images. In Bolivia, the universal has been rejected in favor of what is distinctive and unique. The all-encompassing sequence shot was proposed as the foundation of its own audiovisual language that allows the Andean reality and the cosmovision of its inhabitants to be better conveyed through the images. It is born from the supposed fundamental oppositions between circular Andean time and linear Western time,

21. Unitel (Universal de Televisión) is one of the largest private television networks in Bolivia, based in Santa Cruz and traditionally close to business groups in the Bolivian East. RTP (Radio Televisión Popular) was founded by the late populist leader Carlos Palenque and maintains strong links with the popular society of La Paz.

22. Valeria Canelas, "Antagonismo e imaginarios de la pluralidad en el cine boliviano" (*Iberoamericana*, vol. 18, no. 67, January-April 2018), 66. Translated for this essay by Almudena Escobar López.

                                                                 Miguel Hilari

between collectivist culture and individualist culture. In this way, cinema, through the all-encompassing sequence shot, would become a bridge between two opposite worlds.

Circular Time

For Sanjinés, western linear time begins with Genesis and is projected into infinity until it meets with the Final Judgment. The past cannot return, and therefore the West is a culture that despises the past and considers it obsolete, useful only to adorn museums. In Aymara cyclical time, on the other hand, the past constantly returns and the future may be behind us. To move forward, we must contemplate the past, and by incorporating it into the present we turn it into the future.[23] This arrangement of the past before us has inspired interesting conclusions. For example, the Argentine filmmaker Lucrecia Martel says:

> The Aymara, among the various representations they have of time, have one in which the future is behind and the past is forward, so that is why they always carry their babies on the back, because they say that if you walk backwards, you walk towards the unknown, which is the future, and instead cannot help but see the actions he has performed. We can imagine that Aymara ethics must be tremendous, because one can never forget their actions; I imagine that the responsibility must be much greater for the Aymara than for us.[24]

Where are these claims coming from? In Aymara, as in all languages, spatial metaphors are used to refer to time. Time as an abstract

23. Informative brochure for the premiere of *La nación clandestina*. Quoted in David Wood, "Andean realism and the integral sequence shot," *Jump Cut*, no. 54, (Fall 2012).

concept needs an anchor in spatial terms to be communicated. When in Spanish we refer to *el año que viene* (the coming year), in Aymara we say *jutir mara*. In this case, in both languages, time is seen metaphorically as a flow that approaches us. There are two concepts in Aymara that have particular spatio-temporal meanings: *nayra* and *qhipa*. *Nayra* is translated as: "Eye. Organ of sight / Before, anterior." *Nayrapacha* (lit. time/seen space) is translated as: "Past. Aforetime."[25] *Qhipa* instead translates as "Behind. After. Latest."[26] *Akat qhiparuw yatiqañani* literally "from here to the back we will learn" refers to "from now on we will learn."[27] In these cases, *nayra* is in the front and refers to the past while *qhipa* is in the back and refers to the future.

However, there are other examples where this direction is reversed. In Aymara we can say *nayrar uñtaña*, literally "look ahead" to say "look towards the future." Also famous is the expression *qhip nayr uñtasis sarnaqapxañani*, literally "let's move forward looking backwards and forwards," to say "let's move forward to the future taking into account the past."[28] In these examples, *nayra* is in the front and refers to the future, while *qhipa* is in the back and refers to the past.

We could guess that the Aymara have serious orientation problems. Perhaps we could also sense that the centuries of coexistence with Spanish are modifying the authentic Aymara conception of time. The scholar Javier Mendoza traces the evolution of the concepts of "atrás" (back) and "adelante" (forward) related to time in Aymara and affirms that *qhipa* comes from Quechua and appears for the first time as such in *Die Aymara Sprache* by E. W. Middendorf in 1891.[29] During the colony, one would have

24. Griselda Soriano, "Esperando a Zama: Charla abierta con Lucrecia Martel," *El Ángel Extermi- nador*, no. 26 (2017). Translated for this essay by Almudena Escobar López.

25. Félix Layme Pairumani, *Dicciona- rio bilingüe aymara castellano* (Bolivia: Consejo Educativo Aymara, 2004), 125.

26. Ibid, 154.

27. Juan de Dios Ya- pita and J.T. Van der Noordaa, *La dinámica aymara, conjugación de verbos* (La Paz: ILCA, 2008), 49.

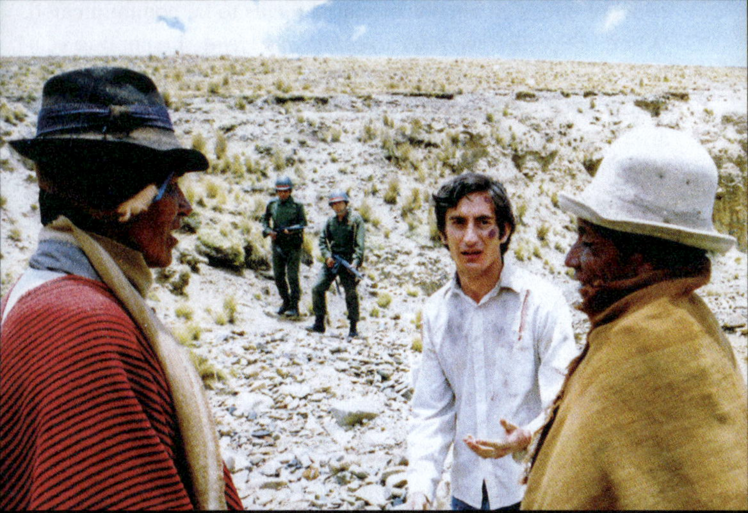

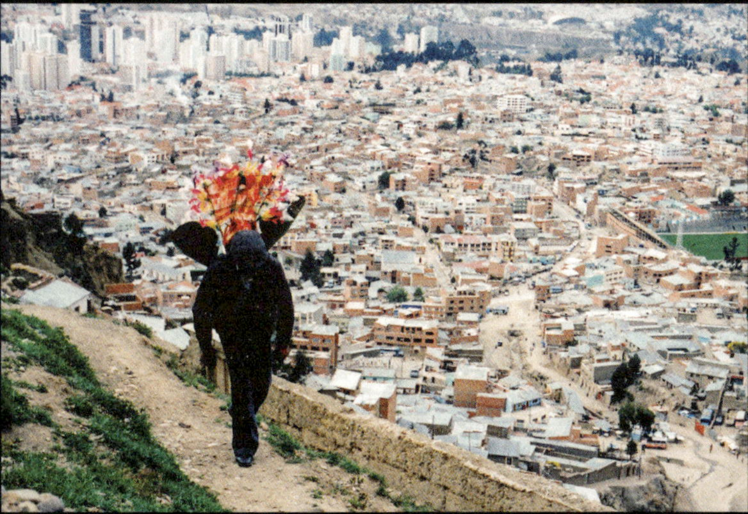

3. *La nación clandestina* (Fundación Grupo Ukamau, 1989)
4. Ibid.

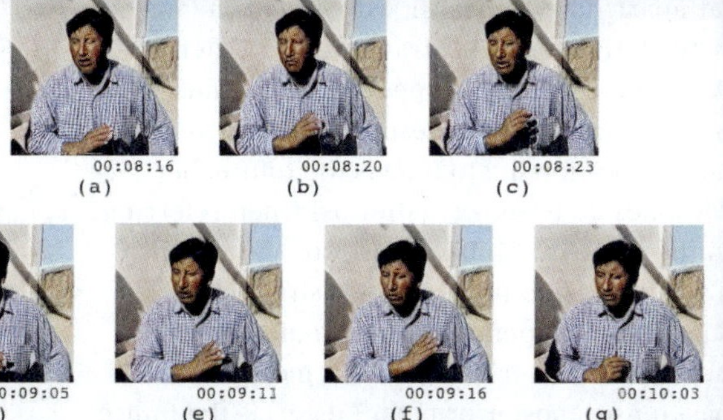

00:08:16
(a)
00:08:20
(b)
00:08:23
(c)
00:09:05
(d)
00:09:11
(e)
00:09:16
(f)
00:10:03
(g)

referred to the future with the word *ch'ina* (rear). In Bertonio, *cchina* appears with a variety of meanings, referring both to the body part and to space and time: *cchina* is the bottom of all animals and *cchina nauna* are the buttocks; *cchina* also means last, and after when it refers to time.[31]

In fact, it seems that the future was located far back. There are some more uses that sound strange in Spanish, but only at first glance. The "Dia del juyzio" (Judgment Day) is translated by Bertonio as *Cchina uru*[32] (literally rear day), which seems even humorous. But if for the same event we use the biblical "last day,"[33] both concepts are no longer so far apart. This is clearer with *cchinassa* (our rear). In Bertonio it is translated as "After us. And all these ways of speaking mean time, and place."[34] In Spanish, "después de nosotros" (after us) referring to time is the future, but "después de nosotros" (after us) when referring to the place is behind. Thus, would the future also appear behind us in Spanish? And if something happened before, would it appear before us? "Anteriormente" (formerly) is the past tense, "posteriormente" (later) is the future tense. If our ancestors were to be resurrected in posterity, who would be behind and who would be ahead? In English we say *Before / After*; *before* refers to the past but also means forward, *after* refers to the future but also means behind. In Old German, *after* had the same meaning as an adverb and a preposition, and both the English and German terms have the same Gothic root: *aftra* (behind). However, in current German this use declines from the seventeenth century due to the predominance

28. Silvia Rivera Cusicanqui, *Oprimidos pero no vencidos* (La Paz: WA-GUI, 2010), 17.

29. Javier Mendoza Pizarro, *El espejo aymara* (La Paz: Plural, 2015), 184.

30. Ludovico Bertonio, *Vocabulario*, Second part, 86.

31. Bertonio, *Vocabulario*, First part, 184.

32. Ibid, 189.

33. Juan 6: 39-54, Reina Valera (1960).

34. Bertonio, *Vocabulario*, Second part, 86.

35. "After," Wolfgang Pfeifer et al., *Etymologisches Wörterbuch des Deutschen* (1993).

of the meaning of the noun: *After* meaning anus.[35] Returning to ancient Aymara, we can affirm that the conception of time is similar in many languages, even in the most unexpected parts.

Abstract concepts like time can only be communicated through metaphors. Linguists Rafael Núñez and Eve Sweetser affirm that there are two multicultural models of the representation of time.[36] If the speaker is understood to be moving through time as moving along a path, the future is ahead and the past is behind. On the other hand, if time is understood as a flow in motion that the speaker observes statically, future events are behind past events. Monday is after Sunday, and before Tuesday. They mention that several studies reached erroneous conclusions by not distinguishing between both metaphors.

In order to define exactly the location of the past and the future in relation to the speaker in the Aymara language, they considered the linguistic evidence they knew to be insufficient and decided to make videotaped interviews to analyze the gestures of the speakers. "The Aymara have been quite isolated from the rest of the world," says *The Guardian* in an article about what appears to have been a tremendous expedition to study an exotic tribe.[37]

Of their twenty interviewees, some placed the past ahead and the future behind, others placed the past behind and the future ahead, and then others placed them to the left and to the right. Although they mention that older and monolingual Aymara people speak more about the past with gestures in a forward direction, and suggest that young Spanish-speakers place the future forward, they also mention that the interviewees in general spoke in more detail

36. Rafael Núñez and Eve Sweetser, "With the Future Behind Them: Convergent Evidence From Aymara Language and Gesture in the Crosslinguistic Comparison of Spatial Construals of Time" *Cognitive Science* 30 (2006), 401-450.

37. Laura Spinney, "How Time Flies" (*The Guardian*, https://www.theguardian.com/science/2005/feb/24/4

38. Rafael Núñez et al., "With the Future Behind Them," 440.

about the past and that some elders refused to talk about
the future "because nothing sensible can be said about it."[38]
This idea coincides with the notion that the main temporal
distinction in Aymara is between seen time, which is the past
and the present, and unknown time, which is the future.[39] It is
debatable whether these interviews allow us to place the
direction of time in Aymara in total opposition to the direction
of time in other languages.

Nonetheless, it was enough for other researchers to cite
their work as a reference and proof that different visions of
progress and development are possible:

> Modern culture favors the conventional image of linear
> time, where the speaker (ego) represents himself facing
> the future. The past is what remains behind, behind
> your back... This is consistent with an ideological
> propensity, founded on the idea of unlimited progress,
> which gives primacy to the figure of "going forward."
> The analysis of the temporal notions of three native
> languages of South America—Quechua, Aymara and
> Toba—offers examples that contradict the above,
> revitalizing the idea that conceptions of time vary
> widely from culture to culture.[40]

In this case, the interest in "exotic" languages in which the direction of time is reversed is based on the desire to find alternatives to the dominant concepts of progress, rather than on an interest in the language itself.

What is discarded by Nuñez and Sweetser is the idea of absolute

39. Marta J. Hardman, Juana Vásquez and Juan de Dios Yapita, *Aymara, compendio de estructura fonológica gramatical* (La Paz: ILCA, 1988), 19. The difference between direct personal knowledge and indirect knowledge is inscribed in the grammar of the language through a great variety of different possible verbal tenses described in Juan de Dios Yapita et al., *La dinámica aymara*, 7-138.

circular time. They affirm that linear temporality coexists and merges with a cyclical structure in all cultures.[41] The anthropologist Alison Spedding mentions that in Andean societies, mainly agrarian, cyclical time refers to the passing of the seasons. The rhythm of the rains is capital and marks the times of the crops, which are repeated year after year. However, she affirms that as in all societies, we live the experience of time in two contradictory ways. On the one hand, there is the time that always passes: we cannot go back in time, people and things wear out, living beings are born, grow, age, and die. On the other hand, time repeats itself in the same way: the sun rises every day and sets. The moon goes from full to waning, disappears and returns as new to grow and become full again. Every year the seasons are repeated. That is the cyclical time that repeats every day, week, month, and year.[42] She also mentions that Christian time is, in principle, linear, because it begins with Genesis, goes through the life and death of Christ, and culminates in the Apocalypse. However, every year the birth of Christ is celebrated at Christmas and his Passion, death and resurrection at Easter. These events are recreated two thousand years later in a ritual to maintain their relevance and value today. The remote past is cyclically brought into the present to influence the future. She concludes that it is false to affirm that Western culture perceives time in one way and Andean culture perceives it in a totally different way.

If in all cultures we live with a mixture of temporal conceptions, and in various languages we have representations of time in which the spatial layout of the past and the future varies,

40. Summary of Gabriel Luis Bourdin's work, "En los tiempos de *ñaupa*: el cuerpo y la deixis temporal en lenguas originarias de Sudamérica" *Peninsula* 9, no. 1, (2014), 33-58. Translated for this essay by Almudena Escobar López.

41. Núñez et al, "With the Future Behind Them," 413.

42. Alison Spedding, *Religión en los Andes. Extirpación de idolatrías y modernidad de la fe andina* (La Paz: ISEAT, 2008), 33-44.

why the desire to place Andean culture in "another time"? It is convenient to begin answering this question by quoting the phrase that appears in the poster for *La nación clandestina*: "Only men and nations that assume their identity can be themselves again." The sentence presupposes that: 1. We are not ourselves; 2. That's a problem; 3. To overcome it, we must assume our identity. But: how to assume our identity, if we are not ourselves? Maybe the movie tells us how to do it? And if so, how have the filmmakers found our true identity?

Sanjinés's under-recognized comrade and wife Beatriz Palacios said in 1979: "Although in *Ukamau* Sanjinés does a profound and poetic work using the classic resources of cinema, the film does not open paths towards our most recondite and true identity. It is not enough that your subject is ours."[43] It is assumed, then, that in *La nación clandestina* they wanted to open paths towards true identity. The use of the adjectives "recondite" and "true" in relation to identity is not without attention. Isn't identity something in constant motion? And is it not possible that in this it resembles time? And cinema?

Using "recondite and true" sounds more like identity takes refuge in a hiding place in the highlands, and that perhaps no one has really discovered it yet. The filmmakers are standing on the edge of the city, with theodolites and bulldozers, ready to blaze the trails. But they are confused, they don't know where to go, because they don't know in which cave the true identity is hidden. Perhaps there are some empty caves, and they will have wasted their resources opening paths to caves with no content. Or worse, perhaps there are caves where false identities are hidden that can deceive the filmmakers like the sirens tried with Ulysses. We do not know. What we do know is that the discovery of our true identity will be

43. Beatriz Palacios, "A propósito de una ponencia sobre el cine boliviano," in *Cine boliviano del realizador al crítico* (La Paz: Editorial Gisbert, 1979), 120. Translated for this essay by Almudena Escobar López.

a moment of revelation for us all. Let's hope that the filmmakers find it soon.

Perhaps this is the reason for placing Andean culture in the greatest otherness possible: the more distant, the more authentic. The more difficult it is to access the cave of identity, the greater the value of its discovery. "Bolivia, donde lo auténtico aún existe" (Bolivia, where the authentic still exists), read a tourist slogan from a few years ago. Etymologically, the Latin *authenticus* (original, recognized, reliable) comes from the Greek *authentikós* (related to the author of an act) and *authéntēs* (author of an act, but also: master, tyrant).[44] Authenticity as a source of political legitimacy runs through the history of the West. Authenticity invents communities, creates nations, or serves to delegitimize other groups or nations. The presentation of authentic national cultures was central to the formation of the nation-state as well as to the self-affirmation of post-communist and post-colonial societies.[45] Just as in politics, authenticity also seems to be the most precious asset in our cinema. The possession of the true identity legitimizes some and delegitimizes others.

Perfidy

Central to scholar Molly Geidel's reading of *La nación clandestina* is the idea of perfidy.[46] She maintains that the protagonist Sebastián's betrayal of his culture is attributed mainly to his mother, who gave the boy Sebastián to the *patrones* (masters) to raise him in the city. Therefore, the woman will bear the guilt of not having raised a good son, while the man has the

44. "Authentizität," Wolfgang Pfeifer et al., *Etymologisches Wörterbuch des Deutschen*.

45. Thomas Noetzel, *Authentizität als politisches Problem*. Quoted by Hito Steyerl, *Die Farbe der Wahrheit* (Vienna: Turia + Kant, 2008), 113.

46. Molly Geidel, "Messing with the Enemy: Movement and Cinematic Representations of the Traitorous Intermediary in Neoliberal Bolivia" (*Latin American and Carribbean Ethnic Studies*, vol. 8, no. 2, June 2013), 140-158.

possibility of redeeming himself through the ritual dance.

The blame scene can have several readings[47] however, it is interesting to highlight the figure of the internal traitor. If in *Ukamau* (1966) the mestizo rapist is executed, in *Yawar Mallku* (1969) it is necessary to castrate the sterilizing gringos. In both films, an external danger threatens a relatively homogeneous Indigenous community. Broadly speaking, this vision is maintained in the following films: *El coraje del pueblo* (The Courage of the People, 1971), *El enemigo principal* (The Main Enemy, 1973), *¡Fuera de aquí!* (1977), and *Las banderas del amanecer* (The Flags of Dawn, 1983). By contrast, in *La nación clandestina*, the protagonist is a traitor within the community. It is no longer a question of expelling evil foreign influences, the question is how to deal with false representatives within one people. The betrayal of one's own culture is a greater danger than foreign evil. We could add that the splitting of false representatives of the community would be directly related to the overcoming of false formal mechanisms for the representation of Andean reality. In this case, the all-encompassing sequence shot would be an analogy to the ritual sacrifice of the protagonist: both signify the birth of a new authentic representation and the overcoming of false representations. Sebastián's dark past, the embezzlement of communal funds and his expulsion from the community are overcome through his ritual death, which signifies his reintegration into the collective. He is once again a true representative. In the same way, alienated and alienating cinematographic forms, which respond to a western and individualistic vision of the world, are overcome by the all-encompassing sequence shot, which represents the Andean reality in an authentic way. Formally, this procedure also becomes a true representative.

We have seen that the all-encompassing sequence shot

was thought as an authentic expression of Andean culture. Through it, the filmmakers tried to develop an own cinema, in form and content. This process would function as an integrating vehicle at various levels: it would bring circular time closer to cinema, the peasant to the gentleman, the collective to the individual, and in short, the Andes to the West. The more marked these borders and the more opposed the sides, the greater the importance of translation.

What the all-encompassing integral sequence shot has shown is that a Westerner can leave his linear time to enter circular time. More or less in the way of abandoning one vessel and getting on another, and perhaps only for a moment. Watching the film is surely the best way to do it. Watching *La nación clandestina*, it seems that many linear people have been able to experience cyclical sensations.

But if one is Aymara, will there be the possibility of abandoning circular time to enter linear time? We have seen that with movies this was difficult, the fragmented montage

47. Although I agree with Geidel, there is a peculiar twist in the translations that deserves attention. The author refers to the first scene of the film, in which Sebastián's grieving family returns home after the funeral. Recalling Sebastián's life, the brother addresses his mother with the words: "*Jumanakamakiw jucha-nipxtax*" (Only you are guilty). The Spanish subtitles say: "*Ustedes han sido los culpables*" (You were the culprits). The second person plural includes Sebastián's father, absent at the burial but pre-sent in the following scene, in which he hands over the child to the *patrón* with servile gestures. In this case, we understand the phrase as the son blaming his parents, a generation claiming its faults to the previous one, specifically, the submissive attitude towards the *patrón*. In English, "you are guilty" can be read as an exclusive complaint to the mother due to the coincidence between the singular and the plural of the second person. Indeed, Geidel then writes: "Sebastián's mother, weeping, her face in shadow, agrees with this assessment of her guilt." *You* and *her* in this case are singular and refer exclusively to the mother. Now the central meaning of the phrase refers to the male child blaming the mother.

made it difficult to enter another time. What if it was just for a moment? Watching *La nación clandestina*, it seems that this will be seen as treason and one will have to dance in circles to death.

Reviewing the readings about *La nación clandestina*, we can understand that the all-encompassing sequence shot worked as the translation of a supposed Andean conception of time for urban audiences, both national and foreign. From the beginning, these audiences assumed that Andean identity was radically different from their own, and wanted to see the "authentic Andean worldview" translated into images. However, the conceptual foundations of the construction of the all-encompassing sequence shot are problematic: we have seen that linear time is not exclusively Western, nor is circular time exclusively Andean. The spatial metaphor of the location of the past ahead and the future behind in the Aymara language has served as the basis for the construction of an authentic otherness. However, we do have similar space-time arrangements in several European languages, which, following Bertonio, should at least inspire caution in the use of metaphors. It must be taken into account that the approaches of Sanjinés date back several decades. The all-encompassing sequence shot was envisioned to bridge spaces and conceptual systems that perhaps at that time seemed more distant than they do today. However, it is unlikely that the notion of a pure and unsullied Andean experience of time and space, radically different, was not anachronistic in 1989. As early as 1612, Bertonio mentioned the contamination of Aymara with Spanish words and advised accommodating to it:

> The Indians already use many words taken from the Spanish language, because there are none in theirs, or because they are stuck in their minds as a result of their relationship with the Spaniards, such as Candelero

(candlestick); Vinagrera (cruet); Sombrero (hat). And if they use them, although incorrectly, I think it is better to accommodate their way of speaking than not to invent new terms in their language. Because they will understand better if we say candelero or candrillo apanima, than not candela saattaaña apanima. Because although this second wording is typical of the language, the first one is more received, and used, and the same happens with the verbs. All the names and verbs taken from Spanish are declined and conjugated in the manner of the Aymara language, such as açothita (to whip), Perditha (to lose), Pacaritha (to pay), and like these there are many others that will be found in various parts of the vocabulary, especially in the first.[48]

It is striking that the verbs borrowed from Spanish are precisely to whip, to lose, and to pay, and one can only wonder if this contamination really meant an enrichment. However, returning to the translations, it is also noteworthy that Bertonio calls for accommodation to contamination, while Sanjinés intends to build an authentic translation of a reality understood as fundamentally alien. Perhaps the search for cultural purity, whether one's own or another's, was always anachronistic.

48. Bertonio, *Vocabulario*, Annotation
2, paragraph 8. Nb. Because this is
an adapted translation from ancient
Spanish, the translator Almudena
Escobar López has retained the old
grammar constructions and meaning,
hence the inaccurate grammar.

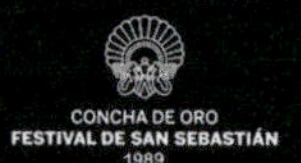

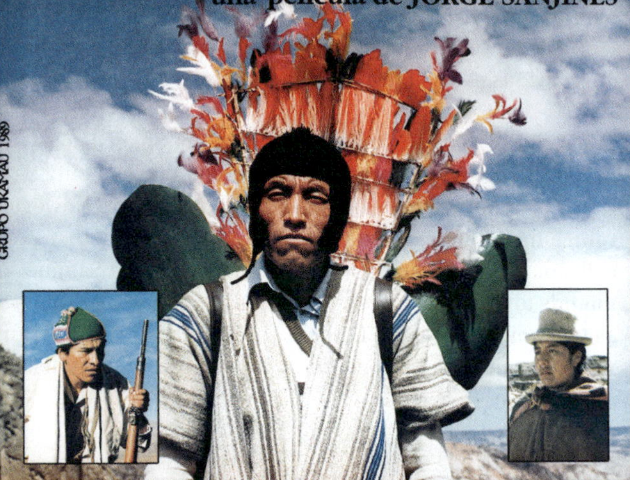

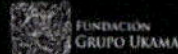

6. Poster for *La nación clandestina* (Fundación Grupo Ukamau, 1989)

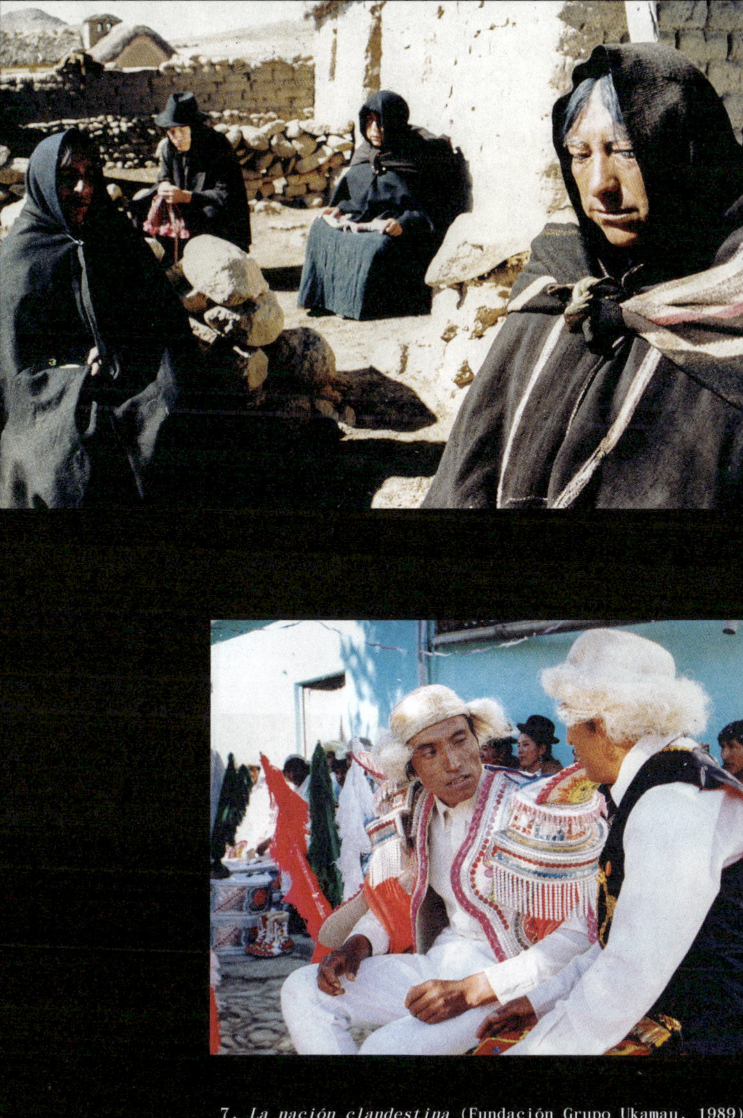

7. *La nación clandestina* (Fundación Grupo Ukamau, 1989)

8. Ibid.

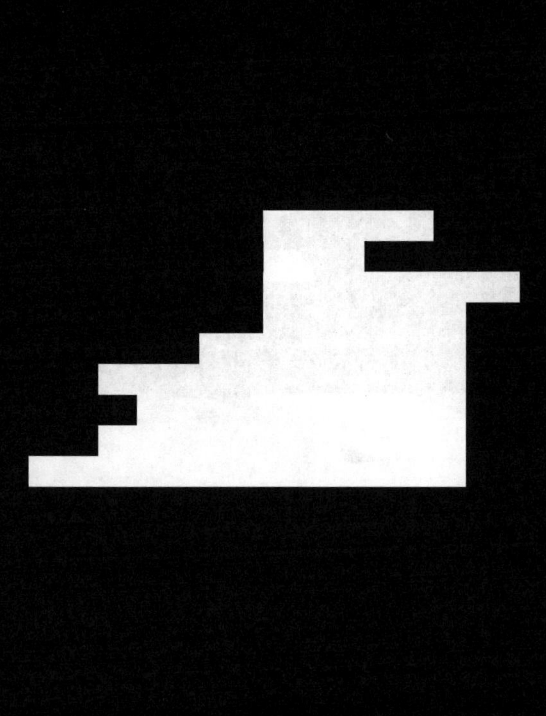

A Conversation
Between
Guillermo Gómez-Peña
and Raven Chacon

We Are All Aliens in Pandemia, or a Navajo and a Mexican Artist, Bonded by Chicanismo, Reflect on Art and Pandemia

In this unique interview, conducted in June 2022, after 24 months of lockdown due to the Covid-19 pandemia and all of its macabre variations, I had the opportunity to speak, Chicano-computer to Chicano-computer, with an artist who has been an important influence to myself and my collaborators in Postcommodity. In a career that spans some forty years, performance artist, spoken word poet, radical pedagogue, and vernacular philosopher Guillermo Gómez-Peña has provided guidance to a generation of artists seeking to complicate their own identities, and for me, a Navajo-Chicano-noise-musico-performer, his work imagines the places where such identifiers are pointless. In 2018, Cristobal Martinez and myself collaborated with Gómez-Peña on a short film, *A Song Often Played on the Radio*, which finds Guillermo retracing the steps of a misguided conquest in Northern New Mexico. Here we talk further about how the grand conquest has been interrupted by a virus, and the work that was made during a forced time of isolation. —*Raven Chacon*

RAVEN CHACON: Tell me about how music has played a part in your work. Whether it is performance, or poetry, or in any other ways the conjuring or implementation of work occurs.

GUILLERMO GÓMEZ-PEÑA: For as long as I can remember, music has been a huge part of my life and artistic practice. I grew up in Mexico City where wild music permeates everyday life, from boleros rancheros, and over-the-top pop, to rock en español. My father collected music. He had over 6,000 albums; music from all over the world was the ongoing sound bed for the household.
Music is also crucial to my performance troupe, La Pocha Nostra. We've always collaborated

with musicians and composers in various
capacities. We often invite them to jam with us
during a live performance or a workshop, other
times we ask them to compose for us, like galindog
and Greg Landau. I think most performance artists
are deeply frustrated rockers, and vice versa.

The sound studio is one of my favorite
homes. During pandemia and confinement, I've
had a regular weekly podcast titled the *Mex
Files*, in which I mix my poetic commentary on
the times with music from my favorite composers
and sound art from my archives. In my podcasts,
I select some of my favorite songs and audio art
from various decades, rolas that I feel can tell the
listener the story of my life and times, and I mix
them with wild spoken word spanglish poetry and
social commentary. It's a memory exercise and an
experiment, a deep dive into the eclectic jukebox
of my life soundtrack. I have discovered that music
is the best communication strategy across national
borders, more efficient than poetry or dance, or
football, soccer... Also, music helps us to not go
mad. I don't know what I would have done without
it during pandemia.

RC: I was in a group exhibition recently in which the title
included the word "Latinx." I have no idea how this
word is pronounced, and am not quite sure what
it really means, though I believe the intentions
are good. If we are talking about the margins or
borders, and the spectrum in-between, what are
better suffixes or hyphen-words to inclusively
describe all possibilities of existence instead of the

awkward, unpronounceable "x"? (And are these designations proper for the techno-future?)

GGP : The US has always had problems with languaging complex identities, especially those of citizens of Latin American descent. There's a long list of highly charged terms attempting to define the Latin American Other inside our borders: some are self-identified—Chicano, Nuyorican, etc.; others are more ideologically driven by marketing experts and electoral politics: Hispanic, Mexican-American, Latino... My understanding is that "Latinx" has been used in social media by activists, students, and academics who seek to advocate for non-binary and gender nonconforming individuals. For me, it's really a question of self-determination: every community, and every individual must choose their own terminology.

Now, as a performance artist, my job is to complicate definitions. Personally, I like to fuck with normative terminology: I often describe myself as neo- or post-Chicano or neo-Mexicano, or "a chicalango in process of Chicanoization," a hybrid vato, a techno-indígena... If you cannot be defined by the mainstream or the art world, you remain independent... that's the core of performance art!

RC : In an interview with Josh Kun in 2000, you discuss how the internet has affected performance art, speaking about the ease of delivery, and that anyone has access to fetishes that were previously concealed. Twenty-two years later, everyone has the pinche internet connected directly to the palms of their hands. How has *this* affected performance art, and language?

GGP : (Chooses to answer this question in Spanish) Con la pandemia y el confinamiento, he re/valorado mi opinión sobre el internet. Creo que el performance y la literatura se adaptan muy bien a nuestros tiempos de aislamiento virtual. Hay movimientos de "poesía digital" en páginas electrónicas y blogs de performance con públicos muy amplios. Mis colegas y yo desde hace diez años tenemos un proyecto de poesía para Twitter. Mis "poetuits" por cierto también funcionan como mini-libretos de performance... El performance también incorpora las nuevas tecnologías de formas muy variadas y complejas. Postcommodity fue un ejemplo muy claro de la relación entre la tecnología compleja y la performance ritual. I call it "High Tech Aztec."

Somos muchos los artistas de performance que estamos haciendo obra para redes sociales y youtube, con mínimos elementos de producción, o por Skype o Zoom, donde la cámara, una cámara ordinaria, incluso de un teléfono toma el lugar del público. En México tengo un amigo, Fernando Llanos, que organiza festivales de cine hecho con celulares (Iphones). Le llegan miles de peliculitas y propuestas de todo el mundo.

Oh and I forgot, let's talk about Zoom in English, the ultimate performance platform in the bizarre post-real world of "pandemia." In the past two and a half years, the imaginary territory of Zoom has been the main virtual stage for performance artists to broadcast our despair and

ambitions. The weird thing about Zoom is that it is
happening in real time and place, but at the same
time it is totally imaginary... and (he reconsiders)
yet it is somewhat "real." It's like a performance
seance, a witchcraft ritual. The liquid screen of our
computer acts as the conduit or cyborg Ouija board
to contact spirits (artists) on the other side.

Yo ahorita estoy haciendo escenificaciones
o reinterpretaciones de mi obra clásica en
video, pensadas para un público joven que ya
no me conoce y que tengo que volver a seducir.
Luego las subo a Youtube y ¡cataplum!, tengo
un público instantáneo de miles de gentes. Se
trata de otra manera mágica de distribuir obra
internacionalmente. Funciona muy bien. Aunque
claro, no es lo mismo acariciar la piel sudorosa
de una persona, que verla en pantalla. El público
virtual no me emociona.

RC: Are there any random objects of power you have recently
discovered, or found then avoided?

GGP: During pandemia and confinement, we were forced to
rethink our homes as performance studios and
vernacular museums. We had no other option but
to reinvent the quotidian realm, and ritualize our
homes and objects in order to not go mad. Part of
this radical reinvention process was to open boxes
and closets, the pandora boxes of our lives and our
hearts. We became domestic archeologists... In this
lonely process, I rediscovered my classic personal
archeology; the power objects that survived the
shipwreck, so to speak.

Some examples come to mind: my original outfits and props for *The Couple in the Cage* (1992) and *The Mexterminator* (1998); the original suits of "El Mariachi Liberachi" and "Supermojado," my collection of shamanic headdresses and skirts from various cultures... My dilemma has been, do I sell these objects to pay the rent and keep the doors of my troupe open? Do I call curators and collectors to help me? Should I donate them to the Smithsonian (ja ja)? I still don't know what to do with them.

Also, during these last years, many objects given to us by friends, colleagues, and relatives have acquired a fetish, or even iconic status in our art. They make us feel grounded and connected to land, community, and history. They become part of our home, traveling altars and recent performances. We also give presents to people who are close to us. We give them books, props, found objects, souvenirs of pandemia... and our friends treasure them. My homes in San Francisco and Mexico City, after confinement, look like thrift shops. I need to edit them down constantly. I have become a border hoarder of power objects.

And you, how do you deal with power objects? Do you give them away? If so, can I have a few? (ja ja je)

RC : Yes, I have a few. Lately I have been reviving some of my broken electronic instruments. Some that I had created myself, and others that were likely broken in a performance. But by reviving, I do not mean I can make them come back to life, but rather, their presence alone still emanates some kind of

     A Conversation Between Guillermo Gómez-Peña and Raven Chacon

vibration, although they no longer make sound.
If they are present on stage or in a video, they don't
even need to make sound.

Sometimes I wear a mask in my performances.
It is made of plastic netting, like the type that
surrounds a construction site. It is shaped like
a diamond and wraps around my face. When it is
on my face, I dump a pile of jewelry on top of it,
and allow the earrings, necklaces, bracelets to
attach themselves to the pores of this mask.
The jewelry comes from many places: thrift shops,
estate sales, some are from loved ones who are no
longer with us. One item is from a former enemy
who is no longer either.

I also used to bury cassette tapes, speakers,
and whistles in the desert, and recover them
months later to hear how their sounds have
changed after being in the earth. I forgot the
location of a particular whistle that I buried 15
years ago, but a few months ago I had a dream that
allowed me to remember where it was. When I find
it, I will give it to you.

GGP : That's a deal, carnal. Like me, you are constantly moving
around from New Mexico to New York State, and
Canada. How do you re/territorialize yourself?

RC : I used to tour constantly—every night would be in a new
city, where there was one task, and it was the
20-minute performance gig. To live like this, you
are not quite a guest, nor a tourist. When I was
sharing my work, there was a feeling that I was
leaving little bits of my true home in those places

of performance when I left town. By "true home,"
I mean the place where I originally created the
work, which was usually Albuquerque, New
Mexico. What eventually happened, though,
was that I never quite fully returned to a stable
geographic location to recalibrate the music set.
So it became a continuous "song." I would play it
slightly differently every night, influenced more
by what happened in the previous city than by the
original version. I am still trying to understand
which provides the better outcome, but I am
leaning toward the idea that artists ultimately need
to return to places of recalibration.

I suppose what I am getting at is that there is
a danger of becoming an artist that is always (and
only) responding to the locales of where one is
visiting. That one puts themself in the position to
have to retell the story of the new place, becoming
a reductive funnel for other tourists. This is the
pitfall of the site-specific artist, who even by
invitation, becomes trapped by this perpetual
formula, instead of drifting through like a ghost,
turning lights on and off.

Tell me about the work you just completed,
We Are All Aliens.

GGP : It's our most recent project, a weird performance opera.
As border artists, we are trying to defy travel
bans, the closing of geopolitical borders, and to
remind ourselves that the border is not just a
dangerous metaphor of fear but a meeting place for
reinvention and exchange. The core of the project
is a music jam between a chic US concert pianist,

who specializes in European classical music made
by immigrants from Eastern Europe to the US, and
a traditional mariachi band specializing in corridos
about the departure and the longing for homeland.
It's interesting, but what people consider "classical
European music" was largely created by Russian
and Eastern European musicians who first migrated
to Paris, and then to New York after the Second
World War. So they were the mariachis of their
time. The project is also a celebration of Otherness
and hybridity in times of pandemia and generalized
panic; the alien inside of us, the internal exile... The
project expanded during confinement to include
more than ten musicians from different subcultures
and genres—a gospel singer, a powwow drummer,
a Mexican rocker, an opera baritone, a soprano,
etc.—jamming with my Pocha performance artists
in an eighteenth-century desacralized church...
It was awesome, a really bizarre concert, a world
populated by radical Pocha Nostra performance
imagery commenting on the history of colonization
by the Church...

RC: Give me some concrete examples, ese.

GGP: A naked green alien crucified on the altar of the church;
a confessional in which audience members got
to confess their racist sins and pandemic fears to
Balitrónica [Gomez] dressed as an S&M nun; an
actor friend of mine who looks like a Franciscan
friar was walking around as a flasher. We set up
a bar, right across from the confessional, where a
bunch of gorgeous drag queens, sex workers,

and go-go dancers were hanging out and discussing the event with audience members.

In the final event of *We Are All Aliens*, we had over 200 people in costumes and masks, willing to play with us. For most of them it was their first outing after Omicron. They were people we've never seen before, those who survived the big city crisis during pandemia. It was pinche exhilarating.

Next, we are organizing a jam between concert pianists and mariachis right at the Tijuana–San Diego border wall; a truly binational concert, an impossible project! When? Impossible to tell. Nowadays, we can't predict anything. I just keep working, imagining a world where everything is possible, hoping for the best in a fucked-up upside down world that feels like an entropic sci-fi movie. It's the era of "the post real."

RC: Well, I guess pandemia is somewhat over, and the expectation to go back on the road to perform is there. I am anxious to see what has changed; do audiences and listeners have the same capacities for attention as before, or is that another casualty of the virus? This pandemia has been a perfect time to hole up in small rooms and make recordings. But I feel like I was losing my mind at some points; pacing my little makeshift recording room like goddamn Bruce Nauman; singing, whistling, banging my coffee cup, recording audio of myself doing nothing but staring at the wall. In other words, I got a lot of work done. But now I am back on the road, and I've moved out of the Southwest also.

It's been nice to follow my friends from afar
still. I saw that Pocha Nostra recently completed
a short film!

GGP : Several, actually. Film has been my salvation during
pandemia. In 2020 and '21, essentially when
I couldn't tour, I was basically just shooting what
I call "quick and dirty" movies, guerrilla movies
about pandemia. I made one in Mexico about the
historical character La Malinche, with a bunch
of performance artists utilizing my house in
Mexico City as a workshopping space and base of
operations. And we were shooting all throughout
Central Mexico, in Teotihuacán, Querétaro,
Puebla, and Guanajuato.

Then I came back to San Francisco, where
I engaged in a similar exercise. We found a toxic
waste site right outside of the city that a bunch
of anarchists had occupied during pandemia and
turned it into an art space. The place includes
a bunch of abandoned train wagons, an old Hells
Angels clubhouse, and a native plants garden
curated by a Lakota couple. It was a beautiful
place. I joined the raggedy collective right
away. And I asked my filmmaker friend Gustavo
Vazquez if he was interested in making a film
there. And he invited Lalo Obregon, one of the
original cameramen for [Alejandro] Jodorowsky.
He shot *El Topo* (1970), *Fando y Lis* (Fando and
Lis, 1968), and *La montaña sagrada* (The Holy
Mountain, 1973). We put out a convocatory, and
about thirty performance artists, dancers, and
musicians showed up. It was wild! We created

a bunch of jam sessions with them, utilizing
the whole anarchist compound. The result was
a half-hour performance movie, a utopian/
dystopian project titled "SF Apocalypse," and the
overall budget was under $500.

In pandemia, you work with whomever is
around and willing to play with you. And this
includes some of my neighbors, the people
who became my friends during the first
confinement in 2020. I started cooking up
ideas with the neighbors in my building in San
Francisco. One of them, Taylor, was this cool
unemployed filmmaker who was getting restless
in confinement and had all this amazing film
equipment. I asked him if he wanted to make
a film series with me. My idea was to create a
series of short "video diaries" on how to survive
pandemia. And he was ecstatic. So we started
knocking at people's doors, dressing up the
neighbors and friends, and creating psychomagic
situations in confinement. The shooting would
last three or four hours, and the editing, a long
session over pizza.

We put them out online and people liked
them a lot. And then artists, poets, dancers, and
musicians from other parts of the city began
to show up during the informal shooting of our
video diaries and we incorporated them in the
experiment. Once we have ten video diaries,
we will begin to formally promote them as a
"Pandemia Project by La Pocha Nostra." For the
moment, they are mere curadas, things to do
when you get restless.

So yeah, performance film has been my
salvation, carnal. I'm very happy with the results.
They're quick and dirty, and self-produced with
very small budgets. And then we edit them
either at my kitchen table or in one of my friend's
living rooms. It's like returning to the origins of
underground cinema.

RC: It's inspiring to think of low budgets and about how we find
ways to improvise around them, finding solutions
for what we need without lots of money.

GGP: It's an old Chicano motto. Minimum budget,
maximum quality.

RC: And fast, right? We can touch on that. I like hearing about
that: who was around, who was roped in? What
tools were there, what accidents happened?

GGP: A lot of accidents. Performance is the art of
the unexpected.

RC: Yeah. And were these films sometimes shot in both
places? Would it start in one place and go to
Mexico City, or vice versa? Or were they made
solely in one spot?

GGP: Yes, for example, the film *Malinche* (2020) was originally
shot in Mexico. But of course in our film version,
La Malinche escapes from Hernán Cortés in
Mexico, crosses the border into the US and
becomes an activist-immigrant. And in the final
scene, which we are shooting next month, you see

La Malinche, a fully tattooed Mexican woman on a motorcycle, driving north into California, and joining the Chicano movement. So the last scene, the redemption of La Malinche, is going to be shot right here in the Mission District of San Pancho. My hope is to hire a group of biker cholas from San Jose to create a delta formation entourage for La Malinche. Their performance action is going to be them driving around Dolores Mission, where the original Ohlone inhabitants of the Bay Area are buried. The serpent is now biting its tail. It's like a fulfilled prophecy; the end of the world as we know it. Wow! I'm beginning to sound like a mad philosopher, coño!

And you carnal, what are you plotting next?

RC: I would love to make more films as well. The medium and the process feels like when I make an album, that there is a composing of the elements that you won't hear or see. To me, these are as important as what appears on-screen or what you can hear on the recording. For example, we are not supposed to know where a particular song was recorded, to understand the reverb of a space. I prefer to imagine that it was recorded in a cave or a void in the universe—there is more information in that mystery than if it were known. To me, cinema and moving image can create other dimensions of unknowable sites. This is in contrast to the art installation work I have been doing for twenty years. Not everything needs to be site-specific. But yes, literal plotting, writing stories. Music rarely lets you do that.

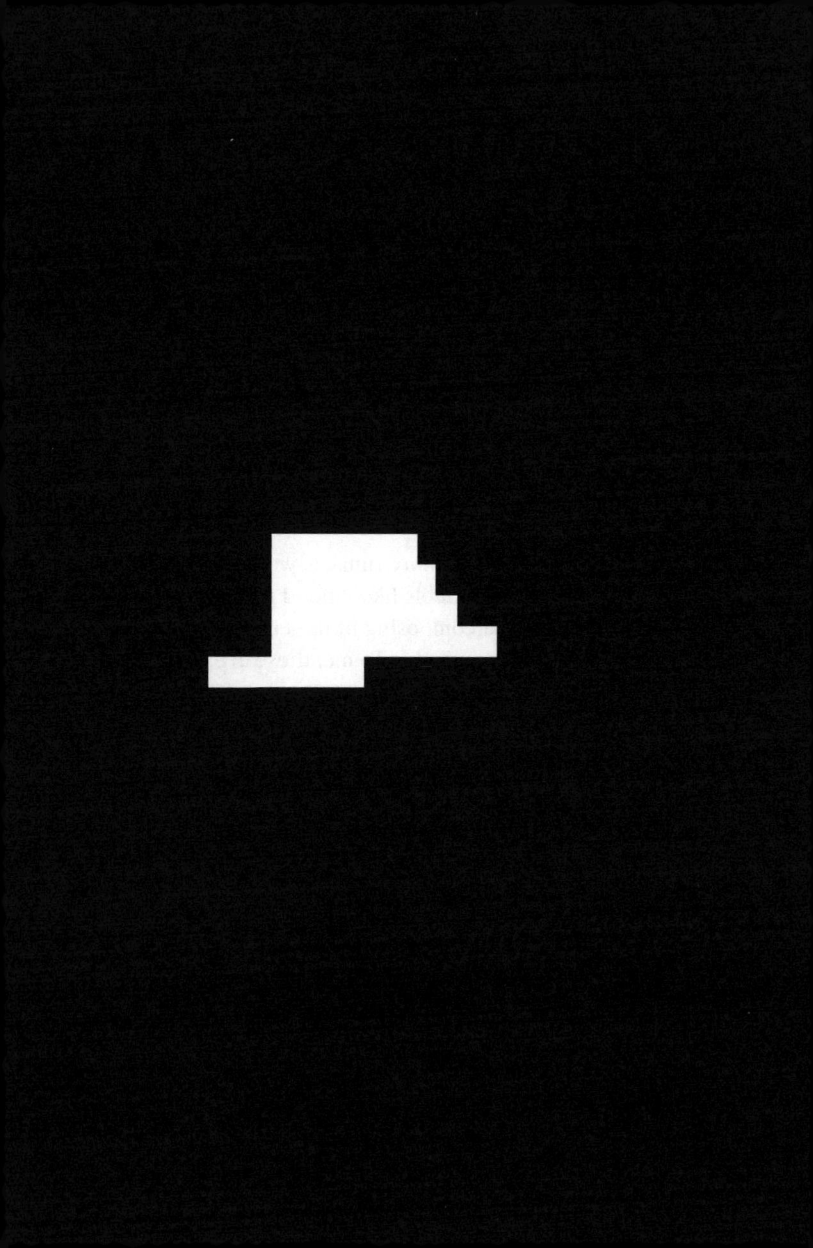

To Weave With Light, Ulana me ka mālamalama

Tiare Ribeaux

Hawaiian Futurism in the Past and Present

If you trace the migratory path of Kānaka Maoli (Native Hawaiians) throughout Polynesia, we were nearly the last to touch down on our islands, finding our unique placement in Hawai'i in Moananuiakea (the Pacific). During a collaborative workshop series that I helped organize in 2021 called Kō Manawa, the Hawaiian artist Solomon Nui Enos memorably described our people as being full of "wanderlust and wonderlust." He said, "The Samoans are the philosophers, the Maori are the pragmatists, and the Hawaiians are the Romantics." As some of the world's greatest navigators, we have always sought to go beyond known horizons.

Kānaka have always been resourceful and future-oriented. Around a thousand years ago, we created one of the world's most advanced aquaculture systems. "As far as is known, fishponds existed nowhere else in the Pacific in types and numbers as in prehistoric Hawai'i," writes scholar Marie Alohalani Brown in her book *Ka Po'e Mo'o Akua: Hawaiian Reptilian Water Deities*. "Only in the Hawaiian Islands was there an intensive effort to utilize practically every body of water, from the seashore to the upland forests, as a source of food." Our loko i'a (fish ponds) were an integral part of the Ahupua'a system, created to maintain the use of our resources within certain districts divided by rivers— from the tops of mountains to the coral reefs—recognizing the boundaries of our land, and out into the ocean.

Kānaka have always been taking on new forms. In Hawaiian cosmology, our akua (deities) are elemental and manifold. Their kinolau (many forms) often represent specific aspects of the biomes they are in, or a whole biome to which all Hawaiians have ancestral ties. Through mo'olelo (storytelling), and thanks to the fact that we have always been soil scientists and marine biologists, our knowledge of hydrological and 'Āina (land) based systems were also told through the relations of akua that live in our stories. Just as the ʻŌlelo noʻeau *"I ka wā ma mua, i ka wā ma hope"* tells us that we must look to our past to inform our future, our moʻolelo continues to evolve.

Three years after the illegal overthrow of the Hawaiian Kingdom by foreign colonizers, armed troops, and sugar barons in January 1893, ʻŌlelo Hawaiʻi (Hawaiian language) was banned from being taught in schools. In 1986, one hundred years after the repression of our language, the ban on teaching ʻŌlelo Hawaiʻi in academic institutions was finally lifted while the Hawaiian Kingdom continued to be illegally occupied. Since then, ʻAha Pūnana Leo Hawaiʻi Immersion Schools have been founded, where children speak and learn primarily in ʻŌlelo Hawaiʻi, while the number of other schools that teach primarily in ʻŌlelo Hawaiʻi has increased to this day.

This revival of language coincides with the Second Hawaiian Renaissance in the 1970s—a movement which saw a revitalization of our cultural practices, pride, and strength in Kānaka Maoli identity, with traditional practices being increasingly integrated into contemporary arts and music. Bands like The Sunday Manoa, The Brothers Cazimero, and musicians Keola and Kapono Beamer gained local and international popularity, adding new melodies and layering slack-key guitars and other instruments over ʻŌlelo Hawaiʻi and traditional ʻoli (chants), inspired in part by folk rock groups on the continent. Around this time in Hawaiʻi, the moving image as an artform started to function in a similar way.

Hawaiian Moving Images Through Spaces: The Eyes of the Land, HIFF, and HUFF

Hawaiian filmmakers pull from a rich legacy of cinema spaces, teachings, and communities. These activities can be traced back to the early 1980s, when Puhipau, a Hawaiian fisherman and storyteller, formed the independent video production team Nā Maka o ka ʻĀina (The Eyes of the Land) with his partner Joan Lander. After Puhipau's forced relocation from Sand Island, and his involvement with *The Sand Island Story* (1981), a documentary that follows the dislocation of Hawaiians like himself, he was moved by the power of storytelling through moving images to shed light on injustices within Hawaiʻi. Through Nā Maka o ka ʻĀina, over one hundred documentary films were created that focus on issues deeply affecting Hawaiians, highlighting our history, as well as our resiliency, sovereignty, culture, and our principles of aloha ʻāina. Their early films were made on a shoestring budget, with an almost guerilla-style approach. In 1993, after one hundred years of illegal occupation of our islands, the production team released *Act of War: The Overthrow of the Hawaiian Nation*, a film which powerfully depicts—from a Hawaiian perspective—the military occupation through archival footage from local and national media channels, alongside re-enactments of the treasonous coup d'état. One of the most important Hawaiian language and culture public broadcast stations, ʻŌiwi TV, aired this and many more of the team's films, as well as other documentaries and programs centering Hawaiian language and cultural practices.

Although at this time documentary films by Nā Maka o ka ʻĀina and ʻŌiwi TV were telling our stories on our terms, Hawaiian narrative fiction films remained dominated by predominantly white culture, and marked by the extractive use of the Hawaiian Islands as a backdrop for an inaccurately whitewashed paradise.

The underground film scene in Hawaiʻi grew out of the need to subvert this colonial perspective. In the late '80s, the punk scene was burgeoning in Hawaiʻi, and DIY filmmakers were busy creating music videos, short narrative and experimental films. There was no film school at the University of Hawaiʻi—though its

East-West Center in Mānoa launched the Hawai'i International Film Festival (HIFF) in 1981. HIFF was groundbreaking for presenting and premiering feature films from East Asia and other countries, and for being a venue for people in Hawai'i to both see and be in dialogue with international films pre-internet. At this time, there still wasn't really a venue for local artists to show or be exposed to short-form or experimental works. Recognizing this, Hawaiian filmmaker Christopher Kahunahana and Marco Corrado founded The Honolulu Underground Film Festival (HUFF) in 1995 as a platform for local artists and to bring more underground and radical films to Hawai'i from the continent. HUFF was extremely countercultural, showcasing everything from experimental art pieces, music video, and suspension video art, to BDSM and protests on Mauna Kea. It featured local filmmaking legends like Jon Moritsugu (*Terminal USA*, 1993; *Mod Fuck Explosion*, 1994), and connected Hawai'i to the larger underground film festival communities in NYC, LA, and around the continent. The first HUFF was spread across fourteen venues, including non-traditional cinema spaces, nightclubs, and cafes; and the festival ran until Kahunahana moved to the continent to pursue a career in film.

Alongside the support given from festivals, screenwriting labs and showcases have helped birth many Hawaiian films since the mid-'90s. When HUFF closed, the `Ohina Short Film Showcase was founded shortly after, in 1999, by Jason Suapaia and Jeff Katts—the same year *Baywatch: Hawaii* began airing on NBC. Focusing on local filmmakers in Hawai'i, Suapaia and Katts hosted the first Showcase out of the Doris Duke Theater, in what was meant to be a one-off event. But as demand for a venue for local cinema continued to grow, they ended up running the `Ohina Short Film Showcase annually, until 2008. It was resurrected in 2010, by filmmaker Gerard Elmore and producer Darrin Kaneshiro, who, in 2017, also began ʻOhina Labs, a screenwriting lab that continues today to provide mentorship and resources for local filmmakers. Also notable today are Hawaiʻi Women in Filmmaking, founded in 2011 by Vera Zambonelli, which runs the Wahine in Film Lab, centering and empowering women and girls, genderfluid and genderqueer filmmakers.

In 2003, Kahunahana moved back to Hawaiʻi to help co-direct the Cinema Paradise Independent Film Festival with filmmaker and photographer Sergio Goes. After watching their favorite venues close down again and again, the pair decided to found their own venue—Next Door—as a cinema lounge and concert hall in Honolulu's Chinatown. The venue screened independent films but also hosted large music acts as a nightclub to pay the bills. Wanting to stay connected to contemporary film, Kahunahana started the Showdown in Chinatown, a bimonthly competition that ran for over a decade, effectively creating a much-needed film community where many people met, talked story, and formed crews that went on to create their own productions.

Paradise Debunked, Reclaimed, Remastered: Hawaiian Cinema Today

The modern Hawaiian experience includes many hybridizations: a forgetting and remembering of traditions; learning to ʻōlelo on our smartphones via apps or TikTok; figuring out what options we have for work, as mahiʻai (farmers) or within the ever-expanding tourist industry, while the cost of living is always rising; as we fight to just stay on the island or against a desire to leave, or as those of us who left struggle to find home again: these entanglements are today being folded into Hawaiian films and visual artworks, which reveal a layered and vast spectrum of experiences.

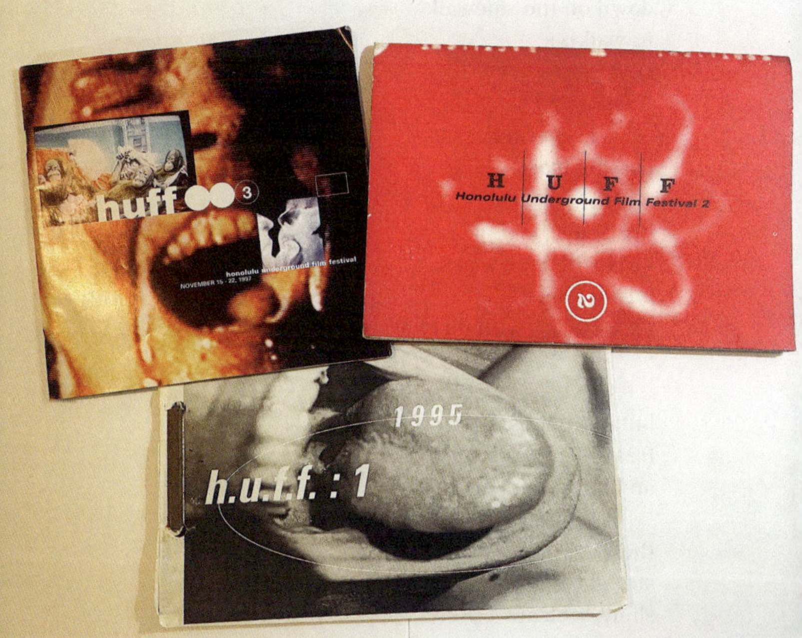

↑ Film programs for HUFF 3, HUFF 2, and HUFF 1.

Down on the Sidewalk in Waikiki (2019), an experimental short directed by the Hawaiian filmmaker Justyn Ah Chong and written by ʻĀina Paikai, is inspired by the work of Hawaiian poet Wayne Kaumualiʻi Westlake. The film follows a janitor who discovers a book of poetry on a man left dead in a bathroom on the notorious Honolulu tourist strip. Through a fast-cut montage of chaotic and almost nightmarish shots of tourist-flooded sidewalks in the night and the day, the film evokes the horror of this now-diluted, glossy capitalist culture of luxury and waste through the janitor's eyes. As goes the Westlake poem of the same title that is voiced by the janitor in the film:

                                        Tiare Ribeaux

down on the sidewalk
in waikiki
I
   SEE
       EVERYTHING
passing me:

lost souls
girls with nice asses,
businessmen
       with dirty assholes
       and shiny suits,

bums   pimps   whores
freaks   junkies   gigolos
and burnt out Amerikans...

they're
straight bent
slimy   clean
women under the
       spell of the MOON
children learning
       the GAME too soon

policemen   hippies
Kahunas (a few)
fat sick Amerikans
and speedy Japanese

studs   cunts
rich   poor

                    perverts   weirdos
                    beggars   fools
                    crazy-men
                    and old people
                              about to DIE...

                    they're all there
                    I tell you,
                              man
                    from my seat
                    down on the sidewalk
                    in waikiki
                    I SEE EVERYTHING
                    this gigantic PIG
                                   PARADE
                              staggering by...

                    and across the street
                    unnoticed,
                    an old Hawaiian
                       slowly sweeps
                     the sidewalk
                              clean
                         with a fallen
                         coconut leaf:

                    away,
                         you fools
                     he whispers,
                              away!

                                    Tiare Ribeaux

This poem appears in the same posthumously published collection of Westlake poetry that also inspired the video art piece *Spouting Water* (2020) by kekahi wahi (Sancia Miala Shiba Nash and Drew Kahu'āina Broderick). Circulating recent video snapshots of a dead-quiet Waikiki during the pandemic, the

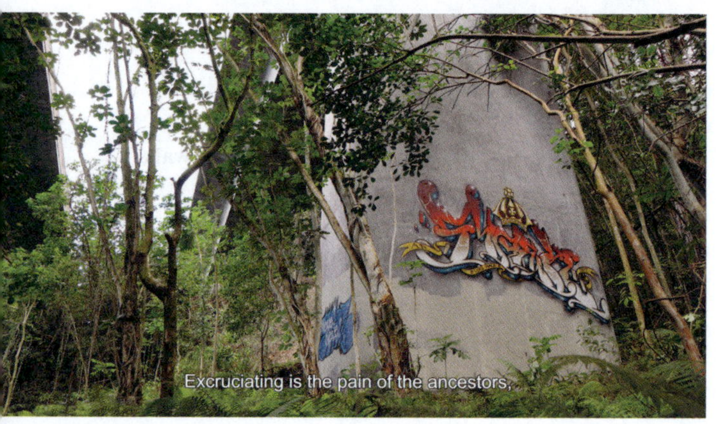

↑ kekahi wahi, *Kau 'eli'eli kau mai, kau 'eli'eli ē* (2020)

video collages storefronts, neon signs, floating trash in water features, tchotchkes for sale aimed at tourists, and chlorinated water pools—a portrait of a toxic industry in decay. Another video work, *Kau 'eli'eli kau mai, kau 'eli'eli ē* (2020), is shot from the perspective of the driver's seat, as a car travels along the Interstate H-3, a highway that connects two military bases (Joint Base Pearl Harbor-Hickam and Kāne'ohe Marine Corps Base). Costing nearly two billion dollars, the highway was built in the late 1980s and '90s amid major protests and controversy. Recordings of activists opposing its construction, and a kanikau (lament) written by Kapulani Landgraf and chanted by Lilikalā Kame'eleihiwa and Keali'i Gora, can be heard as the car cuts through the Koʻolau mountains, former sites of heiau (temples, sacred sites) that were destroyed or relocated for the highway's construction.

But not all films are focused on the struggles of our people—others aim to uplift and reclaim our way of life and our practices, through retellings which emphasize their significance, and by expanding into other mediums, spaces, and forms. The short *Kālewa* (2018) by Mitchel Merrick imagines a Hawaiian astronaut discovering a new planet while recording his ancestral names in that site, while the short animated work *Kapaemahu* (2020) focuses on the little-known but deeply significant healing stones in Waikiki, revived by filmmaker and kumu hula Hinaleimoana Wong-Kalu, also known as Kumu Hina, in collaboration with the filmmakers Dean Hamer and Joe Wilson. The film focuses on Māhū (neither male nor female) healing practitioners from Tahiti who bestowed healing knowledge upon Hawaiians, and imbued pohaku with the power to hold this knowledge.

Reimagined as a large-scale exhibition at Honolulu's Bishop Museum, *Kapaemahu* is groundbreaking in its mission to revive Māhū culture and to de-weaponize and de-stigmatize the term within both Hawaiʻi and the world. In the decades prior, the word "Māhū" was often used out of context. With the arrival of missionaries in the early 1800s, māhū became a role that was misunderstood and misinterpreted by Western missionaries and settlers and was suppressed, oftentimes violently. The term māhū still carried stigmatization up until the 2000s and 2010s, and was often weaponized as a slur/insult against LGBTQ+ folks. Now, it has reclaimed its place amongst our people as a respected role, a pillar of Native Hawaiian culture to heal and balance energies in Hawaiian society, largely thanks to Kumu Hina's and others' decades of activism. The power of media to help normalize something that our ancestors practiced, by showing our ancestors practicing it through story and visualization, has also really helped to reclaim and illuminate our way of being as māhū.

Kumu Hina's work has allowed a new generation of Māhū in Hawai'i to feel empowered, such as Kālikopuanoheaokalani Aiu, an artist who creates video essays with their poetry, video documents, and collages of their dance performances. We collaborated on my short film *Ulu Kupu* (2021, co-directed by Jody Stillwater), which follows a performance of harvesting materials from the 'āina: hala, wauke, and hau to make textiles and other crafts in both an honoring, remembrance of, and dance with the 'āina. The kapa artist Nanea Lum, who co-wrote that film with me, also helped in writing *Pō'ele Wai* (2022) in which both Lum and Aiu feature. *Pō'ele Wai* (As the Water Darkens) is a short narrative work that employs magical realism and horror to express concerns about political and environmental issues on O'ahu. It follows a weaver who experiences a transformation when they find out their drinking water has been poisoned by the petroleum leaking in from the Red Hill Bulk Fuel Storage Facility at Kapūkakī.

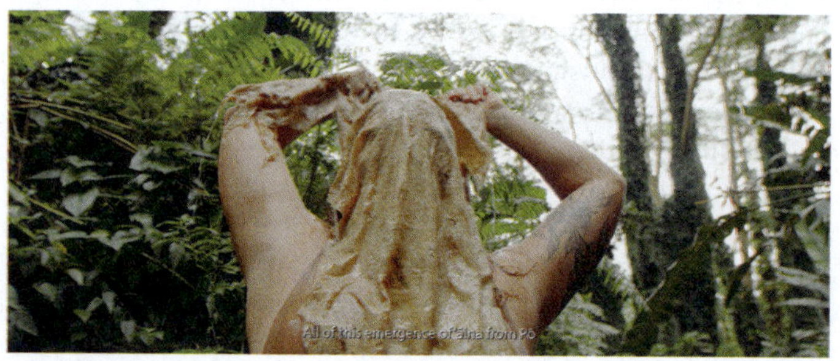

↑ Photo Credit: Tiare Ribeaux, *Pō'ele Wai* (As the Water Darkens)

Polyfantastica and *PIKO*: Centering Reality Through Hawaiian Lenses

In 2010, the current director of ʻŌiwi TV, Naʻalehu Anthony (who has also crafted a large body of video and documentary work) created the documentary *Papa Mau: The Wayfinder*, a film which chronicles the influence of Mau Piailug, a master navigator from the Federated States of Micronesia who shared his knowledge of wayfinding with Hawaiians—to teach them how to remember—to sail the *Hōkūleʻa*. The *Hōkūleʻa* is a replica of a Polynesian waʻa (voyaging canoe) that was built in 1975 to revive the tradition of wayfinding. At that time, wayfinding techniques for open ocean voyaging were nearly lost; less than a dozen native Hawaiians still possessed this navigational knowledge. Anthony's film honors Piailug's efforts in our navigational revival, and underlines our debt to him, as well as the journeys of the *Hōkūleʻa*, which has since sailed all around the world with the goal of not only reviving wayfinding as a practice, but to share and exchange cultural knowledge and practices of kānaka ʻōiwi.

The power of moving images now bridges generations and geographies of storytellers, traveling globally across oceans like the *Hōkūleʻa* via transpacific submarine cables that carry our contemporary moʻolelo. Similar to the way that The Sunday Manoa and The Brothers Cazimero added contemporary melodies and instrumentation to traditional chants in their songs in the 1970s, which was radical at that time, the artforms which allow Hawaiian ʻike (knowledge) and moʻolelo to be shared has continued to evolve and hybridize today, expanding to include multimedia works, projections, websites, augmented and virtual reality.

In a virtual reality bridge to the *Hōkūleʻa*, artist Kari Kēhau Noe (alongside Patrick Karjala, Anna Sikkink, and Dean Lodes), created the simulation *Kilo Hōkū VR* which allows users to be immersed in the experience of being on board the *Hōkūleʻa* (a Hawaiian double-hulled sailing canoe) at night out on the ocean, gaining navigational knowledge of modern Hawaiian wayfinding within a virtual environment. "By developing the simulation," the team wrote in 2016, "we aimed to assist in the education of the celestial navigation portion of modern Hawaiian wayfinding knowledge, and to help educate future generations of navigators."

Another notable work is Solomon Enos's multi-form visual timeline *Polyfantastica* (2006—) which imagines how Hawaiians might have continued to evolve as a people over a span of 40,000 years, and the technology they might have created, if contact with Westerners and colonization had never happened. Inside his "paraverse" of illustrations, multi-headed, multi-limbed akua live alongside robots and cyborgs, warriors in armored suits built from bio-materials, techno-nativational instruments, and spaceships modeled after our waʻa (canoes like *Hōkūleʻa*) that travel to other galaxies. Enos's work is so important because it also illustrates the inherent inventiveness of Hawaiians, and our desire to expand beyond known terrains.

The artist and architect Sean Connelly takes a different approach to futurism with new media websites that he calls "digital land art projects," which feature experimental cartography, moving diagrams accompanied by open access essays, and visions to bring back ahupuaʻa systems on Oʻahu. In particular, projects such as Hawaiʻi Futures (hawaii-futures. com) and Ala Wai Memorial project (alawaicentennial.org) offer professional, time-based climate recovery plans that he describes as an "ecological revolution" to restore the more comprehensive systems of the island's built environment, using the past as a baseline for Indigenous Futures. These projects outline detailed strategies that imagine permeable urban

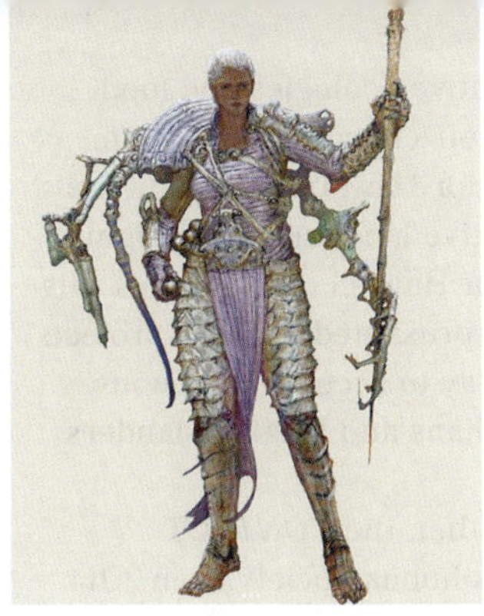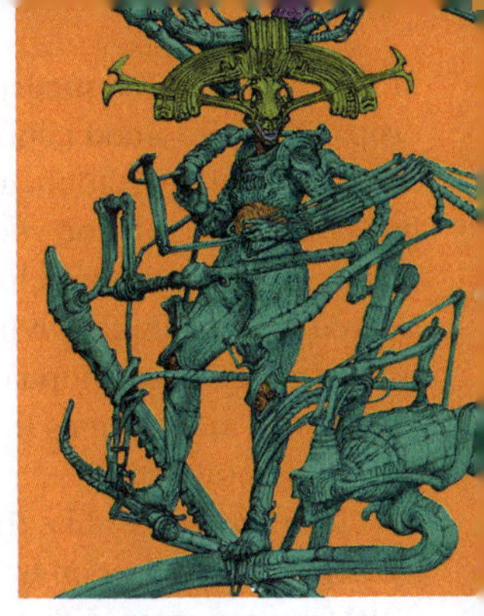

↑ Solomon Enos, *Polyfantastica* (2022). I ka wā ma mua, ka wā ma hope—at the time ahead of us, is the time behind us: a manifestation of the paradox of walking backwards into the future.

→ Solomon Enos, *Polyfantastica* (2022). *Hoʻomau ka pūkaʻina: Nā Hoʻokele Mua*, The Future Navigators!

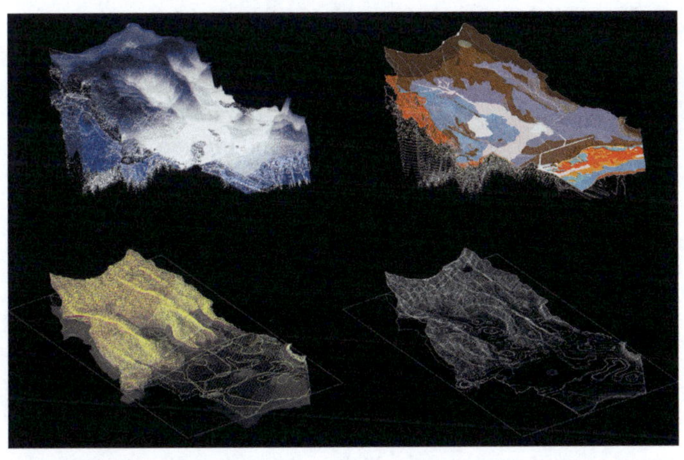

↑ Sean Connelly's Hawaiʻi Futures. This project includes an archive of animated 3D models generated in architectural software from satellite data, and includes information on soil drainage, rainfall, and cloud cover simulating systems and cycles of the oceanic environment, like cloud-to-aquifer (top left); ground and soil (top right); rainfall, wind, and forest (bottom left); and lunar motion (bottom left).

landscapes and that incorporate native ecologies and food
crops, consider flood control and soil/climate stabilization,
address demilitarization, advocate for Hawai'i History in the
built environment, and reclaim Native land and water rights
for regeneration and reciprocity for Hawai'i communities. His
approach to the built environment presented in these projects
is informed by the ahupua'a as a way to access Indigenous
knowledge and systems that Hawaiians and Pacific Islanders
have long practiced.

Bringing artists like these together, the *CONTACT*
exhibition series put on by The Pu'uhonua Society from 2014–
2019 featured many different Hawaiian and local artists to,
as described in the exhibition catalog, "parse the legacies of
contact and settler colonialism." The third curated annual group
show, *CONTACT 3017*, asked artists to imagine Hawai'i 1000
years in the future; the final iteration, *CONTACT: Acts of Faith*,
explored contemporary Hawaiian spirituality and practices at
the Hawaiian Mission Houses— the controversial site where the
first missionaries settled on O'ahu.

My two-channel video work *Pele and Plastiglomerate* (2019-
2020), also a part of *CONTACT: Acts of Faith*, juxtaposes the
techno-colonial gaze of Hawai'i Island and the two belief systems
at play: video projections of satellite monitoring via LiDAR footage
of Halema'uma'u crater at Kilauea's summit (an invasion of our
spiritual realm) are set against footage of Kilauea's magma flows
destroying buildings and technological devices like iPhones, and
chants honoring Pelehonuamea (our deity associated with the
active volcano).

In a similar reclaiming of the site, artist Nicole Naone used
large-scale projection in her work *Kalaoke o Makua* (2019) as
a means to combine footage of the 1983 Mākua Valley evictions
with a chant that honors the Makua ahupua'a with captions
of the 'oli, allowing it to be sung through karaoke by anyone

passing by. In an article on Naone's work and visual politics in the Pacific, the scholar Courtney Sato speaks to the power of projection as an artistic medium: noting Naone's comments in 2022 that the creative and subversive potential of projection lies in its capacity to place incongruent or uncanny images in unsettling proximity, Sato writes, "This capacity to unsettle is precisely why Naone and other contemporary Kānaka Maoli artists have harnessed projection as modes of artistic resistance."

Naone's earlier work, *Mauna Fiji* (2014, for the exhibition *Mauna Kea* as part of the Honolulu Biennial), projects documentation of Mount Fuji over her Hawaiian-Korean father, a former Parker Ranch cowboy, superimposed with imagery from the Subaru telescope on Mauna Kea, layering the absurdity of misplaced value systems and the desecration of sacred spaces. As Sato writes in the same article, "Centuries of genocide and settler colonial violence has, in Naone's estimation, only reiterated the importance of scale for Indigenous artists. Not only do expansive scales garner increased visibility, but these opportunities to 'speak louder and bigger' amplifies Indigenous resistance."

Speaking to the power of large-scale projection, and continuing the work that focuses on Mauna Kea, the work *PIKO*—by Christopher Kahunahana, Lanakila Mangauil, and Naone—uses VR and dome projection as a tool to immerse audiences using 360 time-lapse video footage. *PIKO* premiered as part of *Artists of Hawai'i Now*, a group exhibition that opened at the Honolulu Museum of Art in September of 2021. The work allowed viewers to experience a full day-and-night cycle at the sacred landscape of Pu'ukohe, situated more than 8,000 feet above sea level on Hawai'i Island. Positioning the 360 video work on this site allowed simultaneous filming of Mauna Kea, Maunaloa, and Hualālai's land and skyscapes, which had not previously been documented. Four different 'oli are recited, and

   Tiare Ribeaux

"booming Hawaiian chants by Mangauil," as the writer Matthew Dekneef describes in an article for the Hawaiian culture journal *Flux*. "The piece forwards both an explicit political thrust and a soulful metaphysical message to right-size another misleading narrative that pertains to Native Hawaiians over the community's embrace of various fields of science and tech."

Standing at the base of Mauna Kea in 2022, imagining the thousands who assembled there in protest of the attempted construction of the Thirty Meter Telescope on our sacred land, I think of the university that was created there—the joy and inspiration that grew out of being in community at Pu'uhuluhulu, learning, and the strength in creating that

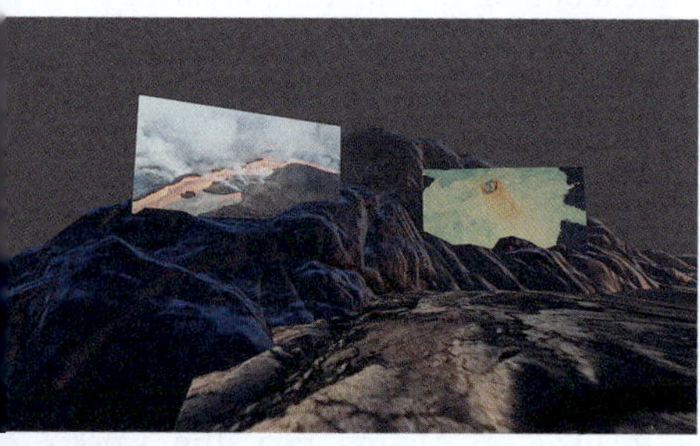

← *Pele and Plastiglomerate* (2020) by Tiare Ribeaux

↓ *Mauna Fuji* (2014) by Nicole Naone

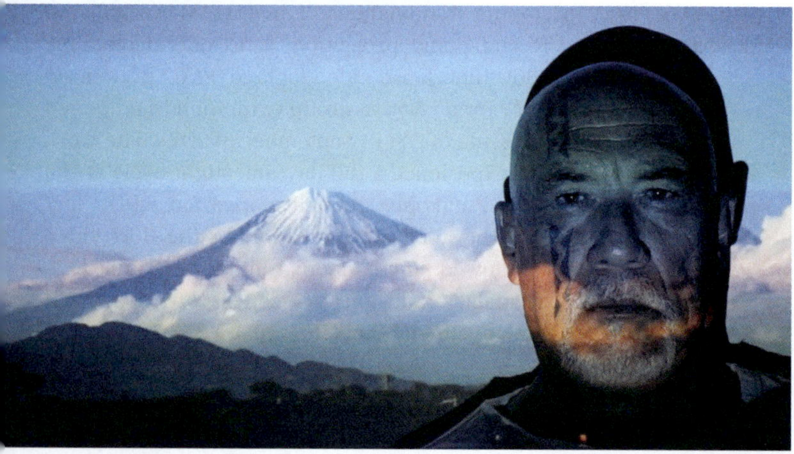

intentional space and Puʻuhonua. I think of Ciara Lacy's film
This is the Way We Rise (2021), featuring poet, artist, and
scholar Jamaica Osorio, and their poems about the Mauna,
read aloud to all who were gathered there. Moving images as
a medium contain powerful messages that call us to action, or
to places we need to be.

Other Hawaiian artists are using video games and
augmented reality as both educational tools and to expand
moʻolelo, such as Daniel Kauwila Mahi's work, one of the creators
of the online game *He Ao Hou*, and his AR and sculptural work
Kūikawalakiʻi. *Kūikawalakiʻi*, also shown at *Artist of Hawaiʻi
Now*, is a 3D-printed decolonial sculptural work that represents
a totem for protest and overthrow against the current governance
of the island, and also a gamified AR experience that takes you
through a colonial history of monuments and architecture in
Hawaiʻi. Mahi states that *"Kūikawalakiʻi* interrogates Hawaiian
ceremonial aesthetics through a 3D-printed Kiʻi (tiki) carved out
by millennia of moʻolelo (stories)."

In 2020, I began the collaborative project Kai 海 Hai
(a hybrid of 'Ocean' in ʻŌlelo Hawaiʻi and Mandarin) in 2020
with Qianqian Ye, a series of virtual and augmented reality
installations that utilize transpacific folklore—remixing
ancestral and speculative narratives to explore environmental
issues, reclamation, and diaspora across the Pacific Ocean. Our
first AR sculpture *Nakili* was spawned on the shores of Waikiki
beaches as a large monumental sculpture to reclaim land and
re-insert moʻolelo about our oceans, and reposition the sacred
over the deeply over-touristed and desecrated wahi pana. As
a future vision—I imagine AR monuments throughout Waikiki
made by different artists focusing on futurity and reclamation.

As of October 2023, the Kapaemahu Stones in Waikiki now
have a plaque with a QR code directing visitors to the website
(kapaemahu.info) as well as an AR app (with the technical

assistance of Kari Kehau Noe) that includes Kumu Hina speaking about the genealogy and history of the stones, and which allows visitors to interact virtually with the stones to access deeper knowledge, expanding their reach and offering a wider context around the pōhaku.

The works presented here all offer a pathway through which digital media and moving images can serve as a means to trace genealogies, and amplify and expand stories that envision resilience and futurity in Hawai'i and greater Polynesia. But then again, we have always been imagining futurity...

While discussing an evolved being that featured in the midpoint of the 40,000-year timeline of *Polyfantastica*, Enos, drawing on a long sheet of paper that wrapped around GRRIC Contemporary gallery during the Kō Manawa workshop, said that there was no way to fit the form on the paper. "It's a paragalactic organism made up of entire stars and galaxies, this being exists in multiple universes at the same time... that's how big they are, and there are all these other dimensions to be discovered." Not surprising. He continued, "My love has gone to all these places... Love can go everywhere throughout space and time. I think that's a more sustainable version of immortality. Don't you?"

In the introduction to her book of collected essays *Ho'oulu: Our Time of Becoming*, the Hawaiian scholar Manulani Aluli Meyer writes:

> We must delve inside ourselves... We were always capable of leading ourselves. We are representations of what is best about life. Aloha teaches us that. Aloha will help us return to that. I believe we're ready. There's no other way because the world needs us now... Aloha is our intelligence... Aloha. Compassion—a sacred idea that connects us to all spiritual traditions, all ancient cultures.

There are many terms for Aloha throughout Polynesia: Aroha, Alofa, 'Ofa. Our work in Hawai'i and this small selection is just a sampling and a branching of the work created by our people throughout what Epeli Hau'ofa has so deftly termed Our Sea of Islands, and of the many incredible moving image and expanded media works and voices that are coming out of Polynesia and Oceania, imagining our present futures—a small slice of a huge movement in which both we and our Pasifika cousins are imagining Aloha in its myriad forms. Aloha as resistance, as our power. Aloha, for us, must persist as our present, and hopefully it can become our world's future.

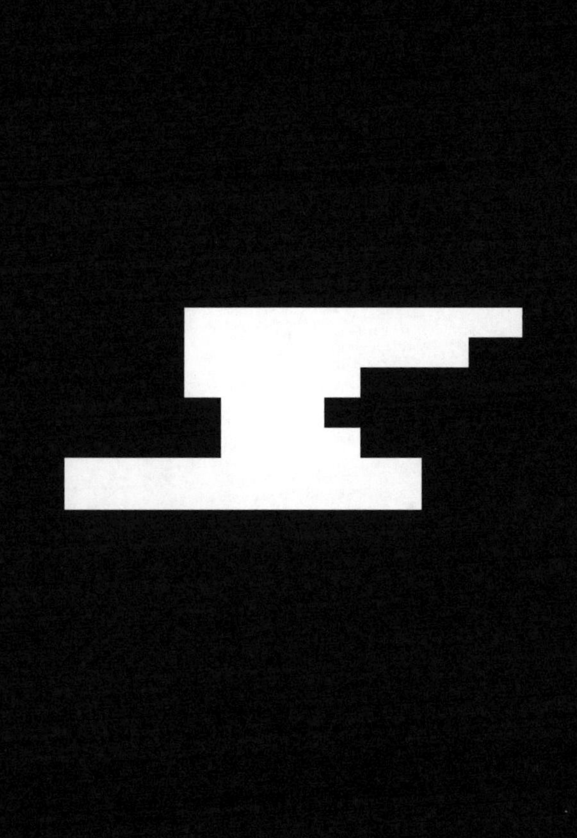

Taking the Fiction Out of Science Fiction:

A Conversation
Between
Grace Dillon
and Pedro Neves Marques
About Indigenous Futurisms

Grace Dillon is an Anishinaabe cultural critic, professor in Indigenous Nations Studies at Portland State University, and a key figure in contemporary conversations about Indigenous Futurisms. Anchored in analyses of science fiction, her work spans literary sources, film, and popular culture. Her edited anthology *Walking the Clouds: An Anthology of Indigenous Science Fiction* (2012) has become an invaluable guide to the growing field of Indigenous Futurisms and its many ramifications in studies and debates about race, gender, geography, science, and the notion of temporality itself. In this sense, Indigenous Futurisms—in the plural, as Dillon reminds us in this interview—encompass Indigenous perspectives on science fiction, speculative storytelling, and world-building through literary, cinematic, and other artistic forms, emphasizing both the colonial role of science and technology and its decolonial uses in affirming Indigenous sovereignty and creativity.

As a filmmaker, artist, and writer who has done extensive work in Brazil, I found myself confronted with the questions of who defines futures, when is the future, and what is futurity itself. This led me to consider the politics behind science fiction—its ideologies and world-building powers. In particular, my work with Indigenous actress and artist Zahy Guajajara, starting with my fiction film *Exterminator Seed* (2017), and my conversations with anthropologist Eduardo Viveiros de Castro, among others, have led me to inquire about the cosmopolitical encounters and mis-encounters between my native Portugal and Brazil—that is, between "parallel futures." Although the notion of futurity itself is part and parcel of normative processes, the reality is that many futures survive and thrive in the present. In this respect, Dillon's work has been particularly important for me. Hers is a voice that helps us navigate the depressing reality of colonial legacies but also the affirmative, empowering magic of storytelling beyond trauma.

In our conversation, Dillon talks about key concepts within Indigenous-led science fiction and offers a genealogy of the term "Indigenous Futurisms," going back to authors like Gerald Vizenor and Diane Glancy; in doing this she provides a precious bibliography at a time when some of the most exciting science fiction writing today is coming from nonwhite authors. She considers stories with topics ranging from technology, environmental justice, and relations between human and other-than-human creatures, showing that thinking with science fiction offers a rich path to decolonize the notion of science itself, freeing up space for political imaginations beyond a one-world future. *—Pedro Neves Marques*

PEDRO NEVES MARQUES: Your seminal anthology *Walking the Clouds: An Anthology of Indigenous Science Fiction* is a collection of science fiction literature by contemporary Native writers from North America, the Caribbean, and Australia. In it, you characterize the term "Indigenous Futurisms" through different categories or concerns, all of which have both aesthetic and political connotations. These categories are: Native Slipstream; Contact; Indigenous Science and Sustainability; Native Apocalypse; and *Biskaabiiyang*, meaning "Returning to Ourselves." Could you describe these ideas briefly and how they might prove helpful to better understand the scope of Indigenous Futurisms?

GRACE DILLON: I want to make clear that, as I was creating these categories, they seemed very flexible and moveable to me. I first asked each writer how they defined science and what they saw as science-

                  A Conversation Between Grace Dillon and Pedro Neves Marques

fictional about their writing, and only then about Indigenous Futurisms. So these categories came to me from their own voices and what was available at the time. It's true that I didn't get everyone in; there were plenty of other voices that should've been a part of the collection. Another thing about the book is that, instead of it really being a story-by-story collection, I was more interested in getting people excited about the authors and their many writings. That's why sometimes there are just snippets of novels, rather than full short stories.

To start, Native Slipstream came from the fact that there were several ways of thinking and writing about space-time—not as separate subjects, like "now let's talk about space" and "now let's talk about time," but rather as space and time flowing together, like currents in the same navigable stream. While sorting through my research, I was also reading the latest physics of that moment, with multiverses and parallel universes actually being verified by scientists. It was an exciting moment, because my own Anishinaabe traditional knowledges, *gikendaasowin*, and even our sacred stories, *aadizookaanan*, were being honored by these scientific discoveries, by "sciences in the making," as Bruno Latour refers to the stage when proofs are still in process or remain an artifact rather than a fact. I took great delight in that and called this aspect Native Slipstream in honor of those much more ancient forms of thinking, and also in honor of writers like Anishinaabe Gerald Vizenor and Cherokee Diane Glancy.

Vizenor and Glancy were writing way back before computers, and were among a bunch of artists and authors who couldn't get published by mainstream presses because their ideas just seemed so strange and unusual. So what they did was to create an exchange of self-publishing called Slipstream Press, borrowing the aeronautical term "slipstream" and then opening it up to experimental forms of writing. This was way before Bruce Sterling is said to have coined the term in the science fiction field. They were viewing and talking about their work as slipstream back in the 1970s, while Sterling only came up with the term during the cyberpunk days, in his 1989 fanzine column for *SF Eye*. What's fascinating is that a lot of science fiction academics will start with Sterling and say that he is where slipstream comes from, overlooking these BIPOC voices that were already writing and sharing it among each other.

For its part, "Contact" was and remains a decolonizing feature of many Indigenous stories because, of course, contact is such a big topic in science fiction, especially in the form of contact with alien peoples. For us Native Americans and/or Indigenous peoples throughout all the Americas—South, Central, and North—contact carries political reverberations. Take these myths that talk about Indigenous peoples having visions or prophecies about white people coming and making contact. White people misunderstood, for example, our Anishinaabe word *manidoo*, which was used during that moment of contact or encounter with others; it can mean "spirits," but it doesn't mean "gods" or "deities." The immediate perception of the white settlers was that somehow they themselves

    A Conversation Between Grace Dillon and Pedro Neves Marques

were the gods who had arrived, whereas for Anishinaabe people like me, *manidoo* means: this is such an amazing event that it will shift our lives irremediably, for all of us, not just for Indigenous peoples, but also for settlers or whoever is involved in that contact. In other words, contact is such a momentous occasion that it will genuinely change relationships within the common pot—I use this term in honor of Abenaki Lisa Brooks's explanation of the common pot as a space-time that is intended for all who come to its area to live relationally and comfortably together. The myths about idealizing settlers and settler nations at the time of contact are a huge misunderstanding that is still promoted today.

PNM: You already mentioned science, but do you mind going back and talking a little bit more about the notion of Indigenous Science and Sustainability?

GD: Nowadays, I think in terms of Indigenous *sciences* rather than science. I feel that's the way we should think about all sciences, as plural, whether we label them Westernized, Indigenous, or whatever form they may take. Let me quote from Gregory A. Cajete, a member of the Santa Clara Pueblo Nation who has worked in the field of Native science or sciences. He asks, "What is Indigenous science?" According to him, "It is knowing how to live in a place sustainably." In his *Indigenous Community: Rekindling the Teachings of the Seventh Fire* (2015), he writes: "Over the years I've developed some working definitions. Here is how I defined that term.

A body of traditional, environmental, and cultural knowledge unique to a group of People that has served to sustain that People through generations of living within a distinct bioregion."

So you have this kind of intergenerational knowledge, but you also know that you're always learning more. This is another definition that he gives: "Indigenous science is founded on a body of practical environmental knowledge that has been learned and transferred over generations of a People through a form of environmental and cultural education that is unique to the People."

Lastly, Cajete says: "Indigenous science can also be described as guiding thoughts and stories about the world uniquely based on the lived experience of a group of People."

Indigenous science, then, is a process for exploring, which reminds me, again, of Bruno Latour's "sciences in the making."

What I love about current Indigenous Futurisms and how they're changing is that they aren't constrained by this binary between Western science and Indigenous or non-Western science. One example is Nalo Hopkinson's novel *The New Moon's Arms* (2007), set in the Caribbean. There's this scene close to the end of the book, after the characters have suffered all of this environmental and extractivist injustice, where the grandmother is passing on her traditional ways of knowledge to her grandson but, since he goes to school, they're actually teaching each other. "Intergenerational" doesn't imply a hierarchical, top-down elders' passing of knowledge only. It's more of an exchange of ideas. This is what I see going on between generations in our Indigenous communities right now. In the science fiction field, my goal is to quietly change the mission for the top-notch journals in the field that are still simply clinging to stories about advanced technology and this linear way of thinking about knowledge as mere accumulation.

PNM: You also speak about Native Apocalypse, which reads to me much like Vizenor's notion of "survivance." In *Manifest Manners: Narratives on Postindian Survivance* (1999), Vizenor explains that the end of the world has already been experienced by many people, mostly nonwhite, and still these people resist, survive, and thrive. It seems like this is something that white people have only recently caught up with, now that we're also somewhat facing our own end of the world. This is quite intriguing, because to me the current obsession with dystopias, in books and television series, reads as a final appropriation of sorts. While Indigenous peoples have lived through apocalypses for centuries, white people now steal even that space, or airtime if you will, of both Native trauma and survivance, only to push their own anguish, seemingly erasing any colonial differences with statements like, "We're all together in this climatic mess."

GD: As Indigenous peoples, we've already experienced forms of genocide, including biowarfare, with blankets being contaminated with smallpox and then handed out as a way to decimate our people. You can connect this with Vizenor's notion of survivance—telling stories to overcome the lived experience of tragedy, dominance, and victimhood. The important thing is not to be subsumed by those experiences. In Waubgeshig Rice's novel *Moon of the Crusted Snow* (2018), you have an Indigenous community where all of a sudden the power is cut off and there's no internet or any connection to the outside world. To help everyone survive, what the community does is return to traditional protocols: if anyone hunts a caribou or a moose they don't hoard but share it with everyone, starting with the elders. To me, that is the hope that underlines the reality of Native Apocalypse: you lived through it, so you may know how to pull together as an Indigenous community through any kind of crisis.

PNM: That connects to how you manage to go back to the community through Indigenous Futurisms, which is what is referred to as *Biskaabiiyang*, an Anishinaabe word meaning "Returning to Ourselves." From what you explain, this implies a sense of reencounter and pride in Native traditions, not simply to preserve them but to push them towards better futures.

GD: For us Anishinaabe, *Biskaabiiyang* is a specific term that means "returning to the woods," because we're woodland peoples. For example, I grew up growing my "three sisters"—that is, corn, beans, and squash—along the edge of the forest, using what people now call sylvan culture or permaculture. It's curious how this counters the perspective of classical authors

like Dante in early modern Europe or, later, Edmund
Spenser, an important Renaissance poet, who view
the woods as this terrifying presence. Why is this
decolonizing? Because through boarding schools
and many other colonial experiences, that fear of
the woods creeps in.

PNM: In Brazil, the word that the postwar fascist regime used
for clearing certain areas of the country to allow
for so-called development was "pacification,"
which was applied to both Native peoples and the
landscape. Instead of saying that they would cut
down a forested region or displace and "educate"
its local Native communities, they'd call the
whole process "pacification." So that's become
an extremely loaded word in the Portuguese
language. Beyond the term's historical associations
with the military fascist regime, it reinforces
the colonial notion that equates Native peoples
with "nature" and a violent wildness, like the
threatening woods that you just mentioned.

Going back to your ideas, it's been almost a
decade since your anthology *Walking the Clouds*
was published. And what a decade it was! We saw
an intense transformation in the field of science
fiction, with a wave of Indigenous, Black, Asian,
and many other nonwhite authors, including
women and queer writers, being published and
offering some of the decade's most challenging
stories. N. K. Jemisin, Stephen Graham Jones,
and Hao Jingfang are well-known examples. At
the same time, there were tremendous political
upheavals and now-iconic Indigenous struggles,

like the NoDAPL movement against the Dakota Access Pipeline in North America. Do you feel certain things have changed in the space both of Indigenous struggle and of science fiction since the book's publication?

GD : A key change has been the integration of racial justice with criminal-justice reform. A good example of a story that portrays the racism of incarceration is Australian First Nations writer and director Wayne Blair's television series *Cleverman*. It tells the story of these supposedly nonhuman people called the "hairies"—and they are hairy!—as a way to exaggerate and exemplify how Australia's First Nations people are treated, especially in urban areas. It really speaks to issues like immigration reform and the caging of people by showing how they are interrelated issues.

Climate justice is another issue that's being addressed in fiction right now. I don't mean that stories are simply talking about climate change, but that the stories themselves become forms of climate justice. Take Waanyi Nation Alexis Wright's *The Swan Book* (2017), which deals with the contamination of First Nations' rivers and waters. Or, also in Australia, the works of Wirlomin Noongar writer and poet Claire G. Coleman, like *Terra Nullius* (2017) and *The Old Lie* (2019), the former a clear take on climate injustices. Anishinaabe Louise Erdrich's novel *Future Home of the Living God* (2017) is a really interesting take on decolonizing the Anthropocene. The main character is a pregnant woman who is ready to have her little one in what other non-Native and non-BIPOC people in the story view as a mutated or regressive state. There's also the novel *Corvus* (2015) by Harold Johnson, who is Cree. The novel is very cyberpunk, with its urban forms of technology, but in this world there's this particular way of traveling where you can climb inside a mechanical bird to glide; the hero picks a raven but soon learns that the raven is actually a bird-person who brings him back to his own Native community out in the mountains and hidden valleys.

PNM: Do you find that multispecies entanglements and the inclusion of nonhuman beings has also grown in visibility, within and outside these stories? I'm asking this because, for instance, in Brazil, debates about the rights of nonhuman or other-than-human beings have been key to Indigenous and anthropological discussions for at least the past two decades. There, the debate mostly centers around plant or animal persons, and moreover the anthropological question of "what is human," from an Indigenous point of view. That is, the knowledge that terms like "animal," "plant," "human," and "spirit" may mean something much broader than how modern sciences define them.

GD: Back in 2012, I was talking about animal persons, rock persons, phenomenological persons, plant persons, and so on, and you could sense a quiet skepticism among some people. They would see it as a form of animism, when in fact I was talking about sciences. For example, plants literally converse among each other; plants that live in toxic areas warn other plants to stay away. There are many examples of nonhuman persons in fiction about sciences. Take Thomas King's novel *The Back of the Turtle* (2014), a story about a First Nations scientist who is developing chemicals for a bioengineering company that is truly extractivist and toxic, until he sees how that's impacting the land, together with its animal and plant persons, and he is thrown into a crisis. Does he want to be a scientist? Or at least a scientist in that kind of context?

PNM : That story reminds me of Larissa Lai's latest novel, *The Tiger Flu* (2018), and its post-hardware future, where plant seeds become technologies and the world has shifted entirely to wetware, cell culture, and herbology. It speaks to what you're saying about fiction that responds to knowledges of the land, rather than science fiction being restricted to "hard" technology like spaceships.

GD : Speaking of outer space, one indication of how much things have changed is the fact that I was invited to the advisory board of what's called ETHNO-ISS, an organization that focuses on the International Space Station and life in outer orbits. They want people working on futurisms, including Indigenous Futurisms. Right now, I'm also working with three other editors, Isiah Lavender III, Taryne Taylor, and Bodhisattva Chattopadhyay, on a Routledge collection on Alternative Futurisms, or "Co-Futures" as Bodhi has coined it. That includes Afrofuturism, African

Futurisms (with Nnedi Okorafor's definition of this in mind), Indigenous Futurisms, Latinx Futurisms, Gulf Futurisms, and Asian Futurisms. The mindset is shifting for the better, I think; it is becoming more inclusive and diverse.

PNM: You always say Indigenous Futurisms, in the plural, rather than in the singular, just as you say "sciences" instead of "science." I'd like to ask about this plurality of futurisms. Connected to this, it comes to mind that instead of painting the rosy multicultural future world imagined by much optimistic science fiction and liberal politicians, many of the writers whom you reference don't shy away from historical, racial, and thoroughly cosmological tensions. Would you like to comment on that?

GD: Indigenous Futurisms, in the plural, was a choice that I made after 2012. Until then I was calling it "Indigenous Futurism." The choice reflects the richness of Indigenous communities globally. I based it on the process and legal struggles that led to the United Nations Declaration on the Rights of Indigenous Peoples, with an *s*. It took about three decades of struggle to get that letter *s* in there. The reason that it's so important is because our nations can cross borders of what are perceived as other nations. My own nations are that way. Bay Mills Nation in the Upper Peninsula of Michigan, in the US, and Garden River First Nation, in Ontario, Canada, belong together, but because of the 49th parallel, it's Canada on one side and the US on the other. We're not just one people, we are *peoples*, and our lands can encompass more than one settler nation. So Indigenous *Futurisms* became a political pushing-forward of decolonization.

Then, talking with other people, they said, "Yes, we should call it African Futurisms, Latinx Futurisms," and so on. It's been very conversational. We left Afrofuturism alone because that was really the starting point, with Alondra Nelson's 2002 *Social Text* issue on Afrofuturism. Mark Dery is given credit for coining the term "Afrofuturism" back in 1994, when he edited the collection *Flame Wars: The Discourse of Cyberculture*, where he interviewed Samuel R. Delany, Greg Tate, and Tricia Rose. Once again, final credit was given to a white man, just like with slipstream. For my part, I start that discussion on Afrofuturism with Nelson; her collection is the first genuine piece of scholarship on Afrofuturism that brings in different African American voices. In 2003, when I coined the term "Indigenous Futurism" (later "Futurisms"), I was doing it as an homage to Alondra Nelson's collection.

PNM : Interestingly, your anthology includes Indigenous writers from across the world, particularly those subjugated by British imperialism and the structures it left behind. To ask for the inclusion of South American Native voices perhaps would have been too much, but I wonder how that speaks to a divide between North and South America. In the North, thanks to voices like yours, Indigenous Futurisms have become a political and aesthetic project.

     A Conversation Between Grace Dillon and Pedro Neves Marques

My knowledge only goes so far, but I haven't seen
much on Indigenous Futurisms in Brazil, which is
what I'm most familiar with. (I'd say it's different
with Afrofuturism though.) In Brazil, you may even
find a certain distrust in the notion of futurity itself.
I can understand that, because the relation between
the future and technological advancement leading
to a "better world" is fundamentally a modern
Western invention. And we know how that future
not only led to but is based on the colonization of
other peoples' worlds, including their particular
perception of technology, humanity, and the
environment. In those techno-scientific, linear, or
messianic terms, Native peoples were and continue
to be robbed of any future, be it access to white
privilege or their own cosmopolitical sovereignty.
How might Native Slipstream and the concept of
survivance respond to this possible frustration
and offer other ways of understanding the future
beyond settler time?

GD: I should apologize, because when I edited *Walking the
Clouds* I really wanted to bring in Indigenous Latinx
authors from countries in South America. I speak a
bit of Spanish but not fluently. I would have needed
someone to translate those stories for me. Now things
have changed. Now there are many more collections
in many languages, and stories are being translated.

In terms of the future, my Anishinaabemowin
language has a word, *kobade*—a very small word,
but in reality an extremely sophisticated concept.
The idea is that everything that's in the past
and the future is also in the now, but it's not as

simplistic as that. It's more like there exists a spiral of intergenerational connections, so that even if you are in the present you have spirit persons at your side; they can be ancient spirits, considered to be from the past or from the future. *Kobade* is the recognition of all persons, not just human persons, and of all the intergenerational connections that we have, which are never linear, but spiral. In my language some people may describe it as a chain, wherein we're connected to each other, so that the future is always containing the past and the present; I don't use the word "chain" because I work in Black Studies and it just feels heavy and inappropriate. I use the image of a spiral. This is very different from the former science fiction model, what was called "extrapolative fiction." This word came directly from Robert A. Heinlein, who took the idea from mathematical equations, where you pull something out of the past or the present and draw this imagined plausible future from one dot to another. That's an extremely linear concept, too simplistic to allow other forms of thinking. For example, we just don't arbitrarily choose a certain point in the past when writing and developing characters; there can be all kinds of remnants of pasts, presents, and futures.

PNM: That's such a fundamental rupture in the practice of science fiction. Of course, the 1960s and '70s New Wave generation already broke with that more messianic, technologically bound view of science fiction. But Indigenous Futurisms introduce, to my mind, a rupture not only in the conceptualization

      A Conversation Between Grace Dillon and Pedro Neves Marques

of time but also within the very topic of science fiction itself. It's science fiction, not future fiction. It's about the science, first and foremost.

GD: When talking about her 2010 short film *The Cave*, Helen Haig-Brown says that what she did in the film was to take the fiction out of science fiction. The film tells the story of a bear hunter who ends up in a cave, inside an alternative world where people speak to one another telepathically and you have these spirit beings floating in the air; in the credits they're actually listed as Spirit Woman 1, Spirit Man 2, and so on! The hunter meets a telepath spirit woman who warns him, "You're not ready for this knowledge, you need to go back," and there's a sudden clap of energy that pushes him back to the woods, where he finds that his horse is now a skeleton, as if he's been gone for decades. What's so interesting is that Haig-Brown was filming a recorded Tsilhqot'in story, which her tribal nation gave permission to adapt, and these were real people from the community who agreed to participate in the film. While the film may appear as science fiction, it's taking the fiction out of science fiction. This is something you see in many Indigenous Futurisms.

PNM: How do you see the relation between science fictions and Native myths and mythology? While the modern mind may eventually recognize the cultural value of Indigenous myths, it refuses to see them as scientific evidence. I wouldn't want to project a meaning onto these stories, so I say this very carefully, but although in Brazil you may not find a great presence of Indigenous science fiction, Native traditions and myths almost seem to perform science-fictionally, in how they both rupture modern categories and expectations and allow for imagination beyond colonial frameworks.

GD : I have a lot to say about this. The first thing I'd like to do is to eradicate the term "myth" or "mythology," because that implies that these stories are false or that they are fictions that should be questioned. Instead, what I do—and this is what I grew up with—is to call them "stories." Everything is storytelling. Indigenous sciences are embedded in stories; this is how we share our Indigenous sciences.

I grew up in a pacifist anarchist community that was Anishinaabe-founded, at least to some degree. So, when I read Ursula K. Le Guin's 1974 novel *The Dispossessed*, I could absolutely understand the whole process of community and of shunning or shaming a person as a form of power and control, but also the recognition of combining art with science, rather than understanding them as separate. Although her story is science fictional, by acknowledging the role of storytelling in this combination between art and science, Le Guin again takes the fiction out of science fiction, and works with other forms of science.

Our word *aadizookaanan* means "ceremonial stories" or "sacred stories." Most First Nations don't share those sacred stories with outsiders. However, in 2012 many of the nations I belong to—and you should know that we Nish peoples are often called

     A Conversation Between Grace Dillon and Pedro Neves Marques

the pacifist-anarchists among other Indigenous nations—got together and decided to share not only our *gikendaasowin*, meaning herbal knowledge and science and how they interact with ceremonies and songs, but also our *aadizookaanan*. We decided that some of our sacred stories needed to be shared globally, because they were necessary right now for dealing with *Mizzu-Kummik-Quae*, Mother Earth. So the reason I'm interested in science fiction is that when I was little and we had firesides, sweats, and other ceremonies, we were telling stories about star peoples that came to Earth in, basically, space canoes. For me, the concept of a spaceship was not unusual. And, of course, we are all star people. We are made of stardust, which is scientifically accurate. Everything is made of stardust.

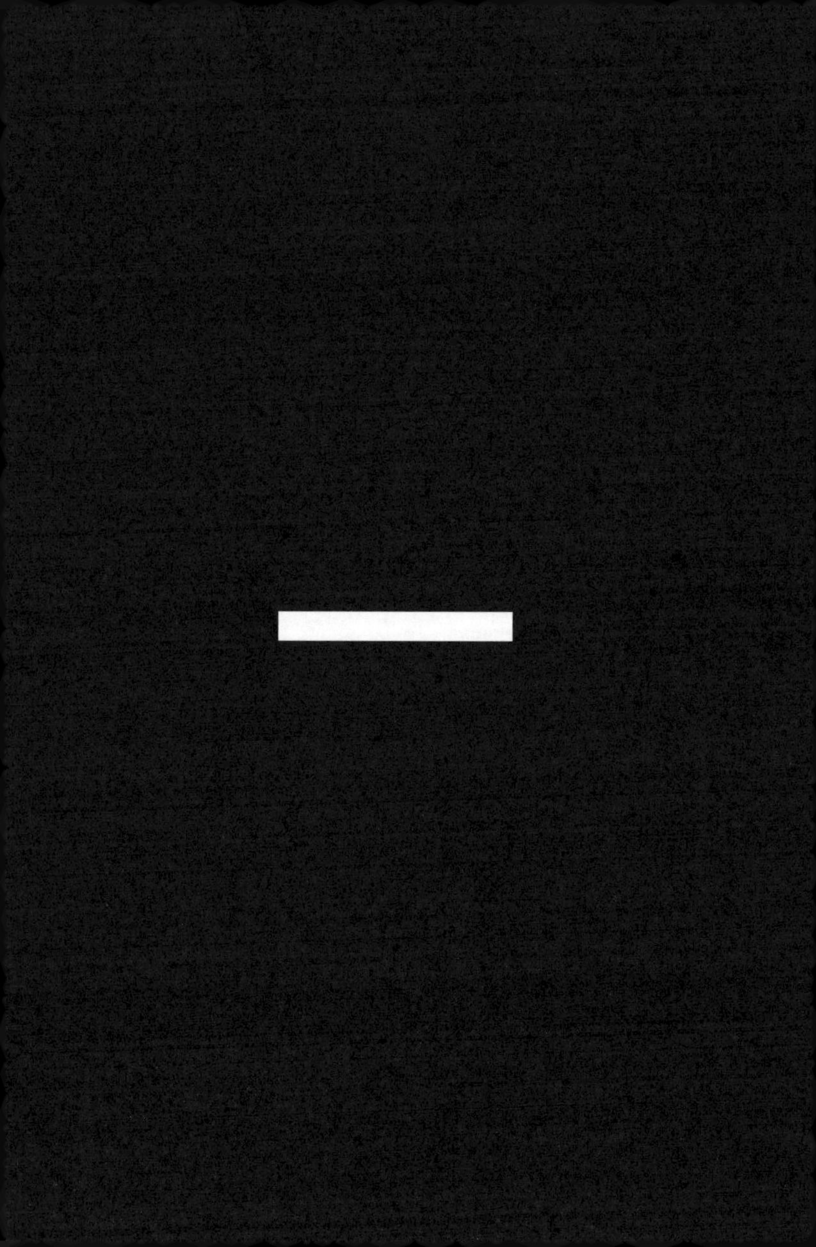

Contributors

RAVEN CHACON is a Pulitzer Prize-winning Diné composer,
    performer, and installation artist from Fort Defiance,
    Navajo Nation. He lives in Red Hook, New York.

COLECTIVO LOS INGRÁVIDOS (Tehuacán) is a Mexican film
    collective founded in 2012 to dismantle the commercial and
    corporate audiovisual grammar and its embedded ideology.

LOU CORNUM is a writer and scholar of Native American
    Studies. They are a member of the Navajo Nation and also
    descended from Irish-Scottish settlers.

GRACE L. DILLON, PhD, is an Anishinaabe scholar and
    Professor of Indigenous Nations Studies at Portland
    State University.

GUILLERMO GÓMEZ-PEÑA is a performance artist, writer,
    activist, radical pedagogue, and artistic director of the
    performance troupe La Pocha Nostra.

MIGUEL HILARI (Aymara/German) is a filmmaker based in La
    Paz, Bolivia. His work centers on migration, history and
    Indigenous identity.

SKY HOPINKA is a member of the Ho-Chunk Nation and a
    Pechanga descendant who is a filmmaker, visual artist,
    and writer.

ADAM KHALIL is an Ojibway filmmaker and artist, his practice
    attempts to subvert traditional forms of ethnography
    through humor, relation, and transgression.

ZACK KHALIL is an Ojibway filmmaker and artist, his work centers Indigenous narratives in the future through the use of innovative nonfiction forms.

KITE A.K.A. SUZANNE KITE is an award-winning Oglála Lakȟóta performance artist, visual artist, composer and academic, known for her sound and video performance with her machine learning hair-braid interface.

ALEXANDRA LAZAROWICH is an award-winning Cree filmmaker from northern Alberta, Canada. She is one of the four founders of COUSIN Collective.

FOX MAXY (Mesa Grande Band of Mission Indians and Payómkawichum) is a filmmaker whose work has screened at places such as MoMA, LACMA, Rotterdam Film Festival, and BlackStar Film Festival. In 2022, Fox was named Sundance Institute's Merata Mita Fellow, and she's also a Vera List Center Borderlands Fellow.

MICHAEL METZGER is the Pick-Laudati Curator of Media Arts at the Block Museum at Northwestern University, where he directs the Block Cinema film series.

CAROLINE MONNET (Anishinaabe/French) is a multi-disciplinary contemporary artist and filmmaker based in Montreal, Canada. She is known for her work in sculpture, installation and film.

DR. JAS M. MORGAN is a Toronto-based Cree-Métis-Saulteaux Assistant Professor in Toronto Metropolitan University's Department of English.

PEDRO NEVES MARQUES is a film director, artist, and writer.
They were the Portuguese Official Representation at
the 59th Venice Biennale (2022); are co-founders of the
poetry press Pântano Books; and write regularly about
art, ecology, and science fiction.

SHELLEY NIRO (Mohawk) is a photographer, painter,
sculptor, bead worker, multimedia artist and independent
filmmaker. She is a member of the Turtle Clan at Six
Nations of the Grand River, Ontario.

ADAM PIRON (Kiowa/Mohawk) is a filmmaker, writer, and film
curator based in Southern California. He currently serves
as Director of Sundance Institute's Indigenous Program
and is a cofounder of COUSIN.

TIARE RIBEAUX is a Kanaka 'Ōiwi filmmaker, writer and
creative producer from Honolulu whose work involves
a magical realist exploration of spirituality, labor, and
the natural environment.

DIANA FLORES RUÍZ is an Assistant Professor in Cinema and
Media Studies at the University of Washington, Seattle.

WALTER SCOTT is an interdisciplinary artist working across
comics, drawing, video, performance and sculpture.
His comic series *Wendy* chronicles the continuing
misadventures of a young artist in a satirical version of the
contemporary art world.

GIRISH SHAMBU teaches at Canisius College in Buffalo. He
is the author of *The New Cinephilia*, and editor of *Film
Quarterly*'s online column, Quorum.

PAUL CHAAT SMITH is a Comanche author, essayist,
and curator. His books and exhibitions focus on the
contemporary landscape of American Indian politics
and culture.

ADAM SPRY (White Earth Anishinaabe) is an Associate
Professor of Literature at Emerson College. His research
focuses on Anishinaabe literary and cultural history.

ELIZABETH WEATHERFORD is the founder and Emeritus
Director of the Film and Video Center of the National
Museum of the American Indian. She is currently creative
director of the consulting organization Indigenous Media
Initiatives.